CRIME
IN A PSYCHOLOGICAL
CONTEXT

CRIME

IN A PSYCHOLOGICAL CONTEXT

FROM CAREER CRIMINALS

TO CRIMINAL CAREERS

GLENN D. WALTERS

Los Angeles | London | New Delhi
Singapore | Washington DC

Los Angeles | London | New Delhi
Singapore | Washington DC

FOR INFORMATION:

SAGE Publications, Inc.

2455 Teller Road

Thousand Oaks, California 91320

E-mail: order@sagepub.com

SAGE Publications Ltd.

1 Oliver's Yard

55 City Road

London EC1Y 1SP

United Kingdom

SAGE Publications India Pvt. Ltd.

B 1/I 1 Mohan Cooperative Industrial Area

Mathura Road, New Delhi 110 044

India

SAGE Publications Asia-Pacific Pte. Ltd.

33 Pekin Street #02-01

Far East Square

Singapore 048763

Printed in the United States of America

Library of Congress Cataloging-in-Publication Data

Walters, Glenn D.

Crime in a psychological context: from career criminals to criminal careers / Glenn D. Walters.

p. cm.

Includes bibliographical references and index.

ISBN 978-1-4129-9608-2 (pbk.)

1. Criminal behavior. 2. Crime—Psychological aspects. 3. Criminal psychology. 4. Criminology. I. Title.

HV6080.W24 2012

364.3—dc22   2011007101

This book is printed on acid-free paper.

11 12 13 14 15 10 9 8 7 6 5 4 3 2 1

Acquisitions Editor: Christine Cardone

Editorial Assistant: Sarita Sarak

Production Editor: Brittany Bauhaus

Copy Editor: Megan Markanich

Typesetter: C&M Digitals (P) Ltd.

Proofreader: Christine Dahlin

Indexer: Diggs Publication Services, Inc.

Cover Designer: Janet Kiesel

Marketing Manager: Liz Thornton

Permissions Editor: Karen Ehrmann

Contents

Preface

This book is the third iteration in a series of three works designed to construct a meaningful and useful theory of criminal behavior. The first iteration occurred over two decades ago with publication of *The Criminal Lifestyle* (Walters, 1990), and the second iteration took place 12 years later with publication of *Criminal Belief Systems* (Walters, 2002). This new book is entitled *Crime in a Psychological Context*, and its purpose is to offer a more compelling exposition of crime than was possible in the first two iterations, in part by showing how the criminal lifestyle is capable of integrating two seemingly incompatible crime paradigms: (1) the career criminal paradigm and (2) the criminal career paradigm.

A working hypothesis was the title of the opening chapter of *The Criminal Lifestyle* and in concert with this sentiment, all future iterations of the criminal lifestyle have taken as their principal function the alteration, clarification, and refinement of ideas, principles, and concepts introduced in *The Criminal Lifestyle*. This first iteration emphasized the role of cognition and behavior in the formation of chronic antisocial behavior, defined the lifestyle, and discussed the interactive and thinking styles that characterize the lifestyle. Some of the assessment devices and intervention strategies used with a criminal lifestyle were also discussed during this opening iteration.

In *Criminal Belief Systems*, the second of three iterations in this series, a number of refinements were made. First, the conceptual roots of the criminal lifestyle were more clearly laid out than they had been previously. Second, the developmental model was altered to bring it into line with general lifestyle theorizing (Walters, 2000a, 2000b). Third, assessment of the eight thinking styles first described in *The Criminal Lifestyle* was enhanced with introduction of the Psychological Inventory of Criminal Thinking Styles (PICTS) (Walters, 1995a). Fourth, a more integrated program of intervention was outlined based on a synthesis of group and individual strategies.

In this book, *Crime in a Psychological Context*, the most recent iteration of the criminal lifestyle construct, the theory has been refined further.

Prominent among these refinements are locating the criminal lifestyle in latent structure space, describing the means by which the primary dimensions of a criminal lifestyle can be assessed, explaining the etiological roots and hierarchical nature of a criminal lifestyle, outlining the parameters of an evidence-based program of intervention, and using important developmental issues to construct an effective program of secondary crime prevention. Finally, this new book gives the criminal lifestyle a decided psychological focus in contrast to the mixed criminological–psychological focus the theory had during its first two iterations. This work covers latent crime-related constructs such as psychopathy, antisocial personality disorder, and criminal lifestyle.

Other features of this book include chapter-opening cases that are referenced throughout the chapter to help illustrate the content being discussed and a list of key terms and concepts at the end of the chapter for easy review. Each chapter ends with a conclusion section that provides further evaluation and context for the chapter material.

As the reader makes his or her way through this book, he or she will hopefully come to appreciate the importance and necessity of the changes that have been made to the criminal lifestyle construct in this third iteration. From proactive and reactive criminal thinking to the retooling of existential fear to accommodate fearlessness, the changes and alterations that have been made to the theory are considered essential to its continued viability as a theory of crime. My intent in making these changes has always been to make the theory easier to understand and apply in both academic and practical settings. This, after all, is the nature of a working hypothesis.

About the Author

Glenn D. Walters received his PhD at Texas Tech University in 1982 with a concentration in counseling psychology and a minor in neuroscience. He teaches undergraduate and graduate courses at The Pennsylvania State University Schuylkill campus and Lehigh University and is also employed as a psychologist in a correctional setting. In addition to Introduction to Forensic Psychology, he teaches Abnormal Psychology, Psychological Assessment, Criminology, and Developmental Psychology. He has written two other books with SAGE: *Drugs & Crime in Lifestyle Perspective* and *The Criminal Lifestyle: Patterns of Serious Criminal Conduct*. The present book is an outgrowth of the author's experiences teaching forensic psychology and criminology courses and the realization that criminal behavior is better understood once students appreciate the context in which criminal behavior takes place.

1

Understanding Crime

The Prime Context

Nothing is easier than to denounce the evildoer; nothing is more difficult than to understand him.

Fyodor Dostoevsky (1821–1881)

Predator

Pete is a 40-year-old single black male serving a 12-year sentence for bank robbery. The only child of an unwed teenage mother, he spent the first 6 years of his life bouncing back and forth between the home of his maternal grandparents and the home of a great aunt who had previously adopted and raised Pete's mother. The great aunt's home was more prosperous than the grandparents' home, and Pete perceived resentment from the relatives who lived with his grandparents full-time. He states that his two adolescent uncles bullied him regularly, often pinning him to the floor to the point where he could not breathe. Pete adds that there was a vague sexual component to his uncles' tormenting, and he openly acknowledges entering into an incestuous relationship with his adolescent aunt. When he was 6 years old, Pete and his mother left the rural area where his great aunt and maternal grandparents lived and moved to a large urban area several hours away. One of his most enduring memories is of his mother inviting strange men into their home and having sex with them in the room next to his. Pete relates that these episodes, like the experiences he had with his adolescent aunt and uncles, both terrified and excited him.

Pete was first arrested at the age of 12 for stabbing another juvenile with an ice pick during an argument. He admits that he and his friends often spoke about the possibility of doing something like this and the opportunity finally presented itself. From this point forward, Pete was repeatedly in trouble with the law. Protected by his mother who would shuttle him from one residence to another to keep him out of the hands of the authorities, Pete failed to learn from his mistakes because he rarely faced the consequences of his actions. The authorities eventually caught up with him, and he was sent to Job Corps at age 16 and then to an adult prison at age 17. Pete admits that he feels more comfortable in jail and prison than he does on the streets, a sentiment supported by his criminal record, which lists prior convictions for burglary, larceny, robbery, and kidnapping. Consequently, Pete has spent 19 of the last 21 years in prison in six different states. Pete is quick to point out that each time he is released from prison he hopes that things will magically work themselves out. They never do, and within several months he finds himself back in jail. In fact, he has never been on the streets longer than 6 months at a stretch since the age of 17.

Pete is driven by fantasies of ultimate interpersonal control. He states that his greatest fantasy is to have a subterranean complex of rooms where he can indulge in fantasies of unlimited power and control. He is particularly interested in women who are vulnerable and states that when he was on the streets he used drugs, in part, to gain access to female drug users whom he found pliable and more than willing to satisfy his sexual fantasies in exchange for drugs. Like a spider weaving a web to trap an unwitting fly, Pete enjoys playing games of intrigue in which his fantasies are played out. His greatest fear is the fear of being exposed. It would appear that he seeks to capitalize on other people's vulnerability before they can spot any weakness in him. Whether in prison or on the streets, Pete masturbates a dozen or more times a day to elaborate fantasies of control and degradation. Armed with the highly fatalistic belief that people do not change and the highly malevolent belief that all women are "whores," Pete maintains that he would be willing to risk lethal injection for the opportunity to have a sex slave who would submit to his every demand.

Given the destructive, self-indulgent, and frightening nature of Pete's thoughts and actions, it is easy to see why some people might consider him mad ("crazy"), bad ("evil"), or worse. Some psychologists would label Pete a psychopath, antisocial personality, or **career criminal**. The purpose of this book is to illustrate how viewing Pete as evil, crazy, or psychopathic impedes our ability to understand him, hinders our ability to effectively intervene with him, and in the long run makes it that much more difficult for him to change. To use such terms to describe Pete or any other offender is to discount the possibility of learning something new about or from him. The words we use, rather than being a simple matter of semantics, reflect our thinking and our thinking influences our behavior. Words like *evil*, *crazy*, and *psychopath* may preemptively reflect the belief that we already know what the problem is and how it should be handled (i.e., incarceration, lethal injection, medication) rather than our willingness to thoroughly investigate the problem, form a complete understanding of it, and find a lasting solution to it.

This book adopts the premise that instead of assigning labels to offenders and conceptualizing them as qualitatively distinct from others, there is a spectrum of criminal behavior and a range of factors that potentially influence the path an offender takes with respect to this spectrum. Rather than focusing on the individual high-rate offender as an accepted category, this book traces the dimensions along which all offenders are arrayed and offers insight into how and why these high-rate offenders assume the highest positions on these dimensions. Likewise, developmental and transitional models, which emphasize age- and state-graded trajectories while contributing valuable information to the study of crime, are no more comprehensive an explanation of crime than the dispositional models that focus on high-rate offenders. The tension between these two models, one of which views high-rate offenders as a distinct category of offender and the other of which views criminals as falling into one or more developmental trajectories, has created a schism in theoretical criminology and clinical forensic psychology. It is the position of this book that integrating the career criminal (high-risk offender) and **criminal career** (age- and state-graded trajectories) paradigms into a single model, referred to here as the **criminal lifestyle** (integrated series of thoughts and actions conducive to habitual criminal behavior), holds promise of mending the career criminal–criminal career schism.

Crime

Lay and scientific explanations of crime can be insightful, intriguing, and—on occasion—misleading. It is imperative, then, that we review some of the more popular lay and scientific theories of crime.

Lay Explanations of Crime

Crime as Evil

Evil is a religio-moral concept that has worked its way into many people's everyday vocabularies. When somebody says or does something with which we do not agree, we conclude that he or she is wrong. When somebody says or does something with which we vehemently disagree, we may punctuate our displeasure by labeling the person evil. Lay explanations of crime are commonly held beliefs about the causes of crime, which while popular, have not been subjected to rigorous scientific investigation. The notion of pure or inherent evil, for instance, not only lacks a clear scientific foundation but conflicts with much of what we know about offenders. Rarely do the perpetrators of evil acts view their behavior as unjustified or gratuitous. More often, the perpetrators of evil acts view their actions as justified and reasonable (Baumeister, 1997). The students who served as guards in the Stanford Prison Experiment (Haney, Banks, & Zimbardo, 1973) viewed the rules laid out by Dr. Zimbardo as reasonable and necessary for the orderly running of their mock jail. By the same token, the students who simulated the role of prisoners in this experiment probably viewed their animosity toward the rules and their captors as justified. When conflict erupted during the experiment, each party attributed the conflict to the other side and considered its own actions a reasonable response to the unreasonable demands or insubordination of its evil opponent. As long as these attitudes persisted, there was little hope for reconciliation, and as long as we subscribe to the view that crime reflects pure or inherent evil, we will continue to fall short in our efforts to understand, predict, and control crime. Pete's thoughts and actions could be construed as evil, but what benefit does this afford us in comprehending and changing his criminal behavior?

Crime as Crazy

Whereas evil is a religio-moral construct, labeling someone crazy because we don't understand his or her thoughts and actions derives from folk psychology. Folk psychology, also known as commonsense psychology, is the study of how we try to predict and understand other people's behavior by cognitively interpreting their behavior and forming attributions or causal inferences for their actions (Heider, 1958). People are often quite adept at predicting other people's behavior and ascribing various mental states to them (Stich & Nichols, 2003). Whether this attributional process is driven by people's knowledge of the inner workings of the human mind (Gopnik & Meltzoff, 1997) or is a form of mental simulation that requires little information on the thinking patterns of others (Gordon, 1986), it can have a profound effect on how people interpret each other's actions. An aspect of attribution that is particularly relevant to the current discussion is people's interpretation of beliefs to which they do not prescribe or cannot relate. These beliefs, sometimes referred to as discrepant beliefs, are the meanings we attach to beliefs that are different from our own. Stich and Nichols (2003) asserted that discrepant belief attribution systems display inaccuracies that reflect a lack of information about certain important aspects of the topic at hand. Attributions of crazy are an example of how we interpret discrepant beliefs.

Some people might classify Pete as crazy because it is difficult for them as outside observers to understand and relate to his actions. The senseless violence in which he has engaged over the course of his life is something we just cannot fathom because it is so alien to our experience. Most people would not think about robbing a bank or plying someone with drugs in order to exploit them sexually, let alone do these things. Just the thought of these actions is enough to make most people cringe. By classifying Pete's behavior as crazy and unexplainable, however, we ultimately shut down important avenues of understanding and potential routes of change. We must understand Pete and how early learning experiences contributed to the formation of his criminal lifestyle before we can understand his behavior. Sexual enticements from his aunt and mother coupled with physical bullying from his uncles resulted in the formation of a worldview based on malevolence and helplessness. To gain control over a malevolent environment, he identified with his aggressors and decided it was better to hurt and control others than wait around for them to hurt and control him. He consequently took a proactive approach to the psychological and physical dangers he perceived in his childhood environment.

It would be a mistake to conclude that Pete is a victim of his early experiences and therefore not responsible for the "evil" and "crazy" things he does. To understand Pete is to put ourselves in a position to help him do something about his self- and other-destructive behavior and prevent other young children from following in his footsteps. Appreciating the early childhood roots of some of Pete's actions and the role his identification with a criminal lifestyle currently plays in the self- and other-destructive path his life has taken does not absolve him of responsibility for these actions. At every point along the path that leads to a criminal lifestyle, Pete made choices, and it is these choices that led him to where he is today. Early environment has an effect on our behavior but it is our interpretation of past and current events that has the greatest impact on our current conduct. Behaviorists have traditionally held that a person is a product of his or her environment. I would modify this statement to say that each of us is the product of our experience (which includes both the environment and our perception of it) as well as various genetic predispositions.

Scientific Explanations of Crime

Crime as a Career

It is easy to see why some social scientists believe crime conforms to a career when we consider the fact that a small fraction of the offender population commits the majority of offenses recorded in any particular jurisdiction. DeLisi (2005) estimated that 10% of the criminal population is responsible for over 50% of all crime and between 60% and 100% of all rapes, murders, and kidnappings. In their classic study on delinquency in a cohort of Philadelphia-born male youth, Wolfgang, Figlio, and Sellin (1972) determined that 6% of their sample accounted for 52% of the delinquent adjudications compiled by the cohort. Using a later born cohort of males and females, also from Philadelphia, Tracy, Wolfgang, and Figlio (1990) ascertained that 7% of the sample accounted for 61% of the delinquencies, 60% of the murders, 75% of the rapes, and 73% of the robberies committed by the cohort. This relationship has been replicated in studies conducted in California (Chaiken & Chaiken, 1982); Racine, Wisconsin (Shannon, 1982); Denver, Colorado; Pittsburgh, Pennsylvania; and Rochester, New York (Thornberry, Huizinga, & Loeber, 1995), as well as in England (Farrington & West, 1993), Denmark (Kyvsgaard, 2003), Sweden (Stattin & Magnusson, 1991), and New Zealand (Fergusson, Horwood, & Nagin, 2000).

The notion of a career criminal is popular in certain quarters of the scientific community and constitutes one of the leading **scientific explanations of crime** espoused by psychologists and criminal justice experts. There are several problems with this conceptualization, however. First, the notion of a career criminal presumes the existence of a qualitatively distinct category of offender. Taxometric research clearly indicates that, contrary to the career criminal paradigm, psychopathy, antisocial personality disorder (ASPD), criminal lifestyle, and other crime-related constructs are quantitatively ordered along a continuum rather than qualitatively organized into distinct categories of behavior. A second limitation of the career criminal paradigm is that it has given rise to a number of negative criminal justice outcomes and policies, from prison overcrowding to California's "three strike" law. The unstated and sometimes stated assumption of the career criminal paradigm is that high-rate offenders do not change and the best way to manage their behavior is to keep them locked up for as long as possible. However, our ability to identify the so-called career offender is far from perfect, and it has been argued that all "three strike" laws, mandatory minimums, and other "get tough on crime" legislation accomplish is an increased tax burden on the citizenry of a society without corresponding reductions in crime or improvements in public safety (Shelden, 2004).

Crime as a Trajectory

In direct contrast to the career criminal paradigm's emphasis on the continuity of criminal behavior, the criminal career paradigm emphasizes change in criminal behavior. Change in criminal behavior, according to the criminal career paradigm, reflects the presence of several crime trajectories. Noted psychologist Terrie Moffitt (1993), for instance, proposed two crime trajectories: a life-course-persistent (LCP) pattern characterized by childhood onset and desistance in middle adulthood, and an adolescence-limited (AL) pattern characterized by adolescence onset and desistance in early adulthood. Additional patterns have also been identified. These include a late-onset chronic group, a low-rate group, and a moderate but declining group (Piquero, 2008). A major component of these trajectory theories, and the reason why they emphasize change over continuity, is the belief that most of the trajectories are state or age dependent and responsive to various life changes such as marriage, military service, and workforce participation (Nagin & Paternoster, 2000). Continuity in crime, according to advocates of the criminal career paradigm, is the result of contagion such that criminal and noncriminal behavior increase or decrease a person's access to certain life conditions, which, in turn, increase or decrease a person's opportunities to engage in further criminal and noncriminal behavior (Sampson & Laub, 1993).

Although popular with both psychologists and sociologists, the criminal career paradigm is limited in several respects. First, there is no general consensus on the number of trajectories. Three to six trajectories have been identified in research using latent growth mixture modeling (Muthén & Muthén, 2007) and semiparametric group-based modeling (Nagin, 1999), procedures designed to uncover the number of unique case clusters in a distribution. However, these cluster-based statistical procedures tend to overidentify the number of categories in a construct (Bauer & Curran, 2003). In fact, when Meehl's (1995, 2004) taxometric procedure was applied to data relevant to Moffitt's two-trajectory theory, the results were more consistent with dimensional latent structure (single trajectory) than with categorical latent structure (two or more trajectories: Walters, 2011a). These findings suggest that Moffitt's LCP and AL patterns fall at different points along one or more dimensions rather than bifurcating into distinct categories. A second limitation of the career criminal paradigm is that it may give too much credence to age- and state-dependent forces in defining people's movements in and out of crime. While it is true that most high-rate offenders significantly reduce their criminality in their late 30s to early 40s, by the time most of these individuals have reached the age of desistance they have gone through several marriages; left a trail of victims; and mishandled numerous educational, military, and job opportunities (Cusson & Pinsonneault, 1986; Shover, 1996). Something more than state dependence, therefore, is encouraging desistance in a large number of these individuals.

Rapprochement

As we have seen, lay explanations of crime, in which crime is equated with evil or craziness, are not particularly helpful in advancing our understanding of crime. Scientific explanations, with their emphasis on continuity (career criminal paradigm) or change (criminal career paradigm), may be more helpful, but even these explanations are lacking in comprehensiveness. Rapprochement between the two scientific explanations is nonetheless possible in that continuity and change need not be antagonistic. The notion that criminal behavior is relatively stable yet subject to change in response to various environmental and personal contingencies is central to the lifestyle theory of criminal behavior (Walters, 1990, 2002). In fact, the principal purpose of this book is to illustrate how the criminal lifestyle, with its emphasis on integrating continuity and change, is capable of mending the career criminal–criminal career schism by melding these two paradigms into a single theory. The criminal lifestyle is one of two bedrocks upon which this book is based. The other is the proposition that crime exists in a psychological context.

In Context

Context can be defined as the background that completes an event or situation—giving the event meaning and making the situation whole. This can perhaps best be illustrated with the analogy of a theatrical play. Most plays have several acts, and within each act are several scenes. The main theme of the story is vital in instilling a sense of continuity in the play, but changes in plot, motivation, and scenery make the play relevant and interesting. Characters come and go, but one or two main characters are usually present throughout the play. Hence, there is both continuity and change in a theatrical play just as there is continuity and change in crime. Continuity in crime is represented by the career criminal paradigm, whereas change in crime is represented by the criminal career paradigm. The main theme of this book is that continuity and change must be integrated before we can understand and alter serious criminal behavior. One way such integration can be achieved is through application of the criminal lifestyle model such that variables, contingencies, and possibilities believed to give rise to crime, help shape its expression, and imbue it with meaning are examined in context. These variable-contingency-possibility contexts of crime include latent structure, diagnosis, assessment, development, phenomenology, intervention, prevention, and application.

In this book, understanding is considered the prime context. Understanding crime means suspending judgment long enough to gather sufficient objective evidence from scientific research and subjective evidence from the people who engage in this behavior to start formulating educated guesses or hypotheses about crime. Accordingly, this text is based on the latest scientific research on crime and supplemented by ample clinical case material. Every chapter in this book begins with a clinical case study that is periodically referenced throughout the chapter in an effort to instill meaning in the context being discussed. The context of understanding is the context from which all other contexts flow. It is, in point of fact, the mother of all contexts. If we do not treat crime as something that needs to be understood rather than as something that needs to be feared, labeled, or exorcised then we will never get to its root; if we never get to the root of crime, we will never find ways to control it. Whereas total eradication of crime is a utopian dream that will likely never be realized, there is no reason why crime cannot be reduced; it is the position of this book, in fact, that understanding is the means by which crime reduction will be achieved.

The Organization of This Book

Each chapter in this book examines crime in a different context, with the overall goal being to facilitate the reader's understanding of crime by fostering an appreciation of the different contexts in which crime exists. The order of contexts in this book is far from random in that later chapters tend to build on the contexts of earlier chapters. For the reader to derive maximum benefit from this book, then, the chapters should be read in the order in which they appear in the book. In Chapter 2, for instance, we examine the latent structure of crime-related constructs such as psychopathy, ASPD, and criminal lifestyle. The bulk of research indicates that the latent structure of these crime-related constructs is dimensional, meaning that individual differences in these constructs are a matter of degree rather than a difference in kind. Psychopathy, ASPD, and criminal lifestyle are ordered along one or more dimensions rather than being divided into distinct groups of psychopaths and nonpsychopaths, antisocials and nonantisocials, or criminals and noncriminals. The implications of dimensionality for diagnosis, assessment, development, intervention, and prevention are discussed in later chapters of this book.

In line with the notion that later chapters build on earlier chapters, Chapter 3 builds on information presented in Chapter 2. Dimensionality has important implications for many aspects of clinical practice, including diagnosis. Whereas a categorical diagnostic scheme makes use of signs and symptoms, a dimensional diagnostic scheme emphasizes trends and patterns. A trend is a person's position on one or more dimensions relative to a normative standard (normative comparison). A pattern is a person's standing on one dimension relative to his or her standing on a second dimension (idiographic comparison). The Lifestyle Criminality Screening Form (LCSF), a measure of criminal behavior styles, and the Psychological Inventory of Criminal Thinking Styles (PICTS), a measure of criminal thinking styles, are introduced in this chapter as procedures that can be used to perform trend and pattern analysis on dimensional constructs like the criminal lifestyle.

Diagnosis, whether performed dimensionally or categorically, provides only a partial assessment of an individual. For both research and clinical purposes, a more comprehensive assessment is required. In Chapter 4, a series of broadband or multiscale clinical forensic assessment procedures (LCSF, PICTS, Psychopathy Checklist-Revised [PCL-R], Level of Service Inventory-Revised [LSI-R]) and narrowband or highly focused/specific clinical forensic assessment procedures (Violence Risk Appraisal Guide [VRAG], HCR-20, Static-99) are introduced and applied to the exemplar case of a female sex offender. The appraisal context for crime exists in the form of two classes of clinical forensic assessment: (1) construct assessment and (2) risk assessment. Construct assessment is performed with broadband procedures for the purpose of evaluating crime-related constructs such as psychopathy, antisocial personality, and criminal lifestyle. Risk assessment is performed with both broadband and narrowband procedures and is designed to answer specific forensic questions involving future risk of violence or recidivism.

Chapter 5 explores the etiological or causal roots of a criminal lifestyle. Returning to the career criminal–criminal career schism, Chapter 5 reviews two propensity theories (Gottfredson & Hirschi, 1990; Hare, 1996) and two developmental theories (Moffitt, 1993; Sampson & Laub, 1993) that correspond reasonably well to the career criminal and criminal career paradigms, respectively. The chapter then describes how features of both propensity and developmental theory can be incorporated into a single paradigm—the criminal lifestyle model—and potentially mend the career criminal–criminal career schism. In outlining the etiological roots of a criminal lifestyle, Chapter 5 hypothesizes that an individual experiments with crime before committing to it and that he or she starts acting like a criminal before he or she starts thinking like one.

The need to understand, not simply condemn, is a theme that runs through the first five chapters of this book. This theme reaches its climax in Chapter 6. A male inmate serving a 32-year sentence for murder is interviewed with Husserl's phenomenological method in an effort to get at the subjective **context of crime**. The subjective context of crime, it should be noted, is a vital link in the sequence of events culminating in a consummate understanding of the criminal lifestyle. By exposing the inner workings of the criminal mind, the phenomenological approach affords the reader a glimpse into the thinking of a criminal and thus a unique opportunity to perceive crime from the perspective of someone who has lived the lifestyle. Gaining insight into the subjective world of someone functioning within the framework of a criminal lifestyle is central to understanding the criminal lifestyle and the behavior of those individuals who adopt this lifestyle.

The notion that nothing works when it comes to changing criminal behavior has been put to rest by a growing body of research showing that evidence-based interventions are effective in reducing future criminal behavior (Andrews et al., 1990). Chapter 7 considers crime in a programmatic context by demonstrating that evidence-based interventions, properly implemented, can substantially increase a person's odds of avoiding future criminal involvement. A program of assisted change or intervention for the criminal lifestyle is constructed from principles derived from the study of individuals who have abandoned crime on their own, a process known as unassisted change. Implementing this program entails selecting a philosophy of change (conflict, moral, fulfillment, learning), accessing an intervention approach (catharsis, interpretation, confrontation, atonement, valuation, empathy, instruction, rehearsal), and evaluating the outcome of the intervention. Like all of the chapters in this book, Chapter 7 builds on several of its predecessors—Chapters 4, 5, and 6 in particular. Chapter 5 (etiology), for instance, informs us that a person acts like a criminal before he or she starts thinking like one; Chapter 7 (intervention) teaches us that a person stops thinking like a criminal before he or she stops acting like one.

Preventing crime is a cost-effective alternative to intervention. Why wait for a criminal lifestyle to develop when it can be prevented? Identifying the key components of a program of prevention, however, is necessary if prevention is to prove cost-effective. Using information from the etiological model of lifestyle criminality described in Chapter 5, the parameters of a secondary prevention program for high-risk youth are outlined. These parameters consist of three levels (incentive, opportunity, choice) and six developmental variables (existential fear, temperament, stress, socialization, availability, decision making). The preventive context shows that an integrated program of secondary prevention capable of addressing all of the social systems in which a child or adolescent functions holds the best chance of preventing high-risk youth from graduating to a criminal lifestyle.

There are many applications that can be made with the information provided in the first eight chapters of this book. Mental illness and malingering are two such applications. Chapter 9 consequently examines the prevalence, latent structure, diagnosis/assessment, development/etiology, and treatment of these two related constructs. Whereas only a relatively small portion of the criminal offending population suffers from serious mental health difficulties, approximately half of those who report mental health problems are either feigning or significantly exaggerating their symptoms. Latent structure, diagnosis, development, and intervention also appear to differ between mental illness and malingering in offender populations.

Rather than exploring an entirely new context, Chapter 10 examines potential future contexts for topics covered in the nine previous chapters. This final chapter deals with future elaboration of the nine contexts examined in this book: (1) the prime context, (2) the dimensional context, (3) the diagnostic context, (4) the appraisal context, (5) the etiological context, (6) the subjective context, (7) the programmatic context, (8) the preventive context, and (9) a range of application contexts. Possible future application contexts include extending the criminal lifestyle model to white-collar crime, organized crime, cyber-crime, mass murder, and serial homicide. Mass murder and serial homicide may provide a particularly interesting link to the complex interaction presumed to exist between Proactive Criminal Thinking (P) and Reactive Criminal Thinking (R).

Conclusion

As discussed in this opening chapter of a book on the psychological context of crime, one of the primary goals of this book is to mend the career criminal–criminal career schism that appears to have inhibited progress in the fields of criminology and forensic/criminal psychology. It was further emphasized that the mending process begins with acquisition of understanding into the behavior of the criminal offender. In its role as the prime context, understanding can illuminate a construct like crime. Once the construct has been defined and clarified, the next step is to apply this understanding to various theoretical, research, and clinical contexts. In fact, understanding and application are inseparable in that understanding crime allows us to predict and eventually manage this ubiquitous social problem. In the absence of such understanding, there is little hope for effective prediction or intervention. Some members of the lay public, law enforcement, or mental health communities may reject the prime context of understanding in the mistaken belief that understanding betokens acceptance or forgiveness (Muslin, 1992), but understanding betokens neither acceptance nor forgiveness, only understanding. Returning to the theatrical play analogy used earlier in this chapter to illustrate how crime interacts with various contexts, it is our ability to understand crime that affects our ability to do something about it and ultimately whether our story will have a sad or happy ending.

Key Terms and Concepts

Career Criminal

Context of Crime

Criminal Career

Criminal Lifestyle

Folk Psychology

Lay Explanations of Crime

Scientific Explanations of Crime

2

Latent Structure

The Criminal Lifestyle
in a Dimensional Context

*I have steadily endeavored to keep my mind free so as to give up
any hypothesis, however much beloved, as soon as the facts are
shown to be opposed to it.*

Charles Darwin (1809–1882)

The Self-Mutilator

Rick is a 23-year-old single white male serving a 6-year sentence for
cocaine distribution. A high school dropout with above average intelligence, Rick has an extensive history of criminal arrest dating back to
age 14 years. His first arrest was for stealing a car, but he has been
arrested for a variety of offenses since then, including assault, robbery,
and drug possession. Rick's current incarceration was preceded by a
1-year stay in a juvenile detention facility at age 16 and a 6-month stay
in an adult facility for youthful offenders. The most noteworthy feature
of Rick's prison adjustment is that it is poor. In less than 2 years, Rick
received 33 disciplinary write-ups for a wide range of institutional
infractions—several of which involved self-mutilation. When frustrated,
Rick will self-mutilate by slicing his arms and legs with a razor blade or
homemade knife referred to as a shank. The self-mutilation can become

so extreme that Rick has had to be tied down in bed with soft restraints. Even then, he will attempt to bite his arms, spitting the flesh and blood out at staff. The **dimensional** nature of the criminal lifestyle, ascertained through an analysis of **latent structure**, may help clarify some of Rick's actions.

What Is Latent Structure?

The latent structure of a psychological construct is how the psychological construct distinguishes or differentiates between entities, whether those entities are people, test items, job titles, or any other phenomena that may be of interest to psychologists. The structure is latent in the sense that it cannot be directly observed. Instead, it must be estimated or inferred from observable variables known as **indicators**. Indicators can be test scores, observer ratings, or behavioral counts designed to represent the psychological construct of interest. Indicators of intelligence, for instance, might include subscale scores on a group-administered intelligence test, observer ratings of a child's ability to solve a series of interpersonal problems in the classroom, or the number of synonyms a child can list for the word *happy*. Each indicator has an outward or surface structure referred to as the **manifest structure**. The manifest structure of an indicator may or may not match the latent structure of the construct it is designed to measure (De Boeck, Wilson, & Acton, 2005; Ruscio & Ruscio, 2002). Consequently, a procedure is required so that researchers can infer latent structure from indicators without having to rely on the manifest structure of the indicators themselves.

Before discussing the manifest-latent distinction further, it is important for the reader to understand that there are three forms of latent structure. First, a construct can place entities along a continuum (**dimensional** latent structure). Second, a construct can assign entities to distinct groups (**categorical** latent structure). Finally, a construct can simultaneously place entities along a continuum and assign them to distinct groups (**mixed** latent structure). Dimensional latent structure is said to make **quantitative** distinctions between entities (differences in degree), whereas categorical latent structure makes **qualitative** distinctions between entities (differences in kind). A psychological inventory that generates a continuous score has a dimensional manifest structure, but this does not mean that the latent structure of the construct the inventory is designed to measure is also dimensional. Likewise, a rating procedure that classifies individuals into mutually exclusive classes has a categorical manifest structure, but this does not mean that the latent structure of the construct the rating procedure is designed to assess is also categorical. The continuous score on a psychological inventory (dimensional manifest structure) may conceal a fundamental discontinuity in the construct (categorical latent structure) just as mutually exclusive groupings on a rating scale (categorical manifest structure) can conceal a fundamental continuity in the construct the rating scale is designed to measure (dimensional latent structure). Height, no matter how it is measured (manifest structure), possesses an underlying dimensional latent structure (feet and inches), and gender, no matter what the manifest structure of the indicators, has an underlying categorical latent structure (male or female). It is the latent structure of the construct and not the manifest structure of the indicators that is of primary concern to research scientists.

There are a number of ways to assess the latent structure of a psychological construct, but most are based either on a factor analytic or clustering algorithm. Factor analysis is a data reduction technique in which a larger number of variables are pared down to a smaller number of factors in an effort to discover the latent dimensional structure of the construct the variables are designed to measure. By contrast, the cluster analytic approach assesses latent structure by creating homogeneous clusters of cases that are maximally divergent from one another. The problem with using traditional factor analytic procedures like confirmatory factor analysis to determine the latent structure of a psychological construct is that these procedures assume a dimensional latent structure and are therefore biased toward a dimensional or continuous solution (Waller & Meehl, 1998). The problem with using cluster analytic techniques to assess latent structure is that they tend to overidentify the number of groups in a distribution and are biased toward a categorical or discontinuous solution (Bauer & Curran, 2003). In addition, neither factor analysis nor cluster analysis make regular use of **consistency testing**. The **taxometric method** (Meehl, 1995, 2004) is an example of a statistical procedure that employs consistency testing (convergence of evidence from several different measures, tests, or sources) and is not biased toward either a latent trait (dimensional) or latent class (categorical) interpretation of latent structure.

The Taxometric Method

Paul Meehl (1995, 2004) developed the taxometric method for the purpose of identifying taxonic (categorical) constructs. Some of the taxometric procedures he and his colleagues developed—mean above minus below a cut (MAMBAC) (Meehl & Yonce, 1994), maximum covariance (MAXCOV) (Meehl & Yonce, 1996), maximum eigenvalue (MAXEIG) (Waller & Meehl, 1998), and latent mode factor analysis (L-Mode) (Waller & Meehl, 1998)—can be used to assess the latent structure of psychological constructs. Each procedure examines the relationship between a series of **quasi-continuous** indicators to determine whether the distribution of scores reveals the presence of a **taxonic boundary** (nonarbitrary distinction or division) between the putative **taxon** (members of a distinct category) and its **complement** class (cases that do not fall into the distinct category). A peaked curve ordinarily suggests the presence of discontinuity (categorical latent structure), whereas a flat or concave curve suggests the presence of continuity (dimensional latent structure). John Ruscio and his colleagues have taken Meehl's approach a step further by introducing the **competing hypotheses approach** to taxometrics in which continuous (dimensional) and discontinuous (categorical) latent structure are viewed as competing hypotheses and the goal is to test the relative fit of the actual data curve to curves formed from simulated dimensional and categorical data (Ruscio, 2007; Ruscio, Haslam, & Ruscio, 2006; Ruscio, Ruscio, & Meron, 2007).

Psychopathy was the first crime-related construct to be assessed with the taxometric method. In an effort to determine whether psychopathy constitutes a **nonarbitrary class** (true category), Harris, Rice, and Quinsey (1994) performed a taxometric analysis of Hare's (1991) Psychopathy Checklist-Revised (PCL-R) using data from a sample of 653 mentally disordered offenders. Subjecting the eight PCL-R items that correlated highest with the total PCL-R score to MAXCOV analysis, Harris et al. (1994) observed results they interpreted as evidence of a taxon or category. Despite its status as one of the most highly cited papers on psychopathy, this study suffers from several serious problems. First, Harris et al. (1994) used summed dichotomous indicators for a procedure (MAXCOV) that calls for nonsummed quasi-continuous (four or more ordered categories) indicators (Meehl, 1995). Walters and Ruscio (2009) noted that dichotomous indicators produce highly unreliable MAXCOV results, a situation made worse by summing the indicators. Second, Harris et al. (1994) included only one taxometric procedure in their analysis, MAXCOV, thus limiting their options for consistency testing. Consistency testing is best realized through the application of quasi-independent and nonredundant procedures like MAXCOV, MAMBAC, and L-Mode. Third, because Harris et al. (1994) failed to employ Ruscio's comparison curve approach, it is possible that certain statistical distributional properties of their data (indicator skew and kurtosis, for instance) were misinterpreted as evidence of categorical latent structure.

Studies that have used quasi-continuous indicators and Ruscio's comparison curve approach have consistently found evidence of dimensional latent structure in psychopathy, whether the indicators come from the PCL-R, Psychopathy Checklist: Screening Version (PCL:SV) (Hart, Cox, & Hare, 1995), Psychopathic Personality Inventory (PPI) (Lilienfeld & Andrews, 1996), or Levenson Self-Report Psychopathy (LSRP) scale (Levenson, Kiehl, & Fitzpatrick, 1995). Table 2.1 provides an overview of taxometric studies on psychopathy and the related constructs of antisocial personality disorder (ASPD) and criminal lifestyle. In 18 out of 19 studies where quasi-continuous indicators and Ruscio's comparison curve approach have been used, the results are consistently dimensional. What this means is that the crime-related constructs of psychopathy, ASPD, and criminal lifestyle are probably ordered along one or more dimensions rather than bifurcating into dichotomous categories of psychopaths and nonpsychopaths, antisocials and nonantisocials, or lifestyle criminals and nonlifestyle criminals. As such, offenders differ quantitatively rather than qualitatively from one another and from nonoffenders and individual variations along these trait dimensions are a matter of degree rather than a difference in kind. Cutting scores may have practical value in identifying certain individuals at risk for future violence or recidivism but they do not mark a taxonic boundary between two qualitatively distinct offender classes.

Identifying the Number of Dimensions or Classes

The taxometric method would appear to be the procedure of choice for determining the presence of a discontinuity or taxonic boundary in a distribution of scores. Once this determination has been made, however, taxometrics cannot be used to accurately identify the number of dimensions or categories in a distribution. This is a job for procedures like confirmatory factor analysis and item response theory in the case of dimensional latent structure and cluster analysis and finite mixture modeling in the case of categorical latent structure. Confirmatory factor analysis and item response theory can be used to identify the number of dimensions in a construct and plot a person's position on each dimension. Cluster analysis and finite mixture modeling can be used to identify the number of classes in a construct and accurately assign a person to the appropriate class. In a series of confirmatory factor analyses, the behavioral and cognitive dimensions of the criminal lifestyle have been identified (Walters, 1997a, 2005b, 2009b).

Table 2.1 Taxometric Studies on Psychopathy, Antisocial Personality Disorder, and Lifestyle Criminality

Study	Sample	Construct	Measure	IND	Procedures	COMP	OUT
Harris, Rice, & Quinsey (1994)	653 mentally disordered offenders	Psychopathy	PCL-R	N	C, BR, BA	N	T
Skilling, Quinsey, & Craig (2001)	1,111 school-age boys	Psychopathy	PCL:YV	N	M, C, G, BR	N	T
Skilling, Harris, Rice, & Quinsey (2002)	684 mentally disordered offenders	ASPD	CATS/AP	Y/N	M, C, G, BR, BA	N	T
Marcus, John, & Edens (2004)	309 jail and prison inmates	Psychopathy	PPI	Y	M, E, L	Y	D
Vasey, Kotov, Frick, & Loney (2005)	386 children and adolescents	CD	APSD	Y	M, C, E, L, BR	Y	T
Edens, Marcus, Lilienfeld, & Poythress (2006)	876 prison inmates/ substance abusers	Psychopathy	PCL-R	Y	M, E, L	Y	D
Marcus, Lilienfeld, Edens, & Poythress (2006)	1,146 prison inmates/ substance abusers	ASPD	SCID-II	Y	M, E, L	Y	D
Guay, Ruscio, Knight, & Hare (2007)	4,865 forensic patients/ prison inmates	Psychopathy	PCL-R	Y	M, E, L	Y	D

(Continued)

19

(Continued)

Study	Sample	Construct	Measure	IND	Procedures	COMP	OUT
Harris, Rice, Hilton, Lalumière, & Quinsey (2007)	512 sexual offenders	Psychopathy	PCL-R	Y/N	M, C, E	N	T
Murrie et al. (2007)	757 delinquent boys	Psychopathy	PCL:YV	Y	M, E, L	Y	D
	489 delinquent boys	CD	APSD	Y	M, E, L	Y	D
Walters (2007b)	771 prison inmates	Criminal Lifestyle	LCSF, PICTS	Y	M, E, L	Y	D
Walters, Diamond, Magaletta, Geyer, & Duncan (2007)	2,135 prison inmates	ASPD	ANT	Y	M, E, L	Y	D
Walters, Duncan, & Mitchell-Perez (2007)	409 prison inmates	Psychopathy	PCL-R	Y	M, E, L	Y	D
Walters et al. (2007)	2,250 forensic patients/ prison inmates	Psychopathy	PCL:SV	Y	M, E, L	Y	D

Study	Sample	Construct	Measure	IND	Procedures	COMP	OUT
Walters & McCoy (2007)	427 prison inmates 393 college students	Criminal Lifestyle	PICTS	Y	M, C, E, L	Y	D
Coid & Yang (2008)	638 general population adults	Psychopathy	PCL:SV	Y	M	N	T
Marcus, Ruscio, Lilienfeld, & Hughes (2008)	6,795 COGA participants	ASPD	AP	Y	M, E, L	Y	D
Walters, Brinkley, Magaletta, & Diamond (2008)	1,972 prison inmates	Psychopathy	LSRP	Y	M, E, S, L	Y	D
Walters (2009b)	637 prison inmates	ASPD (P & R Dimensions)	ANT, LSRP, PICTS	Y	M, E, L	Y	D
Walters & Ruscio (2009)	327 prison inmates	ASPD	SCID-II	Y	M, C, E	Y	D
Walters, Ronen, & Rosenbaum (2010)	1,005 Israeli schoolchildren	Aggression	AQ, ECBI	Y	M, C, L	Y	D

(Continued)

21

(Continued)

Study	Sample	Construct	Measure	IND	Procedures	COMP	OUT
Edens, Marcus, & Vaughn (2011)	723 delinquent youth	Psychopathy	APSD, PPI	Y	M, C, L	Y	D
Walters, Marcus, Edens, Knight, & Sanford (2011)	503 sexual offenders	Psychopathy	PCL-R	Y	M, C, L	Y	D

Note: ANT = Antisocial Features scale of the Personality Assessment Inventory; AP = diagnostic criteria for antisocial personality disorder (ASPD); APSD = Antisocial Process Screening Device; AQ = Buss-Perry Aggression Questionnaire; ASPD = antisocial personality disorder; BA = Bayesian analysis; BR = base rate consistency; C = maximum covariance (MAXCOV); CATS = Childhood and Adolescent Taxon Scale; CD = conduct disorder; COGA = Collaborative Study on the Genetics of Alcoholism; COMP = use of taxonic and dimensional comparison curves; Construct = construct assessed in study; D = dimensional; E = maximum eigenvalue (MAXEIG); ECBI = Eyberg Child Behavior Inventory; G = goodness of fit index (GFI); IND = quasi-continuous indicators containing at least four ordered categories; L = latent mode factor analysis (L-Mode); LCSF = Lifestyle Criminality Screening Form; LSRP = Levenson Self-Report Psychopathy scale; M = mean above minus below a cut (MAMBAC); Measure = assessment measure from which indicators were constructed; N = no; OUT = outcome; P = proactive; PCL-R = Psychopathy Checklist-Revised; PCL:SV = Psychopathy Checklist: Screening Version; PCL:YV = Psychopathy Checklist: Youth Version; PICTS = Psychological Inventory of Criminal Thinking Styles; PPI = Psychopathic Personality Inventory; Procedures = taxometric procedures; R = reactive; S = maximum slope (MAXSLOPE); SCID-II = antisocial personality disorder (ASPD) module of the *Structured Clinical Interview for DSM-IV Axis II Personality Disorders (SCID-II)*; T = taxonic; Y = yes

22

Behavioral Dimensions of a Criminal Lifestyle

Walters (1990) identified the behavioral characteristics of a criminal lifestyle in a rational analysis of criminal history variables obtained from a large sample of penitentiary inmates. The results of this analysis showed evidence of four behavioral styles: (1) irresponsibility, (2) self-indulgence, (3) interpersonal intrusiveness, and (4) social rule breaking. A subsequent taxometric investigation using these four behavioral styles as indicators showed evidence of dimensional latent structure (Walters, 2007b), and two different factor analyses have generated support for the four-dimensional structure of the criminal lifestyle (Walters, 1995a, 1997a). The four behavioral dimensions that constitute the **behavioral definition of a criminal lifestyle** are briefly described next.

The irresponsibility dimension is characterized by poor accountability, weak reliability, and an inability or unwillingness to meet personal obligations. As with any dimension, it is not a simple matter of being completely responsible or completely irresponsible but the degree to which one is responsible or irresponsible. A review of Rick's file indicates a high degree of irresponsibility. Rick started skipping school at the age of 9 and dropped out of school midway through the tenth grade. He has never been married but acknowledges fathering three children with two different women. A review of the record indicates that he is in arrears for failing to pay child support and that he has had minimal contact with all three children. In addition, he was fired from the longest job he ever held (11 months) for being late and showing up for work drunk. These behaviors, taken as a whole, place Rick at the upper end of the irresponsibility continuum.

The self-indulgence dimension is marked by the pursuit of immediate gratification. At the extreme end of the continuum are those individuals who seek pleasure irrespective of the consequences. Drug use, sex, and gambling, are common expressions of self-indulgence when observed through the lens of a criminal lifestyle. Rick began drinking alcohol and smoking marijuana in early adolescence, but it was not long before he was abusing both substances. He graduated to ecstasy and PCP when he was 16 years old and was using cocaine on a regular basis by the time he was 18. Sexual promiscuity and gambling were additional self-indulgent activities that Rick engaged in regularly. Although he has never been married, Rick has had many short-term relationships and one-night stands. Accordingly, he has been treated twice for sexually transmitted diseases. Tattoos, because they are designed to garner attention, are also scored on the self-indulgence dimension. Rick has several tattoos on his arms and torso, the content of which reflect strong antisocial identifications.

The third dimension of a criminal lifestyle, interpersonal intrusiveness, embodies the tendency to violate the rights and personal space of others. Interpersonal intrusion can either be verbal or physical, but it nearly always involves at least one other person. Rick's current offense is not intrusive, but he has engaged in at least two prior intrusive felonies: assault and robbery. In neither of the two intrusive offenses did Rick use a weapon, and he has no history of domestic violence, both of which run counter to the notion of interpersonal intrusiveness. It would appear that interpersonal intrusiveness is the dimension on which Rick is least extreme. It is important to understand that even though the four behavioral dimensions are correlated they are far from identical and as with any dimensional system a person can be high on one dimension and low on another. Rick is high on the irresponsibility and self-indulgence dimensions and moderate on the interpersonal intrusiveness dimension.

Social rule breaking concerns the chronic violation of societal norms and rules. Like the irresponsibility, self-indulgence, and interpersonal intrusiveness dimensions, the social rule breaking dimension has its roots in early developmental processes. What may start out as insubordination and defiance at home often becomes disobedience in school and eventually violation of societal rules and laws. Social rule breaking constitutes a disregard for authority. For as long as his parents could remember, Rick was a problem at home and at school. At age 6, he was evaluated for hyperactivity and placed on Ritalin. Although the medication appeared to calm him down, it did nothing to curb Rick's evolving oppositional-defiant and conduct disordered behavior. Disciplinary problems in school led to three suspensions, the first one coming at age 14 and the final one occurring just before Rick dropped out of school at age 16. Rick's initial arrest occurred at age 14, and he was sent to a juvenile facility at age 16 for the same incident (assault) that led to his third suspension from school.

Cognitive Dimensions of a Criminal Lifestyle

The **cognitive definition of a criminal lifestyle** assumes the presence of a criminal thinking hierarchy. Factor analytic research indicates that criminal thinking is very likely hierarchically organized (Egan, McMurran, Richardson, & Blair, 2000; Walters, 1995a, 2005b). General **belief systems** are found at the top of the hierarchy, specific criminal thoughts (schemes) are found at the bottom of the hierarchy, and several layers of **schematic subnetwork** (thematically related clusters of schemes) are sandwiched in between. Figure 2.1 depicts the hierarchical nature of criminal thinking and how the schematic subnetwork level of the hierarchy is broken down further into sublevels. A belief system, in this case the **self-view**, sits at the top of the hierarchy, three representative schematic subnetworks (goals, outcome expectancies, and thinking styles) fall in the middle, and nine criminal schemes lie at the bottom. The thinking style schematic subnetwork is divided further into Reactive Criminal Thinking (R), which breaks off into cutoff (Co), discontinuity (Ds), and cognitive indolence (Ci), the last of which is broken down further into impulsivity, weak critical reasoning, and short time horizon. Notice also that the criminal thinking system is dynamic in the sense that influences flow in both directions, going from general to specific (deduction) and from specific to general (induction). Hence, general belief systems give rise to specific criminal thoughts or schemes by way of the intermediary action of schematic subnetworks and specific criminal thoughts help shape general belief systems through this same intermediary pathway.

Figure 2.1   Hierarchical Organization of Criminal Thinking

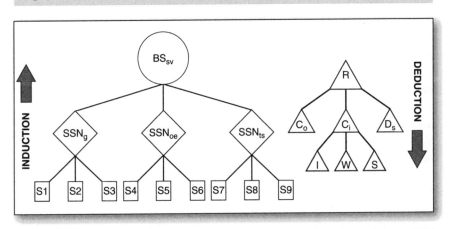

Note: BS_{sv} = belief system–self-view; Ci = cognitive indolence; Co = cutoff; Ds = discontinuity; I = impulsivity; R = Reactive Criminal Thinking; S = individual schemes; S (in second, smaller drawing) = short time horizon; SSN_g = schematic subnetwork-goals; SSN_{oe} = schematic subnetwork-outcome expectancies; SSN_{ts} = schematic subnetwork-thinking styles; W = weak critical reasoning

General Belief Systems

Lifestyle theory proposes five general belief systems formed by dividing the space-time continuum into five parts. Space is divided into the space that is me (self-view) and the space that is not me (**worldview**), whereas time is divided into the past (past view), the present (present view), and the future (future view). It may seem contradictory that as much as I've emphasized the dimensional nature of the criminal lifestyle, I have opted for five categories of belief system when there is no evidence of a taxonic boundary between any of the proposed belief systems. There is nothing wrong with creating categories out of dimensions as long as the boundaries are identified as practical conventions rather than taxonic realities. With the arbitrary yet practical nature of the divisions among the five general belief systems firmly in mind, we now move into a brief description of each of the general belief systems that contribute to the development and maintenance of a criminal lifestyle.

The self-view is a person's overall sense of himself or herself. Lifestyle theory arbitrarily divides what is probably a dimension or series of dimensions into five components: (1) reflected appraisals, (2) social comparisons, (3) self-representations, (4) role identity, and (5) possible selves (Walters, 2002). From the perspective of Cooley's (1902/1964) "looking glass self" and Mead's (1934) self as object, reflected appraisals are how the person believes he or she is perceived by others. Social comparisons are how people view themselves relative to others for the purpose of self-enhancement (upward comparisons with an admired other), self-protection (downward comparisons with a despised other), and self-improvement (parallel comparisons with those at the same level). Self-representations are aspects of one's physical appearance or external environment (including peer relations and religious affiliations) that provide one with a sense of identity. The roles a person assumes in life, whether familial, vocational, or avocational, can also shape a person's self-view. Finally, possible selves are positive (hopeful) and negative (feared) future selves the person strives to either attain or avoid. Rick's self-view is marked by a reflected appraisal of "being a loser," upward comparisons with famous criminals and downward comparisons with child molesters and "snitches," self-representations of the scars on his arms where he has cut himself, a role identity as a hustler, and a feared self of being like his father. The dimensions that underlie these five components of the self-view remain to be identified and explored.

Unlike the self-view, the dimensional underpinnings of the worldview have already been mapped out. Lifestyle theory proposes four worldview dimensions: (1) mechanistic–organismic, (2) fatalistic–agentic, (3) justice–inequality, and (4) malevolence–benevolence. Worldview beliefs on the mechanistic side of the mechanistic–organismic dimension conceptualize the world as a machine that can be broken down into its constitute parts, whereas worldview beliefs on the organismic side of the mechanistic–organismic dimension conceive of the world as a living object composed of complex, interrelated processes. Beliefs near the fatalistic pole of the fatalistic–agentic dimension emphasize powerlessness and the inevitability of negative events in one's life, while beliefs near the agentic pole of the fatalistic–agentic dimension highlight personal choice and responsibility. The third worldview dimension, justice, is marked by the belief that the world in which one lives is just (e.g., "Good things happen to good people, and bad things happen to bad people"), whereas inequality is marked by the belief that the world in which one lives is unjust (e.g., "Bad things happen to good people, and good things happen to bad people"). The final dimension, malevolence–benevolence, contrasts the belief that the world is a dangerous place filled with people of ill will (malevolence) with the belief that the world is a safe place filled with people of goodwill (benevolence). Rick's worldview is weighted toward the mechanistic, fatalistic, just (for other people), unjust (for self), and malevolent poles of each dimension (Walters, 2002).

Compared to the space-divided belief systems (i.e., self-view and worldview), the time-divided belief systems (i.e., past, present, and future views) are more nebulous. Past memories and recollections make up the past view. The present view is hypothesized to have a dual function, one involving perception and the other executive function. The future view is composed of goals and future anticipations. However, the latent structure of these three belief systems is currently unknown, although the assumption is that all three are dimensional in nature. Rick's past view is dominated by thoughts of physical abuse from his father, psychological abuse from his mother, and crimes for which he has never been caught. His present view is marked by perceptual distortions (hostile attribution biases in which he believes others are deliberately "messing" with him or out to harm him) and executive function deficits (poor impulse control and lack of foresight). Like many offenders, Rick's future view is rudimentary and almost exclusively comprises thoughts and questions about what he will do once he is released from prison.

Schematic Subnetworks

A **scheme**, or schema (Piaget, 1963), is defined by lifestyle theory as a single isolated thought. Individual schemes are postulated to cluster into conceptually unified groups of schemes known as schematic subnetworks. There are six types (an arbitrary/practical breakdown rather than a taxonic division in that schemes and schematic subnetworks appear to be dimensional) of schematic subnetworks, which are of primary interest to practitioners of the lifestyle approach: (1) attributions, (2) outcome expectancies,

(3) efficacy expectancies, (4) goals, (5) values, and (6) thinking styles. Attributions are schematic subnetworks designed to explain the causes of one's own or another's behavior and can be organized into four dimensions: (1) internal–external, (2) global-specific, (3) stable–unstable, and (4) controllable–uncontrollable (Weiner, 1990). Outcome expectancies are the anticipated consequences of a particular course of action like crime, whereas efficacy expectancies are the anticipated likelihood of achieving a desired outcome. Goals are the objectives that guide a person's actions, and values are the priorities that guide a person's decisions. Thinking styles are cognitive processes designed to defend and maintain a lifestyle. As previously mentioned, Rick demonstrates a hostile attribution bias in which he frequently misinterprets innocuous events (e.g., someone inadvertently bumping into him) as deliberately hostile. Rick's outcome expectancies for crime encompass the desire for power and control over others and the ability to do what he wants whenever he wants. Like the character played by Nicolas Cage in the movie *Lord of War*, he has a great deal of perceived efficacy in his ability to commit crime (e.g., "I'm good at it"), whereas his goals are mostly short term and his priorities centered around the hedonistic pleasure he gains from crime and the use of drugs.

The schematic subnetworks that have received the most attention in research on the criminal lifestyle are the thinking styles. Lifestyle theory proposes that a criminal lifestyle is supported and maintained by a group of eight thinking styles. Brief descriptions of these eight thinking styles, several of which were originally developed, suggested, or coined by Sykes and Matza (1957) and Yochelson and Samenow (1976), are provided in Table 2.2. Seven of these eight thinking styles contribute to the development of higher-level factors in the criminal thinking hierarchy: Proactive Criminal Thinking (P) and Reactive Criminal Thinking (R). P reflects the planned, devious, and cold-blooded aspects of criminality, whereas R reflects the spontaneous, impulsive, and hot-blooded aspects of criminality. Mollification (Mo), entitlement (En), power orientation (Po), and superoptimism (So) are features of P; Co, Ci, and Ds, on the other hand, are features of R. Rick's criminal thinking tends to be more reactive than proactive, with an emphasis on the thinking styles of Co (e.g., "They don't want to hire me, then fuck it. I'll rob 'em instead"), Po (e.g., "They want to mess with me, then I'll show them the meaning of pain"), and Ds (e.g., "I tend to lose interest in activities, and I have trouble focusing on my goals"). Aspects of Hare's (2003) psychopathy construct may also load differentially onto proactive and reactive criminality, with Factor 1 (selfish, callous, and remorseless use of others) being more indicative of proactive criminality and Factor 2 (chronically unstable antisocial lifestyle) being more indicative of reactive criminality.

Table 2.2   Descriptions of the Eight Thinking Styles

Thinking Style	Description
Mollification	Externalizing, rationalizing, or justifying one's criminal actions in order to relieve guilt over the consequences of these actions (e.g., "It wasn't my fault. He made me do it").
Cutoff	Eliminating deterrents to crime with a single word or phrase (e.g., "Fuck it"), musical theme, or the use of alcohol and drugs.
Entitlement	Maintaining that one is different from others and therefore deserving of special attention and favors; it is often expressed as a misidentification of wants as needs (e.g., "I need an expensive car and a new wardrobe").
Power Orientation	Asserting power and control over the social environment in an effort to ease feelings of powerlessness; it is often accomplished by putting others down (e.g., "When I feel down, I feel better when I take control of a situation").
Sentimentality	Compensating for the negative consequences of a criminal lifestyle by performing various good deeds (e.g., handing out turkeys on Thanksgiving in the neighborhood where one sells drugs).
Superoptimism	Believing that one can indefinitely avoid the negative consequences of a criminal lifestyle (loss of family, freedom, or life) despite observing others experiencing these same consequences (e.g., "It can't happen to me").
Cognitive Indolence	Failing to critically evaluate one's ideas and plans, making impulsive decisions, and taking frequent shortcuts (e.g., "Why do today what I can put off until tomorrow?").
Discontinuity	Lack of consistency in thought and action, leading to weak accountability and failure to follow through on promises, commitments, and initially good intentions (e.g., "I start out with the best of intentions, but then something happens").

Schematic subnetworks are both a cause and effect of belief systems. Goals, values, and outcome expectancies are instrumental in creating and constructing belief systems, whereas efficacy expectancies, self-attributions, and thinking styles are instrumental in maintaining and defending belief systems. All six schematic subnetworks are, in turn, shaped and influenced by these same belief systems in a reciprocal effects model of causality. In a recent study on the relationship between worldview dimensions, as measured by the World View Rating Scale (WVRS) (Walters, 2005a), and criminal thinking styles, as measured by the Psychological Inventory of Criminal Thinking Styles (PICTS) (Walters, 1995a), Walters (2007a) discovered that several of the PICTS thinking style scales correlated with a mechanistic, unequal, and malevolent worldview.

Schematic subnetworks correlate moderately with each other. P, for instance, correlates differentially with positive outcome expectancies for crime, and R correlates differentially with an attributional style in which ambiguous interpersonal actions are often misinterpreted as signs of hostility (Walters, 2007c). Goals and values may also be meaningfully linked and it is frequently the case that positive outcome expectancies influence a person's estimated chances of success in any criminal venture (i.e., efficacy expectancies). A great deal more research is required on the six schematic subnetworks before we can fully understand their interrelationships.

Specific Criminal Thoughts

Individual criminal thoughts are the schemes found at the bottom of the criminal thinking hierarchy. As was mentioned earlier, a scheme is defined by lifestyle theory as a single specific criminal thought. The merging of individual schemes gives rise to schematic subnetworks by way of induction, although these individual schemes are also a product of the deductive influence of these same subnetworks. As should hopefully be clear by now, reciprocity is the name of the game when it comes to understanding the criminal lifestyle. Each scheme can be ordered along three dimensions: (1) valence, (2) complexity, and (3) focus. Valence is the degree to which the person evaluates the object or subject of the scheme in either favorable or unfavorable terms. Some schemes are more complex (contain more nuances or are better integrated) than other schemes, the essence of the complexity versus simplicity dimension. Finally, focus is the degree to which a scheme covers a narrow versus a broad range of topics.

Why Should We Care About Latent Structure?

It would be easy to write latent structure off as an "ivory tower" concern with no real-world relevance to crime, criminals, or the criminal justice system. Nothing could be further from the truth, however. Knowing the latent structure of a construct can have an important bearing on theory, research, and practice with respect to that construct. Several of the more salient implications of latent structure for theory, research, and practice are discussed next.

Theoretical Implications

One of the principal theoretical implications of latent structure is that it can provide clues on causal process. Evidence of a clear taxonic boundary, for instance, supports one of four causal pathways: (1) specific etiology, (2) threshold effect, (3) nonlinear interaction, or (4) developmental bifurcation (Meehl, 1977, 1992). Specific etiology implies that a set of necessary and sufficient conditions is responsible for the development of the behavior in question. A threshold effect occurs when a dimension transforms into a category once the dimension reaches a critical level of vulnerability or severity. Nonlinear interaction involves a synergism of two or more causal influences that produces an effect greater than the sum of the two individual variables alone. Finally, a dimensional state can give way to a categorical state over time by way of a process known as developmental bifurcation. Dimensional latent structure, by comparison, implies that the causal process is additive and that various combinations of relevant risk factors can lead to the behavior in question (Ruscio et al., 2006).

Research Implications

Latent structure also has implications for research. Categorical constructs can be dichotomized at the taxonic boundary and then entered into an analysis of variance or logistic regression analysis as the independent or dependent variable, respectively. In the case of a dimensional construct, the entire range of scores should be included in a research study because dichotomizing a continuous variable can lead to a significant loss of information. The statistical technique of choice with dimensional constructs is therefore regression analysis. Taxometric research can also have important implications for the selection of participants in a research study. College students have traditionally served as subjects in psychological studies, a practice that has become much maligned in recent years. However, if the construct is dimensional, we can often learn something of value from data obtained in subclinical samples and populations. In situations where the construct is categorical, it makes little sense to study subclinical populations because there is a clean break between those above and below the taxonic boundary.

Practical Implications

Latent structure has important implications for classification and diagnosis. A categorical construct can be divided into categories without significant loss of information. Most diagnostic schemes make use of this categorical approach to classification. Based on an analysis of specific diagnostic signs and symptoms, a person is placed in one of two mutually exclusive categories: i.e., either diagnosed with the syndrome or not diagnosed with the syndrome. Dimensional constructs do not conform well to the tenets of categorical classification and there is often a significant loss of information when dimensional constructs are dichotomized. Cutting scores can sometimes be of practical value with a dimensional construct but often it is like trying to fit a square peg into a round hole. A different kind of classification system, one that makes use of the entire range of scores, is required with a dimensional construct. In the next chapter, a dimensional diagnostic system based on trends and patterns in thinking and behavior will be examined.

Latent structure can also aid in the development of certain assessment techniques. The most efficient way to assess a categorical construct is with items that maximally discriminate between the taxon and complement classes. As such, the items on a measure of a categorical construct will be concentrated around the taxonic boundary and may be scored in more complex ways than the typical summed-item dimensional scale (Ruscio et al., 2006). Scales designed to assess a dimensional construct, on the other hand, must discriminate along the full length of the dimension or continuum. Such scales accordingly require items at different points along the continuum. As one might anticipate, measures of dimensional constructs normally require more items than measures of categorical constructs. Another assessment application of the taxometric method is using latent structure to establish the construct validity of a psychological assessment procedure provided the latent structure of the construct is known. Most psychologists would agree that intelligence is a dimensionally distributed ability when biologically based causes of mental retardation (e.g., Down syndrome) are removed. Consequently, indicators from an intelligence test that fail to produce clear evidence of dimensional latent structure in a taxometric analysis would be suspect from a construct validity point of view.

Prevention and intervention are other areas of clinical practice where knowing the latent structure of a construct can be helpful. If a construct is categorical, depending on whether the etiological process is specific etiology, a threshold effect, nonlinear interaction, or developmental bifurcation, one can use this information to develop techniques designed to prevent the onset of the behavior. This could entail genetic counseling for disorders with specific etiology like Huntington's disease (Walker, 2007) or the prevention of childhood abuse as a potential cause of the developmental bifurcation that can lead to dissociative disorder (Waller & Ross, 1997). If the construct is dimensional then prevention needs to be directed at reducing as many risk factors as possible rather than focusing on any one particular risk factor. To the extent that dimensional latent structure suggests an absence of necessary and sufficient conditions for the development of a behavior, the criminal lifestyle is best prevented by reducing as many of the associated risk factors as possible. The implications of latent structure for intervention remain to be worked out, although it may be wise to avoid the use of labels when dealing with a dimensional construct. In light of the fact that the latent structure of psychopathy appears to be dimensional, the practice of labeling someone who scores high on this dimension a psychopath is probably inappropriate and potentially destructive (see Edens, Marcus, Lilienfeld, & Poythress, 2006).

Conclusion

The purpose of this chapter was to introduce the reader to the notion of latent structure and its application to the crime-related constructs of psychopathy, antisocial personality, and criminal lifestyle. Additional discussion showed that with the help of the taxometric method it is possible to determine whether the latent structure of a construct is dimensional, categorical, or mixed. In the case of crime-related constructs, we learned that the underlying or latent structure of these constructs appears to be dimensional. A four-dimensional model of criminal lifestyle behavior (irresponsibility, self-indulgence, interpersonal intrusiveness, social rule breaking) and a hierarchical model of criminal lifestyle cognitive dimensions (belief systems, schematic subnetworks, schemes) were then laid out. As a dimensional construct, we can anticipate that the etiology of the criminal lifestyle is additive and that prevention efforts will need to adopt a wide focus and encompass a broad range of risk factors relevant to the development of a criminal lifestyle. As far as classification is concerned, the signs and symptoms approach used to make categorical diagnoses does not fit a dimensional construct like the criminal lifestyle. Finding a diagnostic model appropriate for use with dimensional constructs will be the principal objective of Chapter 3 as will efforts to ascertain how the behavioral and cognitive dimensions interact to form a criminal lifestyle.

Key Terms and Concepts

Behavioral Definition
of a Criminal Lifestyle

Belief Systems

Categorical

Cognitive Definition
of a Criminal Lifestyle

Competing Hypotheses
Approach

Complement

Consistency Testing

Dimensional

Indicators

Latent Structure

Manifest Structure

Nonarbitrary Class

Qualitative

Quantitative

Quasi-Continuous

Schematic Subnetwork

Scheme

Self-View

Taxometric Method

Taxon

Taxonic Boundary

Worldview

3

Classification

The Criminal Lifestyle
in a Diagnostic Context

*Ignorance is the curse of God; knowledge is the wing whereon
we fly to heaven.*

William Shakespeare (1564–1616)

Mr. Consistency

Will is a 25-year-old single black male serving a 9-year sentence for
bank robbery. As a juvenile, Will had numerous run-ins with the law.
He fought in school regularly and was expelled midway thought the
ninth grade. Despite this, he earned his GED while serving time in an
institution for young adult offenders. Will's two previous adult arrests,
one for possession with intent to distribute heroin and the other for
strong-armed robbery, resulted in jail and prison sentences of 6
months and 3 to 5 years, respectively. Between the ages of 18, when
he first went to jail, and 25, when he was 3 years into his 9-year sentence for bank robbery, Will has spent no more than 8 months in the
community. In a sample of over 500 federal prison inmates followed
for a period of 2 years as part of a study on predicting disciplinary
infractions (Walters, 1996), Will received more disciplinary reports

than any other inmate. He eclipsed Rick's second-best total (33) by seven and had 33 times more total incident reports and 62 times more physically violent incident reports than the average inmate in the sample. Will's 40 infractions included write-ups for fighting, assaulting others, threatening, destroying government property, being insolent, refusing an order, and engaging in a group demonstration. Needless to say, Will spent nearly the entire 2 years of the study in disciplinary segregation.

Diagnostic Functions

Diagnosis serves several interrelated functions. One of the most important functions of diagnosis is to condense and summarize a complex set of behaviors or observations into a format that can be used by researchers, theoreticians, clinicians, and policy makers. Researchers include diagnoses as both independent and dependent variables in their studies. The degree to which a diagnosis is reliable and valid helps maximally differentiate the groups being contrasted (independent variable) and maximally identify an effect in situations where an effect is present (dependent variable). Theoreticians use diagnoses to investigate the etiology of various behavioral disorders. Without reliable and valid diagnoses, it would be difficult if not impossible to systemically investigate the causes of these behaviors. Clinicians are interested in matching diagnoses to interventions because it has been demonstrated that certain interventions are more effective with certain diagnoses than others. Administrators and policy makers are attracted to diagnosis for the purpose of predicting behavior, making release decisions, and assigning inmates to different security level institutions. Two outcomes of great interest to administrators and policy makers are institutional adjustment and recidivism.

There are two types of diagnoses available to researchers, theoreticians, clinicians, and administrators/policy makers: categorical and dimensional. Categorical diagnoses assign cases to mutually exclusive categories (psychopath vs. nonpsychopath), whereas dimensional diagnoses order people along one or more dimensions (degree of psychopathy). A principal advantage of categorical diagnoses is their simplicity and lack of ambiguity. Surveys indicate that most clinicians, particularly those trained in medicine, prefer categorical diagnoses (Sprock, 2003). One advantage dimensional diagnoses have over categorical diagnoses, however, is that they frequently account for significantly more variance in external correlates and future outcomes than categorical diagnoses.

Studies conducted on both Axis I (Rosenman, Korten, Medway, & Evans, 2003) and Axis II (Ullrich, Borkenau, & Marneros, 2001) disorders indicate that symptom data assessed dimensionally are more accurate and precise than the same symptom data organized categorically. Analysis of data from a recent study by Walters and Knight (2010) indicates that a **dimensional diagnosis** of antisocial personality correlated significantly better with self-reported criminal thinking and antisociality than a **categorical diagnosis** of antisocial personality disorder (ASPD) (see Table 3.1).

Table 3.1   Correlates of Categorical and Dimensional Diagnoses in a Group of Criminal Offenders

Variable	Categorical Diagnosis r	Dimensional Diagnosis r	Difference t(326)
Prior Convictions	.144	.170	0.72
Incident Reports	.146	.160	0.39
PICTS GCT Score	.314	.398	2.51*
PICTS P Scale	.310	.419	3.29**
PICTS R Scale	.298	.383	2.52*
ANT Total Score	.338	.488	4.73***
ANT Antisocial Behaviors	.260	.371	3.28**
ANT Egocentricity	.211	.372	4.80***
ANT Stimulus Seeking	.289	.366	2.27*

Note: All correlations are statistically significant ($p < .01$). ANT = Antisocial Features scale of the Personality Assessment Inventory; Categorical Diagnosis = antisocial personality disorder (ASPD) diagnosis with childhood conduct disorder (CD); Dimensional Diagnosis = total symptom count for the SCID-II Antisocial Personality Diagnosis; GCT = General Criminal Thinking; P = Proactive Criminal Thinking; PICTS = Psychological Inventory of Criminal Thinking Styles; R = Reactive Criminal Thinking; t(326) = T-test with 326 degrees of freedom

*$p < .05$; **$p < .01$; ***$p < .001$.

Essentials of Categorical Diagnosis

Categorical diagnosis is grounded in **signs** and **symptoms**. Signs are outward expressions or observable behaviors associated with a particular diagnostic category. A sign of depression might be a sad expression or blunt affect, whereas a sign of attention deficit disorder/hyperactivity could be an out-of-control child running around your office. Symptoms, on the other hand, are maladaptive internal experiences, which, while unavailable to the outside observer, are reported by the client. A symptom of schizophrenia would be auditory hallucinations or the delusion of being controlled by outside forces, whereas a symptom of mania would be flight of ideas that the client describes as racing or crowded thoughts. In a categorical diagnostic system like the fourth edition of the *Diagnostic and Statistical Manual of Mental Disorders (DSM–IV–TR)* (American Psychiatric Association [APA], 2000), clients are assigned to one of two mutually exclusive categories (e.g., depressed–nondepressed, hyperactive–nonhyperactive, schizophrenic–nonschizophrenic, manic-nonmanic) after being assessed on a series of signs and symptoms. Different rules and criteria are used to make each diagnosis, but all divide people into categories based on the number and configuration of various signs and symptoms.

DSM–IV–TR lists seven "adult" criteria (unlawful behavior, deceitfulness, impulsivity, aggressiveness, recklessness, irresponsibility, and lack of remorse) and 15 "conduct disorder" (CD) criteria (bullying others, initiating fights, using a weapon, being physically cruel toward people, being physically cruel toward animals, stealing while confronting a victim, forcing someone into sex, fire setting, destroying property, breaking into someone's house or car, conning others, stealing items of nontrivial value, staying out against parental prohibitions before age 13 years, running away from home overnight at least twice, being truant beginning before age 13 years) for ASPD. At least three adult criteria and three CD criteria must be present since age 15 years and before age 15 years, respectively, for a diagnosis of ASPD to be made. Will satisfies five of the adult criteria (unlawful behavior, impulsivity, aggressiveness, recklessness, and irresponsibility) and six of the CD criteria (initiating physical fights, being physically cruel to people, deliberately destroying other's property, breaking into someone's house or car, stealing items of nontrivial value, and running away from home and staying out overnight at least twice) for ASPD and can be categorically diagnosed as suffering from ASPD.

Essentials of Dimensional Diagnosis

Dimensional diagnosis, rather than being based on signs and symptoms, is grounded in **trends** and **patterns**. Trends measure a person's position on one or more dimensions relative to a population of others (**normative comparison**). A dimensional diagnosis of anorexia nervosa might be constructed from an analysis of a person's position on three dimensions (actual body weight as a proportion of expected body weight, fear of fatness, and undue influence of body weight/shape on self-evaluation). Four dimensions could be used to construct a dimensional diagnosis of generalized anxiety disorder (degree of anxiety and worry, ability to control anxiety/worry, anxiety-related physical symptoms, level of distress created by anxiety/worry/physical symptoms). Both examples illustrate how trends are measured in dimensional diagnoses. Patterns assess a person's standing on one dimension relative to his or her standing on another dimension (**idiographic comparison**). In making a differential diagnosis between mania and schizophrenia, for instance, we might contrast an individual on four dimensions: (1) thought disorder, (2) auditory hallucinations, (3) grandiosity, and (4) flight of ideas. Someone who achieves higher standing on the thought disorder and auditory hallucinations dimensions relative to the grandiosity and flight of ideas dimensions would receive a diagnosis of schizophrenia, whereas someone who achieves the opposite pattern would receive a diagnosis of bipolar disorder. Trends reflect the commonalities, and patterns represent the differences that go into dimensional diagnoses.

Extending the dimensional diagnostic scheme to Will, I would ask the reader to conceive of a dimensional diagnosis of ASPD composed of two dimensions: (1) adult antisociality and (2) childhood CD. I would start by administering Will the *Structured Clinical Interview for DSM–IV Axis II Personality Disorders (SCID-II)* (First, Gibbon, Spitzer, Williams, & Benjamin, 1997) and conducting a review of available records. Identical to the results reported in the categorical diagnosis section, Will met five of the adult criteria for ASPD (unlawful behavior, impulsivity, aggressiveness, recklessness, and irresponsibility) and six of the CD criteria for ASPD (initiating physical fights, being physically cruel to people, deliberately destroying other's property, breaking into someone's house or car, stealing items of nontrivial value, and running away from home and staying out overnight at least twice). Trend analysis reveals that Will demonstrates moderately high standing on both the adult antisocial and childhood CD dimensions. Pattern analysis indicates that Will achieves roughly equal standing on the two dimensions believed to contribute to ASPD.

Constructing a Dimensional Diagnosis for the Criminal Lifestyle

An oft-repeated statement in texts on diagnostics and psychopathology is that a diagnosis that incorporates elements of both a categorical and dimensional nature should be superior to a diagnosis, which considers only categorical or dimensional elements alone. However, when the latent structure of a construct is known to be categorical or dimensional then the diagnostic system should fall in line with the known structure of the construct. In light of the consistent dimensional results obtained in taxometric research on the criminal lifestyle and other crime-related constructs, a dimensional diagnostic system is required. The dimensional model of criminal lifestyle diagnosis makes use of two assessment devices, (1) the **Lifestyle Criminality Screening Form** (LCSF) and (2) the **Psychological Inventory of Criminal Thinking Styles** (PICTS), which are designed to analyze trends and identify patterns.

Lifestyle Criminality Screening Form

The LCSF (Walters, White, & Denney, 1991) is a 14-item chart audit procedure used to assess the four behavioral styles of a criminal lifestyle: (1) irresponsibility, (2) self-indulgence, (3) interpersonal intrusiveness, and (4) social rule breaking. The LCSF produces a total score (range = 0 to 22) and four subsection scores (ranges = 0 to 5 or 0 to 6). As a chart audit procedure, the LCSF is scored from information found in an offender's central file or presentence investigation (PSI) report. One advantage of the LCSF is that it does not require direct contact with the individual being evaluated; one disadvantage is that it cannot be scored without adequate file data. The irresponsibility subsection of the LCSF is composed of four items (failure to provide child support, school dropout, longest job ever held, fired from job or quit without another job to go to), the self-indulgence subsection is composed of three items (drug/alcohol abuse, marital background, tattoos), the interpersonal intrusiveness subsection is composed of four items (intrusive instant offense, history of prior intrusive offenses, use of a weapon during instant offense, domestic violence), and the social rule breaking subsection is composed of three items (prior arrests, age at first arrest, history of disruptive behavior in school). Five items from the irresponsibility and self-indulgence subsections form an impulse (I) factor, and six items from the interpersonal intrusiveness and social rule breaking subsections form a violation (V) factor (range of scores = 0–9 for both factors).

Reliability

The **reliability** of a psychological test is the consistency of measurement between groups of items, raters, or time periods. Analyses conducted on a large sample of LCSF protocols (N = 1,153) reveal that the full 14-item LCSF possesses moderate **internal consistency** (correlations between items). The internal consistency of the four LCSF subsections, however, is poor to low-moderate. Whereas the internal consistency of the V factor is comparable to the full scale, the internal consistency of the I factor is weak. The **interrater reliability** (agreement between raters) of the full LCSF scale is high. In a combined sample of 40 males independently rated by two coders with approximately one-half hour of training each in scoring the LCSF, absolute agreement was high for the total score and V factor score and moderate to moderately high for the I factor score and four subsection scores.

Content Validity

Validity is the extent to which a test measures what it purports to measure. **Content validity** is the degree to which a test appraises the entire domain of content encompassed by the construct the test is designed to assess. Whereas the content validity of the LCSF instrument has not been formally evaluated, the fact that the LCSF covers the four behavioral styles that define a criminal lifestyle implies that the LCSF does, in fact, possess content validity.

Predictive Validity

The ability of a test to predict future outcomes is an important indicant of its validity. Over a dozen studies have examined the **predictive validity** of the LCSF, the results of which are summarized in Table 3.2. The weighted and unweighted effect size estimates—correlation coefficient (r) and area under the curve (AUC) of a receiver operating characteristic (ROC) curve—indicate that the LCSF is a low-moderate predictor of institutional adjustment and recidivism. Correlations (association between two variables) of .10, .24, and .37 are said to represent small, moderate, and large effect size estimates, respectively, whereas AUC (classification accuracy) values of .556, .639, and .714 are said to represent small, moderate, and large effect size estimates, respectively (Rice & Harris, 2005). It should be noted that the V and I factor scales tend to predict different outcomes. Whereas the V scale appears to do a better job of predicting institutional infractions and recidivism, the I scale does a better job of predicting poor social and occupational adjustment. The total LCSF score is still a better predictor of institutional misconduct and community recidivism than either of the two factor scores, however.

Table 3.2 The Lifestyle Criminality Screening Form as a Predictor of Institutional Adjustment and Recidivism

Study	Location	Subject Characteristics			Description[1]	Outcome	Average Follow-Up	r^2	AUC^3
		N	Sex	Age					
Walters, Revella, & Baltrusaitis (1990)	USA	79	M	20–68	federal probationers/ parolees	general recidivism	12 mos.	.37	.724
Walters (1991) study 1	USA	40	M	Adult	maximum security federal prisoners	disciplinary report	6 mos.	.13	–
		40	M	Adult	minimum security federal prisoners	disciplinary report	6 mos.	.39	–
Walters (1991) study 2	USA	50	M	Adult	maximum security federal prisoners	disciplinary report	6 mos.	–.08	–
		50	M	Adult	minimum security federal prisoners	disciplinary report	6 mos.	.59	–
Walters & Chlumsky (1993)	USA	100	M	19–71	released state prisoners	reincarceration	18 mos.	.56	.851
Walters (1996)	USA	542	M	19–72	medium security federal prisoners	disciplinary report	24 mos.	.23	.630
Walters (1997b)	USA	63	M	21–53	released federal prisoners	revocation/new arrest	27 mos.	.39	.722
Walters & Cosgrove (1997)	USA	50	M	Adult	federal probationers/	revocation/ technical violation	30 mos.	.09	.584

Study	Subject Characteristics				Description[1]	Outcome	Average Follow-Up	r^2	AUC[3]
	Location	N	Sex	Age					
Walters & McDonough (1998)	USA	52	M	23–70	federal probationers/ parolees	revocation/ technical violation	36 mos.	.34	.733
Walters & Elliott (1999)	USA	100	F	22–61	federal prison inmates	disciplinary report	18 mos.	.18	.629
Kroner & Mills (2001)	Canada	87	M	18–55	federal prison inmates	minor misconduct	307 days	.21	.611
						major misconduct	307 days	.13	.527
						total convictions	307 days	.22	.620
						violent convictions	307 days	.12	.617
						revocations	307 days	.15	.591
Wexler, Melnick, & Cao (2004)	USA	679	M	Adult	released state prisoners	general recidivism	36 mos.	.08	–
Walters (2005c)	USA	102	M	21–55	maximum security federal prisoners	disciplinary report	24 mos.	.25	.662

(Continued)

(Continued)

Study	Location	Subject Characteristics			Description[1]	Outcome	Average Follow-Up	r^2	AUC[3]
		N	Sex	Age					
Walters & Kotch (2007)	USA	114	M	23–67	federal probationers/ parolees	technical violation	21 mos.	.30	.672
						general recidivism	21 mos.	.19	.662
Meta-analysis effect sizes (k = 17/12)									
Unweighted effect size (r or AUC)								.25	.671
Unweighted 95% confidence interval								.21–	.642–
								.29	.699
Weighted effect size (r or AUC)								.21	.662
Weighted 95% confidence interval								.17–	.631–
								.25	.690

[1]Description of the sample.

[2]Point-biserial correlations between continuous variable (LCSF) and a dichotomized outcome measure, except for Walters (1991) study 2 in which Pearson Product Moment Correlations were calculated between the continuous LCSF score and the total number of disciplinary reports received in a 6-month period.

[3]Area under the curve (AUC) using the receiver operating characteristics (ROC) approach.

Construct Validity

Construct validity is an estimate of the theoretical integrity of a psychological test or procedure. Often phrased as a question, construct validity asks how well a test measures the theoretical construct it is designed to measure. One way to establish the construct validity of a psychological test or procedure is through factor analysis. A confirmatory factor analysis of the LCSF on a group of 542 male medium-security federal inmates revealed the superiority of the theoretical four-factor model (irresponsibility, self-indulgence, interpersonal intrusiveness, social rule breaking) over alternative one- and two-factor models (Walters, 1997a). The results of this study are limited, however, by the fact that the statistical procedure used, standard structural equation modeling (SEM), requires continuous indicators and the LCSF items are categorical (two or three ordered categories).

To correct for the limitations of the Walters (1997a) investigation, a second confirmatory factor analysis was performed using a procedure from *Mplus* (Muthén & Muthén, 2007), which makes allowances for categorical indicators. After an exploratory factor analysis on an independent sample of LCSF protocols revealed the presence of two factors, violation (interpersonal intrusiveness and social rule breaking) and impulse (irresponsibility and self-indulgence), when three LCSF items were removed (school dropout, longest job ever held, use of a weapon during instant offense) a confirmatory factor analysis was conducted. This confirmatory factor analysis revealed that the theoretical four-factor model achieved a significantly better fit than a general one-factor model, although the V-I two-factor model achieved a significantly better fit than both the one-factor and four-factor models.

Another way to assess the construct validity of a psychological procedure is to correlate it with measures of the same or related constructs. Being a chart audit form, the LCSF would show proof of construct validity if it were to correlate with chart audit, interview, and self-report measures of criminality, psychopathy, and antisocial personality. The LCSF total score has been found to correlate substantially with the Salient Factor Score (SFS) (Hoffman & Beck, 1985), Psychopathy Checklist-Revised (PCL-R) (Hare, 2003), and a clinical diagnosis of ASPD. Specifically, the total LCSF score correlated –.54 with the SFS (which is negatively coded for risk, as opposed to the LCSF, which is positively coded for risk) in a group of 24 U.S. federal probationers (Walters & McDonough, 1998), .61 with the PCL-R total score in a group of 108 Canadian prisoners (Walters & Di Fazio, 2000), and .64 with a clinical diagnosis of ASPD in a group of 100 New Mexico state prison inmates (Walters & Chlumsky, 1993). The LCSF also correlates with self-reported antisocial personality and criminal thinking but at a significantly lower level ($r = .18–.22$) than it correlates with chart- and interview-based measures of antisocial personality, psychopathy, and criminal risk (Walters, 2010a; Walters & Geyer, 2005).

Walters and Di Fazio (2000) observed an interesting relationship between the LCSF and the two PCL-R factor scores when the PCL-R was divided into its two principal components. The LCSF, in fact, correlated two and one-half times higher with Factor 2 of the PCL-R (chronically unstable and antisocial lifestyle) than with Factor 1 of the PCL-R (selfish, callous, and remorseless use of others). What this means is that the LCSF is more strongly allied with the impulsive and antisocial features of the PCL-R than with the interpersonal and affective features. Behavioral impulsivity and antisociality consequently figure more prominently in the criminal lifestyle than do the personality characteristics emphasized by Cleckley (1941/1976) and Hare (1996) in their theories of psychopathy.

Interpretive Process

The LCSF can be hierarchically organized (see Figure 3.1). At the top of this hierarchy sits the total LCSF score. A practical breakdown of the total LCSF score into three categories of lifestyle involvement—high (LCSF total score = 10–22), moderate (LCSF total score = 7–9), and low (LCSF total score = 0–6)—has been proposed and can be useful in managing risk (Walters, 1997a). In the LCSF normative sample ($N = 1,153$), the greatest number of protocols fell into the low involvement/risk category (38.7%), the second largest number of protocols fell into the high involvement/risk category (35.6%), and the smallest number of protocols fell into the moderate involvement/risk category (25.8%). It should be kept in mind, however, that because valuable information can be lost when a score designed to represent a dimensional construct is sectioned into categories, the total score should also be reported. What I have learned in over 25 years of clinical practice is that a large difference within a category (e.g., 10 and 17) is usually more significant than a small difference between categories (e.g., 9 and 10).

The second step of the LCSF interpretive process involves comparing the LCSF V factor score with the LCSF I factor score in what has become known as the V-I index. The two LCSF factor scores, although not as reliable nor as internally consistent as the total LCSF score, are significantly more reliable and internally consistent than the four subsection scores, a consequence of the fact that they comprise twice as many items as the subsection scores. By comparing the two factor scores, a clinician can get

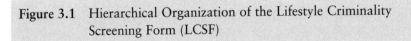

Figure 3.1 Hierarchical Organization of the Lifestyle Criminality
Screening Form (LCSF)

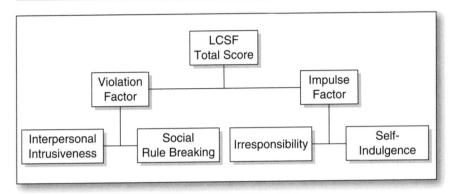

a sense of the offender's primary mode of behavioral deviance. A V-I difference of at least 3 raw score points (population base rate = 30.9%) is said to be significant, a V-I difference of 2 raw score points (population base rate = 23.7%) is said to be suggestive, and a V-I difference under 2 raw score points (population base rate = 45.4%) is considered nonsignificant. A difference that favors V is likely to be manifest in behavioral deviance of an aggressive or violating nature, whereas a difference that favors I is likely to be manifest in behavioral deviance of a social, academic, or occupational maladjustment nature.

The third step of the LCSF interpretive process is to examine the four subsection scores. Given the moderate reliability and low to modest internal consistency of the four subsection scores, I would recommend restricting interpretation to very high (5–6) and very low (0) subsection scores. For subsections i, ii, and iv, low (0) scores range in frequency from 11.0 to 23.6% and high (5–6) scores range in frequency from 2.8 to 7.0%. For subsection iii, a score of 0 is common (42.9%) but a high score should be considered 4 to 5 given the relative infrequency of a score of 4 or higher on subsection iii (9.0%).

Psychological Inventory of Criminal Thinking Styles

The PICTS (Walters, 1995a) is an 80-item self-report inventory designed to assess the eight thinking styles believed to be instrumental in maintaining a criminal lifestyle. Each item on the PICTS is rated on a 4-point scale: *strongly agree, agree, uncertain,* and *disagree.* Strongly agree responses receive 4 points, agree responses receive 3 points, uncertain responses receive 2 points, and disagree responses receive 1 point on all scales except Defensiveness-revised (Df-r) where point values are reversed (strongly agree = 1, agree = 2, uncertain = 3, disagree = 4). The PICTS produces two 8-item validity scales—(1) Confusion-revised (Cf-r) and (2) Df-r—and eight nonoverlapping 8-item thinking style scales— (1) mollification (Mo), (2) cutoff (Co), (3) entitlement (En), (4) power orientation (Po), (5) sentimentality (Sn), (6) superoptimism (So), (7) cognitive indolence (Ci), and (8) discontinuity (Ds). It also produces four nonoverlapping 10-item factor scales—(1) Problem Avoidance (PRB), (2) Infrequency (INF), (3) Self-Assertion/Deception (AST), and (4) Denial of Harm (DNH)—two content scales—(1) Current Criminal Thinking (CUR) and (2) Historical Criminal Thinking (HIS)—two composite scales— (1) Proactive Criminal Thinking (P) and (2) Reactive Criminal Thinking (R)—and one general score—General Criminal Thinking (GCT), which is the sum of the raw scores for the eight thinking style scales.

Reliability

Internal consistency is moderate for the thinking style scales, high for the composite scales, and very high for the GCT score. **Test-retest reliability** (correlation between two different administrations of the same test) for the eight thinking style scales is moderately high after 2 weeks and moderate after 12 weeks. For the P and R composite scales, test-retest reliability is high after 2 weeks and moderate after 12 weeks. The most stable results are obtained by the GCT score with high test-retest reliability estimates after 2 weeks and moderately high estimates after 12 weeks.

Content Validity

To the extent that the PICTS is designed to assess the eight thinking styles believed to support and maintain a criminal lifestyle, it would seem to possess content validity. In addition, inmates familiar with the lifestyle concept were instrumental in the development of PICTS item content and professionals familiar with lifestyle theory have verified the relevance of many of the PICTS items. These three factors suggest that the PICTS possesses a reasonable degree of content validity.

Predictive Validity

Point-biserial correlations calculated from 12 different samples have examined the ability of the PICTS to predict either institutional adjustment or release outcome. The results of these analyses are reported in Table 3.3. Whereas the PICTS thinking style scales, composite scales, and GCT score have registered significant mean weighted and unweighted effect sizes, the effect sizes are, for the most part, modest. ROC analyses also denote a modest level of predictive efficacy for many of the PICTS scales, with Co (mean AUC = .626), Ds (mean AUC = .636), P (mean AUC = .616), R (mean AUC = .642), and GCT (mean AUC = .643) achieving the best results. Owing to the fact that the rate of false positive determinations using a cutting score of 60T on most PICTS scales is two and one half times higher than the rate of false negative determinations (Walters, 2010a), a low score on a PICTS scale will normally do a better job of predicting good outcomes than a high score does of predicting poor outcomes.

Construct Validity

An exploratory factor analysis with image extraction and oblimin (oblique) rotation performed on the 450 male inmates from the original PICTS derivation sample revealed the presence of four factors. These four factors were subsequently labeled (1) problem avoidance (PRB), (2) infrequency (INF), (3) self-assertion/deception (AST), and (4) denial of harm (DNH) (Walters, 1995a). The factor structure of the PICTS was cross-validated in an exploratory factor analysis of 227 female state and federal inmates (Walters, Elliott, & Miscoll, 1998). However, other investigators using different methodologies have proposed alternative factor structures for the PICTS. In a second-order factor analysis of correlations from the original derivation sample, Egan, McMurran, Richardson, and Blair (2000) uncovered two factors: (1) "lack of thoughtfulness" and (2) "willful criminality." Administering the PICTS to a group of adult male English prisoners, Palmer and Hollin (2003) found support for a single general PICTS factor but were unable to cross-validate this pattern in a group of young adult male English offenders (Palmer & Hollin, 2004b). In separate confirmatory factor analyses of male and female PICTS profiles, Walters (2005b) uncovered support for the original four-factor (PRB, INF, AST, DNH) and eight-factor (Mo, Co, En, Po, Sn, So, Ci, Ds) models. The general consensus at the present time is that the PICTS factor structure consists of two major factors (PRB or lack of thoughtfulness and AST or willful criminality) and two minor factors (INF and DNH).

Table 3.3 The Psychological Inventory of Criminal Thinking Styles as a Predictor of Institutional Adjustment and Recidivism

Participant Characteristics							Correlations[a]										
Study	Location	N	Sex	Description[b]	Outcome	Average Follow-Up	Mo	Co	En	Po	Sn	So	Ci	Ds	P	R	GCT
Walters (1996)	United States	536	M	Federal inmates[1]	Disciplinary reports	23 mos.	.05	.11	.12	.14	.11	.06	.08	.08	.10	.11	.12
Walters (1997b)	United States	63	M	Federal inmates[1]	Recidivism	27 mos.	.10	.31	.17	.15	.16	.03	.06	.26	.22	.25	.25
Walters & Elliott (1999)	United States	118	F	State inmates	Recidivism	60 mos.	.17	.16	.20	.13	.38	.10	.19	.20	.19	.19	.26
	United States	100	F	Federal inmates	Disciplinary reports	18 mos.	.25	.33	.37	.35	.22	.24	.28	.32	.29	.35	.38
Palmer & Hollin (2004a)	Great Britain	174	M	Prison inmates	Recidivism	24 mos.	.09	.10	.09	.09	-.01	.23	.05	.12	–	–	.13
Walters (2006b)	United States	226	M	Federal inmates[1]	Recidivism	30 mos.	.11	.25	.26	.17	.16	.16	.24	.26	.25	.26	.26
Walters (2006d)	United States	219	M	Federal inmates[1]	Disciplinary reports	24 mos.	.09	.27	.14	.11	.10	.05	.16	.16	.14	.24	.18
		191	M	Federal inmates[2]	Disciplinary reports	24 mos.	.11	.08	-.02	.10	.09	.08	.08	.10	.00	.13	.10
Walters & Mandell (2007)	United States	136	M	Federal inmates[1]	Disciplinary reports	24 mos.	.10	.16	.22	.14	.07	.11	.20	.20	.26	.19	.19

	Participant Characteristics						Correlations[a]										
Study	Location	N	Sex	Description[b]	Outcome	Average Follow-Up	Mo	Co	En	Po	Sn	So	Ci	Ds	P	R	GCT
Walters & Schlauch (2008)	United States	159	M	Federal inmates[1]	Disciplinary reports	24 mos.	.08	.21	.28	.15	.12	.20	.21	.21	.26	.21	.23
Gonsalves, Scalora, & Huss (2009)	United States	117	M	Forensic patients	Recidivism	49 mos.	.17	.27	.28	.24	.16	.28	.16	.20	.29	.23	.27
Walters (2009c)	United States	107	M	Federal inmates[1]	Recidivism	24 mos.	.12	.26	.19	.12	.24	.10	.22	.25	.21	.28	.25
Walters (2011b)	United States	178	M	Federal inmates[1]	Recidivism	32 mos.	.11	.19	.19	.10	.12	.23	.16	.25	.20	.23	.22
Meta-analysis effect sizes (k = 12)[c]																	
Unweighted effect size (r)							.12	.21	.19	.15	.15	.14	.16	.20	.20	.22	.22
Unweighted 95% confidence interval							.08–	.16–	.13–	.11–	.09–	.09–	.12–	.16–	.15–	.18–	.17–
							.15	.26	.25	.20	.20	.19	.20	.24	.26	.26	.26
Weighted effect size (r)							.10	.18	.17	.14	.13	.13	.15	.17	.18	.20	.19

(Continued)

51

(Continued)

	Participant Characteristics							Correlations[a]										
Study	Location	N	Sex	Description[b]	Outcome	Average Follow-Up		Mo	Co	En	Po	Sn	So	Ci	Ds	P	R	GCT
Weighted 95%								.06–	.14–	.13–	.10–	.09–	.09–	.11–	.13–	.13–	.16–	.15–
confidence interval								.14	.22	.21	.18	.17	.17	.19	.21	.22	.24	.23

Note: Ci = cognitive indolence; Co = cutoff; Ds = discontinuity; En = entitlement; GCT = General Criminal Thinking; Mo = mollification; P = Proactive Criminal Thinking; Po = power orientation; R = Reactive Criminal Thinking; Sn = sentimentality; So = superoptimism

a. Point-biserial or Pearson product moment correlations between the continuous Psychological Inventory of Criminal Thinking Styles (PICTS) scales and dichotomized or continuous measures of outcome.

b. Description of the sample.

c. k = number of effect sizes compiled.

1. Medium security; 2. Maximum security

The construct validity of a psychological test or procedure can be further evaluated by calculating convergent and discriminant validity coefficients between the measure and a series of outside criteria. Walters and Geyer (2005) computed correlations between the Personality Assessment Inventory (PAI) (Morey, 2007), Antisocial Features (ANT), Somatic Complaints (SOM), Anxiety (ANX), Depression (DEP), Mania (MAN), Paranoia (PAR), and Schizophrenia (SCZ) scales, on the one hand, and the PICTS Mo, Co, En, Po, Sn, So, Ci, and Ds scales, on the other hand, for the purpose of assessing the convergent and discriminant validity of the PICTS thinking style scales. ANT-PICTS coefficients in the .30 to .50 range suggest moderate convergent validity (Fiske & Campbell, 1992), whereas 6% to 33% comparison violations (SOM/ANX/DEP/MAN/PAR/SCZ-PICTS correlations that equal or exceed ANT-PICTS correlations) indicate moderate discriminant validity (Bagozzi & Yi, 1991). Six out of the eight ANT-PICTS correlations fell into the moderate range of convergent validity whereas the presence of relatively few comparison violations (18.8%) denoted moderate discriminant validity.

Additional studies have examined the manner in which the PICTS correlates in theoretically meaningful ways with other psychometric indices. Studies relating the PICTS to the NEO-five factor model (Costa & McCrae, 1992), for instance, have found that the PICTS thinking style scales correlate positively with neuroticism and negatively with agreeableness and conscientiousness (Bulten, Nijman, & van der Staak, 2009; Otter & Egan, 2007). The construct validity of the PICTS composite scales has been verified in a series of studies where the P scale has been found to correlate with positive outcome expectancies for crime and prior arrests for instrumental/proactive crimes like robbery and burglary and the R scale has been found to correlate with hostile attribution biases and prior arrests for hostile/reactive crimes like assault and domestic violence (Walters, 2007c; Walters, Frederick, & Schlauch, 2007). Healy and O'Donnell (2006) administered the PICTS to a group of Irish probationers and discovered that the R scales of Co, Ci, and Ds were the only PICTS scales to correlate (negatively) with secondary desistance (long-term cessation of offending). Finally, a study correlating the PICTS with worldview beliefs showed that several of the PICTS thinking style scales correlated with a mechanistic, unequal, and malevolent worldview (Walters, 2007a).

Interpretive Process

The first step in the interpretive process is to eliminate invalid PICTS protocols by examining the T-score levels (a T-score is a normalized score with a mean of 50 and standard deviation of 10) of the Cf-r and Df-r scales. T-scores of 80 or higher on the Cf-r denote that the PICTS may have been compromised by a "fake bad" response style, reading/language difficulties, or haphazard responding. T-scores of 100 or higher are clearly invalid and suggest that the protocol cannot even be used for research purposes. Conversely, T-scores of 65 or higher on the Df-r suggest that the PICTS has been unduly restricted by a defensive or "fake good" response style and that the thinking style and other clinical scales have probably been suppressed as a result. In the event any of these validity configurations are observed, extreme caution should be exercised when interpreting the GCT score, P and R composite scales, or PICTS thinking style scales.

Once it has been determined that the PICTS profile is valid the next step is to interpret the GCT score. The GCT lies at the top of the PICTS hierarchy (see Figure 3.2), much like the total LCSF score sits on top of the LCSF hierarchy and belief systems are on the top tier of the criminal thinking hierarchy. T-scores of 50 or higher on the GCT (top half of the normative sample) denote the presence of a belief system supportive of crime and signal significant commitment to and identification with a criminal lifestyle. Scores below 50 on the GCT do not necessarily mean that the individual is free of a criminal lifestyle but they do imply that the criminal belief system is weak, absent, or hidden. Most of the time when the GCT score is below 50 none of the composite or thinking style scales will be elevated. On rare occasions, however, a composite or thinking style scale will be elevated even though the GCT is below 50. Consequently, the remaining steps of the interpretive process should not be skipped simply because the GCT score is below 50.

The third step of the interpretive process is to compare the two composite scales: (1) P and (2) R. When P is greater than or equal to a T-score of 55 and 10 or more T-score points higher than the R scale, there is a high probability that the individual's criminal thinking is deliberate, planned, and goal-directed (proactive-oriented). When R is greater than or equal to a T-score of 55 and 10 or more T-score points higher than the P scale, there is a strong likelihood that the individual's criminal thinking is impulsive, disorganized, and aimless (reactive-oriented). Positive outcome expectancies for crime seem to drive P, whereas hostile attribution biases are more often the impetus behind R. A possible pattern is inferred when P or R is between 50 and 54 and 6 to 9 T-score points higher than the alternate composite scale.

The fourth step of the interpretation process is to review elevations on the eight thinking style scales. The recommended procedure is to identify the T-score elevations ≥ 60 for the top one to three thinking style scales. These are the thinking styles most apt to influence the respondent's actions and decisions. Averaging the T-scores of the one to three most highly elevated

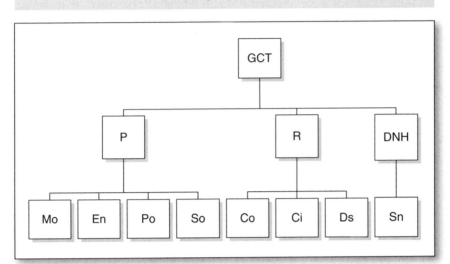

Figure 3.2   Hierarchical Organization of the Psychological Inventory of Criminal Thinking Styles

Note: Ci = cognitive indolence; Co = cutoff; DNH = Denial of Harm; Ds = discontinuity; En = entitlement; GCT = General Criminal Thinking score; Mo = mollification; P = Proactive Criminal Thinking; Po = power orientation; R = Reactive Criminal Thinking; Sn = sentimentality; So = superoptimism

thinking style scales and contrasting this average with the mean T-score of all remaining thinking style scales at or above a T-score of 50 reveals whether the PICTS thinking styles form a differentiated or undifferentiated pattern. Take, for instance, the following thinking style T-score configuration: Mo = 55, Co = 66, En = 46, Po = 58, Sn = 59, So = 58, Ci = 60, Ds = 64. A three-scale elevation (Co + Ci + Ds/3) yields an average T-score of 63 and a contrast average T-score (Mo + Po + Sn + So/4) of 58. Because these figures do not differ by more than 5 T-score points, this is an undifferentiated profile. However, when we contrast the two-scale elevation (Co + Ds/2) with the average of the remaining thinking style scales with TS > 50 (Mo + Po + Sn + So + Ci/5) we get average T-score values of 65 and 58, respectively, which do differ by more than 5 T-score points, thus making the Co/Ds two-scale elevation a differentiated profile.

An undifferentiated profile can still be analyzed but the interpretation is often less precise than interpreting a differentiated profile. Regardless of whether the profile is differentiated or undifferentiated the examiner provides the respondent with information about the one to three most highly elevated thinking style scales with suggestions on how these thoughts and beliefs might best be managed. According to lifestyle theory, one or two thinking styles are easier to manage than all eight. Therefore, by disputing the top one to three thinking styles the individual can prevent an avalanche of negative consequences created when all eight thinking styles become active at the same time. It is hypothesized that the most elevated thinking styles will typically appear in one's thinking before the other five to seven thinking styles and that by challenging these more central beliefs the "snowball effect" that leads to relapse can be prevented.

Analyzing Trends and Identifying Patterns

Trends indicate movement in a particular direction—in this case up and down a continuum. Patterns, on the other hand, focus on the relationship between components—in this case differences between dimensions. Trend analysis of the LCSF begins with the total LCSF score, moves through I and V, and ends with the four subsection scores, although only extreme scores on the subsections are included in the analysis because of low reliability in two of the LCSF subsections. Trend analysis with the PICTS begins with the GCT, moves through P and R, and ends with the eight thinking style scales. The focus of trend analysis for both the LCSF and PICTS, however, is the upper tier of each hierarchy, the LCSF total score with respect to the LCSF and the GCT score with respect to the PICTS. Pattern identification can include comparing individual LCSF subsections or individual PICTS thinking style scales, but the two patterns that should always be examined when conducting a lifestyle assessment are the difference between the V and I factor scales of the LCSF (V-I index) and the difference between the P and R composite scales of the PICTS. Trend and pattern analysis of the three individuals profiled in the first three chapters of this book—Will (this chapter), Pete (Chapter 1), and Rick (Chapter 2)—serve to illustrate how the lifestyle assessment process works.

Trend and Pattern Analysis of Will's Lifestyle Criminality Screening Form and Psychological Inventory of Criminal Thinking Styles

Will's LCSF and PICTS results are reproduced in Table 3.4. In Will's case, as well as in the other two cases, the validity scales were within normal limits and for the sake of simplicity will not be considered further. Trend analysis of the LCSF indicates that Will's overall level of criminal lifestyle involvement is high as represented by a total LCSF score of 12 (82nd percentile). Pattern analysis of the LCSF V-I index suggests that Will's criminal involvements are roughly equally split between impulsive actions and violating behavior. The consistency or absence of patterning in his criminal involvements is further evidenced by his scores on the four LCSF subsections (i.e., three in all four cases). Trend analysis of the PICTS indicates a significant level of criminal lifestyle commitment and identification as measured by a T-score of 65 on the GCT score and elevations of 60 or higher on seven of the eight thinking style scales. Patterns are more difficult to decipher, however, because Will's scores on the P and R composite scales are identical, and his thinking style profile is undifferentiated. Will is the picture of consistency in the sense that he demonstrates a consistent trend toward involvement in, commitment to, and identification with a criminal lifestyle but no differential patterns within these involvements, commitments, and identifications.

Table 3.4 Will's Lifestyle Criminality Screening Form and Psychological Inventory of Criminal Thinking Styles Results

Lifestyle Criminality Screening Form (LCSF)	
Overall Involvement	
Total score	12 (82nd percentile)
Risk level	High
Factor Scores	
Violation (V) factor score	5
Impulse (I) factor score	5
V-I index	5:5
Subsection Scores	
Irresponsibility	3
Self-indulgence	3
Interpersonal intrusiveness	3
Social rule breaking	3

(Continued)

(Continued)

Psychological Inventory of Criminal Thinking Styles (PICTS)	
Higher-Order Factor	
General Criminal Thinking (GCT)	65
Composite Scales	
Proactive Criminal Thinking (P)	56
Reactive Criminal Thinking (R)	56
Thinking Style Scales	
Mollification (Mo)	63
Cutoff (Co)	66
Entitlement (En)	64
Power Orientation (Po)	67
Sentimentality (Sn)	62
Superoptimism (So)	52
Cognitive Indolence (Ci)	62
Discontinuity (Ds)	61

Note: LCSF scores are raw scores, and PICTS scores are T-scores.

Trend and Pattern Analysis of Pete's Lifestyle Criminality Screening Form and Psychological Inventory of Criminal Thinking Styles

Pete's total score on the LCSF (11, 73rd percentile) indicates a clear trend toward criminal lifestyle involvement (see Table 3.5). The V-I index (8:3) shows a strong pattern of V over I. Hence, the nature of Pete's criminal involvement is to violate the rules of society and the rights of others rather than engage in reckless and impulsive behavior. His elevated score on the interpersonal intrusiveness subsection of the LCSF implies a propensity for encroaching on the rights of others. The trend observed on the PICTS reveals

Pete's strong commitment to and identification with a criminal lifestyle (GCT = 71), whereas the 28-point gap between P and R in favor of the former connotes that Pete's pattern is to scheme, plot, and plan (P) rather than react on impulse (R). In addition, positive outcome expectancies for crime, probably some combination of excitement and power, likely fuel the majority of his criminal actions. Pete displays a differentiated PICTS profile with marked elevations on En and Po. This thinking style pattern implies that Pete often misidentifies wants as needs and tries to exert power and control over others. Pete's relatively low score on the Co scale indicates that he can be patient when casing a target or selecting a victim. His relatively high score on the So scale indicates that he believes in the ultimate success of his criminal ventures and his relatively high score on the Sn scale indicates that he probably understands the terror he inflicts on his victims, which may be a driving force behind some of his crimes.

Table 3.5   Pete's Lifestyle Criminality Screening Form and Psychological Inventory of Criminal Thinking Styles Results

Lifestyle Criminality Screening Form (LCSF)	
Overall Involvement	
Total score	11 (73rd percentile)
Risk level	High
Factor Scores	
Violation (V) factor score	8
Impulse (I) factor score	3
V-I index	8:3
Subsection Scores	
Irresponsibility	1
Self-indulgence	2
Interpersonal intrusiveness	4
Social rule breaking	4

(Continued)

(Continued)

Psychological Inventory of Criminal Thinking Styles (PICTS)	
Higher-Order Factor	
General Criminal Thinking (GCT)	71
Composite Scales	
Proactive Criminal Thinking (P)	84
Reactive Criminal Thinking (R)	56
Thinking Style Scales	
Mollification (Mo)	53
Cutoff (Co)	48
Entitlement (En)	90
Power Orientation (Po)	75
Sentimentality (Sn)	65
Superoptimism (So)	69
Cognitive Indolence (Ci)	66
Discontinuity (Ds)	68

Note: LCSF scores are raw scores and PICTS scores are T-scores.

Trend and Pattern Analysis of Rick's Lifestyle Criminality Screening Form and Psychological Inventory of Criminal Thinking Styles

Trend analysis of Rick's LCSF results, as reflected in Table 3.6, reveals that Rick demonstrates strong prior involvement in a criminal lifestyle (total LCSF score = 12, 82nd percentile). Pattern analysis of the LCSF, however, provides little useful information in that Rick's V-I index is 5:5. Fortunately, the PICTS offers more information than the LCSF, which is often the case when self-report measures like the PICTS are compared to static risk procedures like the LCSF. On the PICTS there is a clear trend in favor of a significant level of commitment and identification with the criminal lifestyle (GCT = 57), particularly the power

(Po = 65) and impulse-irresponsibility (Co = 60; Ds = 60) aspects. Like Pete, Rick produced a differentiated PICTS profile in that the average of the top three thinking style scales (Po, Co, Ds) is 6 points higher than the average of the remaining thinking styles scales > T-score of 50 (En, So, Ci). Pattern analysis of the PICTS reveals that Rick's criminal commitments and identifications are more impulsive and spontaneous than they are thought out and planned (R > P by 12 T-score points). As was noted previously in my discussion of Pete's PICTS results, low scores on a PICTS thinking style scale can sometimes be as significant as high scores on a PICTS thinking style scale. Rick's low scores on Mo and Sn indicate that he generally does not rationalize his actions by blaming others (Mo) or performing various good deeds (Sn), though his lack of empathy (Sn) can result in inadvertent harm to others in comparison to Pete who seems to enjoy the terror he inflicts on others.

Table 3.6   Rick's Lifestyle Criminality Screening Form and Psychological Inventory of Criminal Thinking Styles Results

Lifestyle Criminality Screening Form (LCSF)	
Overall Involvement	
Total score	12 (82nd percentile)
Risk level	High
Factor Scores	
Violation (V) factor score	5
Impulse (I) factor score	5
V-I index	5:5
Subsection Scores	
Irresponsibility	4
Self-indulgence	3
Interpersonal intrusiveness	1
Social rule breaking	4

(Continued)

(Continued)

Psychological Inventory of Criminal Thinking Styles (PICTS)	
Higher-Order Factor	
General Criminal Thinking (GCT)	57
Composite Scales	
Proactive Criminal Thinking (P)	49
Reactive Criminal Thinking (R)	61
Thinking Style Scales	
Mollification (Mo)	43
Cutoff (Co)	60
Entitlement (En)	54
Power Orientation (Po)	65
Sentimentality (Sn)	44
Superoptimism (So)	56
Cognitive Indolence (Ci)	58
Discontinuity (Ds)	60

Note: LCSF scores are raw scores and PICTS scores are T-scores.

Conclusion

Categorical (signs and symptoms) and dimensional (trends and patterns) models of diagnosis were compared in this chapter. Given strong evidence of dimensional latent structure for crime-related constructs, a dimensional diagnostic system was proposed for the LCSF and PICTS. Despite this, the LCSF and PICTS are far from perfect. One of the principal limitations of the LCSF (its foundation in static indicators and consequent lack of sensitivity to change) is what gave rise to the development of the more dynamic PICTS. The results of a recent study by Rozycki-Lozano, Morgan, Murray, and Varghese (2011) showed that prison and antisocial tattoos are more crimi-nogenic than the amount of skin covered by tattoos, the focus of the third item of the LCSF self-indulgence subsection. If these preliminary results are replicated in future studies, then the LCSF will need to be modified accordingly. In the meantime, one of the principal goals of dimensional assessment with the LCSF and PICTS is finding ways to integrate the static information produced by the LCSF with the dynamic information provided by the PICTS to promote accurate classification, comprehensive assessment, and effective intervention.

Key Terms and Concepts

Categorical Diagnosis

Construct Validity

Content Validity

Dimensional Diagnosis

Idiographic Comparison

Internal Consistency

Interrater Reliability

Lifestyle Criminality
Screening Form

Normative Comparison

Patterns

Predictive Validity

Psychological Inventory of
Criminal Thinking Styles

Reliability

Signs

Symptoms

Test-Retest Reliability

Trends

Validity

4

Assessment

The Criminal Lifestyle in an Appraisal Context

The power of accurate observation is commonly called cynicism by those who have not got it.

George Bernard Shaw (1856–1950)

Tuesday's Child

Grace is a 21-year-old single white female serving an 8-year sentence for child molestation and sexual misconduct with a child. The abuse occurred over a 6-month period when Grace was 20 years old and the two adolescent male victims were 13 and 14. Child molesters are adept at finding jobs and volunteering for positions (e.g., Little League coach, scoutmaster, teacher) that place them in close proximity to children, and Grace was no exception. She gained access to the two boys she abused through her work as a Sunday school teacher at a local church. After developing a relationship with the boys, she invited them over to her apartment and plied them with alcohol. What began as heavy petting soon evolved into oral sex and sexual intercourse. The abuse was discovered when one of the boys told a classmate that he was having sex with his Sunday school teacher. The classmate then reported the abuse to the principal. The police were initially hesitant to arrest Grace, but after speaking with the two boys and their parents they concluded that there was sufficient evidence to make an arrest.

A high school graduate, Grace was attending community college and working part-time as a waitress when she was arrested. She is bright, articulate, and attractive. People who come into contact with Grace are impressed with her manners and seeming maturity. Several of them acknowledged hiring Grace to babysit their children. Quite obviously, they now feel betrayed, although a few of them still believe that Grace is innocent of the sexual abuse charges. Beyond superficial appearances, however, there were several warning signs to suggest that things were not quite as they seemed with Grace. First, when she was growing up, she had many acquaintances but few close friends. Second, although she was never expelled or suspended from school, Grace was often in the vicinity of trouble. Typically she was able to manipulate or maneuver her way out of trouble, letting others take the blame for her misconduct. Third, even though she dated frequently in junior and senior high school, she has never had a serious long-term relationship. Some of the girls accused Grace of being promiscuous, but the rest of the student body assumed the accusations were simply rumors brought on by jealousy.

Psychologically, Grace is guarded when talking about herself, but her defensiveness cannot conceal the cracks in her armor. First of all, she has an arrest record. A review of her file indicates that she was arrested three times before the instant offense. At the age of 16, she was arrested for shoplifting. A year later, she came to police attention for making terroristic threats over the phone. Neither offense resulted in jail time. When she was 19, however, she spent 2 days in jail and received 6 months' probation for theft. The record indicates that Grace stole a little over a $1,000 in jewelry and clothing from a department store. She had successfully completed probation by the time she was arrested on the sexual abuse charges. Grace reports that she has tried both alcohol and marijuana but has never used either substance regularly and gave the impression of looking down on drug users. Grace maintains that she was sexually abused by an adolescent uncle when she was a child. The family could not verify the abuse but neither could they rule it out. Grace always received above average grades in high school and was only a few weeks short of receiving her associate's degree in psychology when she was arrested for the instant offense. She states that her life goal is to work with children.

Clinical Forensic Assessment

Clinical forensic assessment serves three primary functions. The first function is to measure important forensic constructs like psychopathy, antisocial personality, and criminal thinking. The second function is to estimate offender risk and need. The third function is to address specific psychological questions in a criminal or civil court context (competency, responsibility, child custody). This third function will not be discussed further in this chapter. I refer to the first function as **construct assessment** and the second function as **risk assessment**. The most common psychological assessment procedure is the clinical interview, but this approach has been criticized for its poor reliability (Shear et al., 2000). General psychological procedures and inventories like the Rorschach Inkblot Test and Minnesota Multiphasic Personality Inventory (MMPI–2) (Butcher et al., 2001) are frequently employed with forensic/correctional populations, and surveys conducted with forensic (Archer, Buffington-Vollum, Stredny, & Handel, 2006) and correctional (Boothby & Clements, 2000) psychologists indicate that the Rorschach and MMPI–2 are two of the more popular assessment tools used in forensic and correctional settings. In my own research and practice, however, I have rarely found these procedures helpful in answering important forensic questions. Hence, a procedure can be reliable and valid yet still not be useful or relevant for a particular assessment purpose or in a particular assessment context.

According to criteria outlined in a recent Supreme Court decision, *Daubert v. Merrill Dow Pharmaceuticals* (i.e., the **Daubert criteria**), scientific procedures must be both reliable and relevant before they can be admitted into evidence in a legal proceeding. Reliability entails psychometric reliability and validity, whereas relevance is a function of the questions a procedure is capable of answering. The questions that are often of greatest interest to forensic and correctional psychologists are those that involve predicting risk and eliminating need. To the extent that interviews may not always be reliable and general psychological procedures like the MMPI–2 may not always be relevant, psychologists have developed specialized procedures designed to assess forensic constructs and address risk and needs factors in offender populations. This chapter consequently consists of a brief discussion of constructs relevant to the criminal lifestyle and of major risk and needs factors in clinical forensic practice. This will be followed by a review of four broadband assessment procedures that can be used for both construct and risk assessment—(1) **Lifestyle Criminality Screening Form (LCSF)**, (2) **Psychopathy Checklist-Revised** (PCL-R), (3) **Psychological Inventory of Criminal Thinking Styles** (PICTS), and (4) **Level of Service Inventory-Revised** (LSI-R)—and five narrowband assessment procedures that can be used to answer more specific questions of a risk/needs nature.

Construct Assessment

Measuring a forensic construct can be a difficult, frustrating, and time-consuming process. The benefits of accurately assessing a forensic construct, however, make the task of conducting a forensic evaluation well worth the effort. Through construct assessment, we should be able to estimate an individual's position on various dimensions of theoretical interest. For example, in conducting construct assessment using the LCSF, we can map out a person's relative standing on the criminal lifestyle construct (total score) as well as his or her standing on the four subconstructs of irresponsibility, self-indulgence, interpersonal intrusiveness, and social rule breaking (section scores). Using the PICTS, we can map out an individual's relative standing on the criminal thinking construct (General Criminal Thinking [GCT] score), as well as the subconstructs of proactive and reactive criminal thinking (Proactive [P] and Reactive [R] Criminal Thinking composite scores) and mollification (Mo), cutoff (Co), entitlement (En), power orientation (Po), sentimentality (Sn), superoptimism (So), cognitive indolence (Ci), and discontinuity (Ds) (thinking style scales).

As was mentioned in Chapter 2 of this text, other crime-related constructs also contribute to the formation of a criminal lifestyle, psychopathy, and antisocial personality in particular. Measures of psychopathy, such as the Hare PCL-R (Hare, 2003) and the Psychopathic Personality Inventory (PPI) (Lilienfeld & Andrews, 1996), and measures of antisocial personality disorder (ASPD), such as the *Structured Clinical Interview for DSM-IV Axis II Personality Disorders (SCID-II)* (First, Gibbon, Spitzer, Williams, & Benjamin, 1997) and the antisocial personality section of the LSI-R (Andrews & Bonta, 1995), may consequently prove useful in conducting a clinical forensic construct assessment. The current chapter makes use of two criminal lifestyle construct measures (LCSF, PICTS), a psychopathy construct measure (PCL-R), and a multiconstruct measure that covers antisocial personality patterns (LSI-R) to provide a broadband assessment of the criminal lifestyle construct as well as answer questions of relative risk and need.

Risk Assessment

Risk assessment is concerned with evaluating **risk factors** and identifying **dynamic needs**. Speaking within a forensic context, risk factors are variables and conditions that increase a person's odds of institutional maladjustment, violence, or recidivism, whereas dynamic needs are variables and conditions that if addressed could theoretically reduce a person's odds of institutional maladjustment, violence, or recidivism. In many respects, risk factors and needs factors are opposite sides of the same coin. If an individual has a risk factor of associating with criminals then the needs factor would be to learn how to resist negative peer pressure and develop the skills and interests necessary to begin interacting with people who are not involved in crime. In situations where a person abuses alcohol or other drugs, the risk factor is substance misuse and the needs factor is substance abuse treatment either in the form of a traditional 12-step abstinence program or a nontraditional harm reduction behavioral self-control program. The risk factor consequently identifies an area requiring attention whereas the corresponding needs factor highlights potential goals for intervention.

According to the results of several meta-analyses, a finite number of risk and needs factors are capable of predicting and reducing, respectively, such behaviors as institutional misbehavior, violence, and recidivism (Bonta, Law, & Hanson, 1998; Gendreau, Andrews, Goggin, & Chanteloupe, 1992; Gendreau, Goggin, & Law, 1997; Gendreau, Little, & Goggin, 1996; Hanson & Morton-Bourgon, 2004; Simourd & Andrews, 1994). Although there is growing consensus that risk and needs factors are important in forensic and correctional psychology, there is no single risk/needs model upon which most forensic and correctional psychologists rely. One of the more popular models of risk and needs assessment, however, holds that there are eight principal or central risk/needs factors, the first four of which are considered the most important: (1) history of antisocial behavior, (2) antisocial personality pattern, (3) antisocial cognition, (4) antisocial associates, (5) family/marital problems, (6) poor school/work performance, (7) lack of leisure/recreation activities, and (8) substance abuse (Andrews, Bonta, & Wormith, 2006).

Taking the first four ("big four") risk/needs factors, the risk of antisocial history is that the best predictor of future behavior is often past behavior, and the need is to develop noncriminal alternatives to past criminality. Risk with respect to an antisocial personality pattern is supported by research showing that those who are impulsive, selfish, and pleasure seeking are also more apt to violate institutional rules, engage in violence, and reoffend (Glenn & Raine, 2009; Walters, 2006c). The need for those high in antisocial personality is to develop self-control, perspective taking, and goal-setting skills. Antisocial cognition creates risk through a criminal belief system, defiance, and an antisocial identity that provides the individual with high self-efficacy and positive outcome expectancies for crime. The need in this case is for a noncriminal belief system, cooperation, and a prosocial identity that provides the individual with high self-efficacy for noncriminal activities and negative outcome expectancies for crime. Finally, the risk of antisocial associates is that people tend to engage in actions they observe in others and from which they believe they will derive a certain measure of social approval. The need in this particular case is to avoid old criminal associates and develop new noncriminal relationships.

Broadband Clinical Forensic Assessment Instruments

In discussing specific assessment instruments capable of both construct and risk assessment, it is important to determine how each addresses the reliability and relevance criteria established by the Daubert ruling. First, reliability is a function of how thoroughly the method has been researched and the degree to which the method has received empirical support. Translating the legal language of reliability into the scientific language of psychology, the Daubert reliability criterion asks whether the method is (1) falsifiable and therefore capable of being tested, (2) psychometrically sound (reliability and validity) as measured by peer-reviewed published research, and (3) amenable to application by virtue of a known error rate and calculation of a confidence interval. Second, the Daubert relevance criterion asks whether the method addresses pertinent issues for a particular purpose, in this case predicting relevant criminal justice outcomes. This second criterion can be measured against the central eight risk/needs factors previously described. The four assessment instruments to be discussed in this section are the LCSF (Walters, White, & Denney, 1991), the PCL-R (Hare, 1991, 2003), the PICTS (Walters, 1995a), and the LSI-R (Andrews & Bonta, 1995).

Lifestyle Criminality Screening Form

The LCSF is a 14-item chart audit form that can be completed in less than 10 minutes by a trained rater. All of the information used to score the LCSF is found in the presentence investigation (PSI) report and unlike many other clinical forensic assessment procedures the LCSF can be scored without talking to the offender. The LCSF is composed of four sections—(1) responsibility, (2) self-indulgence, (3) interpersonal intrusiveness, and (4) social rule breaking—which, when summed, yield a total LCSF score. On the responsibility section scores range from 0 to 6, on the self-indulgence section scores range from 0 to 6, on the interpersonal intrusiveness section scores range from 0 to 5, and on the social rule breaking section scores range from 0 to 5. The total score on the LCSF can range from 0 to 22, with a cutting score of 10 signaling significant involvement in, commitment to, and identification with a criminal lifestyle. A more useful approach is to organize the LCSF into risk levels: 0–6 = low risk, 7–9 = moderate risk, and 10–22 = high risk.

The reliability and validity of the LCSF for clinical forensic assessment is well documented (see Chapter 3). The relevance of the LCSF for construct assessment is that it measures the four behavioral styles that define a criminal lifestyle (irresponsibility, self-indulgence, interpersonal intrusiveness, social rule breaking). The relevance of the LCSF for risk/needs assessment is that it addresses one of the "big four" risk/needs factors (history of antisocial behavior) and touches on three of the remaining "central eight" risk/needs factors (family/marital problems, school/work problems, and substance abuse) as summarized in Table 4.1. Further support for the relevance of the LCSF for risk/needs assessment can be found in Table 4.2. In this table, each section of the LCSF is reviewed with respect to the risks it presents and the needs it presumes. Hence, for irresponsibility the risk is poor accountability and weak responsibility skills leading to future criminal or violent behavior. The needs that are implied by this section of the LCSF are accountability and responsibility and learning to meet one's obligations. The table not only describes the relevance of the LCSF to risk assessment but also illustrates how needs are often counterpoints to risk. Certain characteristics imply risk and the alteration of these characteristics can lead to positive change, which, in turn, lowers a person's future risk of criminal involvement.

Table 4.1   Issues Addressed by the Four Specific Risk/Needs Procedures

Central Eight	LCSF	PCL-R	PICTS	LSI-R
History of antisocial behavior	X	x		X
Antisocial personality pattern		X	x	X
Antisocial cognition			X	X
Antisocial associates				X
Family/marital problems	x	x		X
Poor school/work performance	x			X
Leisure and recreation activities				X
Substance abuse	x			X

Note: LCSF = Lifestyle Criminality Screening Form; LSI-R = Level of Service Inventory-Revised; PCL-R = Psychopathy Checklist-Revised; PICTS = Psychological Inventory of Criminal Thinking Styles; X = major emphasis; x = minor emphasis

Table 4.2   Risk and Needs Factors Identified by the Lifestyle Criminality Screening Form

LCSF Section Score	Risk Factors	Needs Factors
Irresponsibility	Poor accountability, failure to meet personal obligations, and weak responsibility skills	Being accountable, satisfying personal obligations, and becoming more responsible
Self-indulgence	Substance misuse, pathological gambling, and sexual promiscuity	Involvement in programs designed specifically for alcohol/drugs, gambling, and sexual problems
Interpersonal intrusiveness	Violating other people's rights, ignoring their feelings, and encroaching on their personal space	Learning to take other people's feelings into account through training in social perspective taking
Social rule breaking	Breaching rules, conventions, and laws set forth by an external authority figure	Following rules established by a legitimate external authority figure while resisting the natural impulse to rebel

Note: LCSF = Lifestyle Criminality Screening Form

The strength of the LCSF is its brevity and low cost. Usually it takes no longer than an hour to train someone to competently administer and score the LCSF, and an experienced user can normally complete the LCSF evaluation in less than 10 minutes. In addition, the LCSF does not rely on offender self-report, either in the form of completing an inventory or cooperating with an interview. This just said, the LCSF cannot be effectively completed if the PSI is cursory or incomplete. Nearly all PSIs contain information on the number and kinds of arrests, use of a weapon during the instant offense, and prior substance abuse history. However, some PSIs have insufficient information on educational/work history, family/marital issues, and noncriminal violence to score certain LCSF items. An additional weakness of the LCSF is that it is a completely static measure and so the results will not change even if the individual does. In sum, the LCSF is a reliable, valid, and quick measure of criminal history and related risk/needs factors that is limited by the information available to score it and by the static nature of its items.

Psychopathy Checklist-Revised

Hare's (1991, 2003) PCL-R is a 20-item inventory designed to assess the personality and behavioral features of psychopathy. Whereas the PCL-R was originally created as a construct assessment procedure for psychopathy, it has also been used for risk assessment and serves as a broadband clinical forensic assessment measure. A thorough review of the individual's file and a 90- to 120-minute semistructured interview are normally required to score the PCL-R. Although the PCL-R can be scored exclusively from file information, this is ordinarily only done for research purposes. The 20 PCL-R items are each rated on a 2-point scale: 0 = does not apply, 1 = may apply or in some respects applies, 2 = does apply. Scores on the PCL-R can range from 0 to 40, with 30 being the traditional cutoff for psychopathy, although other cutoff scores have been proposed (Simourd & Hoge, 2000). Early factor analyses revealed a two-factor structure for the PCL-R (selfish, callous, and remorseless use of others; chronically unstable and antisocial lifestyle), but more recent studies have suggested three- (arrogant and deceitful interpersonal style, deficient affective experience, impulsive and irresponsible behavioral style) (Cooke & Michie, 2001) and four- (interpersonal, affective, lifestyle, antisocial) (Hare, 2003) factor solutions.

More research has been conducted on the PCL-R and its 12-item screening version, the Psychopathy Checklist: Screening Version (PCL:SV) (Hart, Cox, & Hare, 1995), than any other measure specifically designed for clinical forensic assessment. Interrater reliability for the PCL-R is comparable to what has been found with the LCSF total, factor, and section scores; the total PCL-R score, Factor 1 and 2 scores, and the Facet 4 score all exhibit high interrater reliability, whereas the Facet 1, 2, and 3 scores all exhibit moderately high interrater reliability (Hare, 2003). The PCL-R predicts institutional adjustment at a slightly higher level than the LCSF but predicts recidivism at a level slightly lower than the LCSF (Walters, 2003a). There is evidence from two meta-analyses (Leistico, Salekin, DeCoster, & Rogers, 2008; Walters, 2003b) that Factor 2 of the PCL-R (chronically unstable and antisocial lifestyle) is a significantly better predictor of general and violent recidivism than Factor 1 (selfish, callous, and remorseless use of others) and from a series of incremental validity analyses (Walters & Heilbrun, 2010; Walters, Knight, Grann, & Dahle, 2008; Walters, Wilson, & Glover, 2011) that Facet 4 (antisocial) may be superior to the other three facets in predicting general and violent recidivism.

Table 4.3   Risk and Needs Factors Identified by the Psychopathy Checklist-Revised

PCL-R Facet Score	Risk Factors	Needs Factors
Interpersonal	Using charm, wit, and deceit to con and manipulate others and get one's way	Dealing honestly with others and telling the truth even when this does not yield immediate results
Affective	Difficulty experiencing anxiety, guilt, or remorse for destructive actions	Emotional awareness and the ability to learn from one's mistakes
Impulsive lifestyle	Boredom, desire for stimulation, and inadequate life direction	Finding prosocial outlets to relieve boredom and developing basic problem-solving skills
Antisocial behavior	Lack of behavioral controls and history of involvement in a variety of criminal activities	Behavioral management and greater consideration of the consequences of one's actions

Note: PCL-R = Psychopathy Checklist-Revised

The relevance of the PCL-R is that it provides a thorough analysis of the personality features associated with antisocial behavior as captured by the two principal factors of the PCL-R: selfish, callous, and remorseless use of others and chronically unstable antisocial lifestyle. On a somewhat smaller scale, the PCL-R assesses the risk/needs domains of prior antisocial behavior and family/marital problems (see Table 4.1). A more fine-tuned analysis can be achieved using the four PCL-R facet scores. The PCL-R interpersonal facet score, for instance, points to the risk associated with manipulative and conning behavior and indicates a need for increased honesty and truthfulness (see Table 4.3). The primary risk presented by the PCL-R affective facet is problems experiencing anxiety and guilt for bad behavior, which suggests a need for greater emotional awareness and the ability to learn from one's mistakes. Boredom and the need for stimulation are risk factors addressed by the lifestyle facet of the PCL-R, and identification of prosocial outlets for relieving boredom and development of problem-solving skills are viewed to be ways of meeting the needs in this domain. Finally, the antisocial facet suggests that poor behavioral controls and prior involvement in criminal activity are risks while behavioral management and learning to anticipate the consequences of one's actions are important needs addressed by this particular domain.

The principal strength of the PCL-R is that it provides a detailed assessment of the personality structure held to be instrumental in the formation and development of criminal behavior. I am referring here not only to the traditional Factor 2 characteristics of impulsivity, irresponsibility, and chronic violation of the laws of society but also to the charming, manipulative, and guiltless qualities tapped by Factor 1. The PCL-R predicts institutional adjustment, general recidivism, and violent recidivism on par with most popular risk assessment procedures and serves as an effective risk/needs measure despite the fact it was never designed for this purpose. One of the primary limitations of the PCL-R is that it requires a substantial amount of time to administer, score, and interpret and a significant amount of time to learn. Of course, one could always use the PCL:SV, which can be completed in half the time it takes to complete the PCL-R, or one of the self-report measures that have been found to generate results that in some ways parallel the PCL-R, such as the PPI (Lilienfeld & Andrews, 1996), Levenson Self-Report Psychopathy (LSRP) (Levenson, Kiehl, & Fitzpatrick, 1995) scale, or the Hare Psychopathy-Scan (P-Scan) (Hare & Hervé, 1999). It would appear that the PCL-R provides perhaps as detailed an analysis of one of the "big four" risk/needs factors (antisocial personality) as is currently available, although such detail may come at the cost of valuable clinician time.

Psychological Inventory of Criminal Thinking Styles

The PICTS is an 80-item self-report inventory designed to measure patterns of criminal cognition believed to support a criminal lifestyle (Walters, 1990). Each item is rated on a 4-point Likert-type scale (strongly agree, agree, uncertain, disagree) with strongly agree responses earning a respondent 4 points, agree responses earning a respondent 3 points, uncertain responses earning a respondent 2 points, and disagree responses earning a respondent 1 point on the scale to which the item is assigned. The PICTS yields scores for two eight-item validity scales—Confusion-revised (Cf-r) and Defensiveness-revised (Df-r)—eight nonoverlapping eight-item thinking style scales—Mo, Co, En, Po, Sn, So, Ci, and Ds—four 10-item factor scales—Problem Avoidance (PRB), Infrequency (INF), Self-Assertion/Deception (AST), and Denial of Harm (DNH)—and two content scales—Current Criminal Thinking (CUR) and Historical Criminal Thinking (HIS).

In recent years, composite scales—P and R—and a general score derived from the sum of the 64 criminal thinking items—GCT—have been added to the PICTS.

The PICTS was created to provide a construct assessment of criminal thinking, but it also addresses the third major risk/needs factor: antisocial cognition (see Table 4.1). Breaking the PICTS down into the eight thinking styles, the instrument was originally designed to measure, we can see that there are risks and needs associated with each thinking style (see Table 4.4). Mo carries the risk of blaming attributions and signals the need for responsibility. The risk of the Co is thinking without acting. Needs demanding attention in someone high on the Co scale involve the acquisition of basic behavioral and self-management skills. Misidentification of wants as needs and a sense of privilege are risk factors for En, the resolution of which requires effective weighing of the long- and short-term costs and benefits of crime. Po presents the risk of exerting power and control over others and is balanced by the need to learn self-discipline as a replacement for external control. Performing good deeds to justify criminality is the risk conveyed by Sn and the need is to learn to realistically self-appraise. An air of invulnerability is the risk of So, and the need is to be more cognizant of the negative consequences of criminal involvement. Taking shortcuts is the primary risk associated with Ci, and the need is to learn how to improve one's critical reasoning skills. Finally, Ds is a risk factor when the individual fails to follow through on initial goals and commitments and a needs factor when calling for greater personal consistency.

Table 4.4   Risk and Needs Factors Identified by the Psychological Inventory of Criminal Thinking Styles

PICTS Scale	Risk Factors	Needs Factors
Mollification	Blaming attributions, externalization, and excuses	Assuming responsibility for one's actions and understanding that behavior is based on choice
Cutoff	Acting without thinking; using a word, phrase, or image to rapidly eliminate natural deterrents to crime	Improved impulse control and the acquisition of basic behavioral self-management and self-control skills

(Continued)

(Continued)

PICTS Scale	Risk Factors	Needs Factors
Entitlement	Sense of privilege or ownership; misidentifying wants as needs	Assessing the anticipated long- and short-term costs and benefits of continued criminal involvement
Power Orientation	Exerting power and control over others as a means of compensating for personal feelings of powerlessness	Dealing with zero state feelings (powerlessness) in ways other than by putting others down and emphasizing self-discipline over environmental control
Sentimentality	Performing good deeds in an effort to justify one's continued involvement in a criminal lifestyle	Conducting a realistic self-appraisal and understanding that a few good deeds do not erase the destruction generated by a life of crime
Superoptimism	Attitude of invulnerability and the belief that one can indefinitely postpone the negative consequences of a criminal lifestyle	Realistic evaluation of the chances of repeatedly experiencing the negative consequences of crime with continued involvement in crime
Cognitive Indolence	Taking shortcuts and failing to critically evaluate one's plans and ideas	Improved critical reasoning and impulse control skills
Discontinuity	Failure to follow through on commitments, goals, and initially good intentions	Goal-setting skills and greater consistency in thought and action

Note: PICTS = Psychological Inventory of Criminal Thinking Styles

A growing body of supportive research indicates that the PICTS satisfies the reliability prong of the Daubert criteria (see Chapter 3), and the measure would appear to be highly relevant to several areas of forensic investigation. One advantage the PICTS has over non-self-report measures like the LCSF and PCL-R is that it provides an in-depth analysis of a "big four" risk/needs factor that is not covered in any meaningful way by the LCSF or PCL-R (i.e., antisocial cognition). The PICTS hierarchical structure is similar in some ways to the PCL-R, and the ability of scales at the upper end of the hierarchy (P, R, GCT) to predict institutional adjustment and recidivism is comparable to the LCSF and PCL-R. Being a self-report measure, the PICTS is in a good position to assess criminal cognition. The principal limitation of the PICTS is that being a self-report measure it is vulnerable to manipulation and response distortion by individuals who respond to the PICTS in a less than honest fashion. Even so, there are two PICTS response style scales (Cf-r and Df-r) that are effective in identifying fake bad and fake good response sets, respectively. An additional limitation of the PICTS is that it appears to do a better job of assessing thought process than of assessing thought content. To remedy this weakness, one could make use of a measure like the Criminal Sentiments Scale (Simourd, 1997), which focuses more on criminal thought content than the PICTS. In summation, the PICTS is an effective self-report measure of criminal thought process, although it may need to be supplemented by other measures if one wants to rule out response distortion and get a complete picture of criminal thought content.

Level of Service Inventory-Revised

The LSI-R is a 54-item interview-based measure designed to assist forensic decision makers in determining the level of supervision and treatment required for a particular offender through a review of static and dynamic risk and needs factors. It measures several relevant forensic constructs (antisocial personality patterns, substance abuse) and is also effective in assessing offender risks and needs. The 54 LSI-R items are organized into 10 domains: criminal history (10 items), education/employment (10 items), financial (2 items), family/marital (4 items), accommodation (3 items), leisure/recreation (2 items), companions (5 items), alcohol/drug problems (9 items), emotional/personal (5 items), and attitudes/orientation (4 items). In addition to a total score, the LSI-R also generates individual scores for each domain. After reviewing the 54 items in an interview with the offender, the test administrator consults relevant records as a check against the respondent's self-report. The interview takes about 30 minutes to complete, and the chart review portion of the evaluation can take anywhere from 15 to 45 minutes. The LSI-R is designed for use by mental health professionals like psychologists and social workers and by correctional professionals like probation officers, parole officers, and correctional workers at jails, prisons, and detention facilities who have been trained to administer, score, and interpret the results of the LSI-R. A screening version of the LSI-R (the Level of Service Inventory-Revised: Screening Version, or LSI-R:SV) (Andrews & Bonta, 1998) is also available.

The interrater reliability of the LSI-R and the majority of its domains is typically high. Lowenkamp, Holsinger, Brusman-Lovins, and Latessa (2004) observed an 85% or higher average rate of agreement between 167 correctional practitioners rating a written vignette on 9 out of the 10 LSI-R domains (the 2-item financial section being the lone exception: 61.5%). In this same study, 86% agreement was achieved between raters in assigning risk level—high, medium, low. For maximum reliability, however, raters need to be well trained. In a study conducted for the Pennsylvania Board of Probation and Parole, interrater reliability was found to be moderate to low, with only a few items meeting the 80% agreement threshold and an overall assignment of risk level of only 71% (Austin, Dedel-Johnson, & Coleman, 2003). The predictive validity of the LSI-R total score, on the other hand, is comparable, if not superior, to the other measures examined in this section. A meta-analysis conducted by Gendreau and colleagues (1997) revealed a mean effect size (r) of .23 for the LSI-R as a predictor of prison misconduct. A more recent meta-analysis by Gendreau, Goggin, and Smith (2002) disclosed a mean effect size of .37 for general recidivism and a mean effect size of .26 for violent recidivism.

The LSI-R is the only measure discussed in this section that addresses the "big four" risk/needs factor of criminal associations (see Table 4.1). Dividing the LSI-R scales into risk and needs factors, prior arrests, convictions, and incarcerations are risk factors for the criminal history domain of the LSI-R, which are then counterbalanced by the need to break the cycle of violence, crime, and coming to prison (see Table 4.5). Unemployment and poor school performance are risk factors for the education/employment domain, and the needs factors are job, academic, and responsibility skills. The financial domain creates the risk of money management problems, which is resolved by developing money management skills. The risk posed by family conflict and nonrewarding family relationships is neutralized by couples/family therapy and the formation of a family support system. Accommodation presents a risk by way of a negative physical and social environment, which may be remedied with public assistance and relocation. Lack of prosocial interests presents a risk for the leisure/recreation domain that can be addressed through development of prosocial hobbies and interests. Antisocial companions are a risk factor that can be managed by replacing antisocial companions with prosocial companions. Alcohol and drug abuse is a risk factor for both institutional infractions and recidivism and calls for some form of alcohol and drug counseling and follow-up. Emotional problems can also create a risk and should be addressed with individual counseling. The attitudes/orientation domain presents a risk through antisocial attitudes and expresses a need for prosocial attitudes and beliefs.

Table 4.5   Risk and Needs Factors Identified by the Level of Service Inventory-Revised

LSI-R Domain	Risk Factors	Needs Factors
Criminal history	Prior convictions; arrested before the age of 16; poor institutional adjustment	Breaking the habit of committing crime and coming to prison
Education/ employment	Currently unemployed; fired from job; expelled/ suspected from school	Job training and the development of academic and responsibility skills
Financial	Difficulty managing money	Public assistance; money management training
Family/marital	Marital/family conflict; nonrewarding parental relationship	Couples or family therapy; formation of new familial and nonfamilial support systems
Accommodation	Inadequate housing; living in a high crime area	Public assistance; relocation
Leisure/ recreation	Poor use of free time; lack of prosocial interests	Identification of physically and psychologically healthy hobbies and recreational activities
Companions	Presence of antisocial companions and absence of noncriminal companions	Avoidance of negative peer associations and pursuit of positive peer associations through social skills training and involvement in prosocial activities
Alcohol/drug problems	Severe alcohol and/or drug problems	Alcohol/drug counseling and follow-up
Emotional/ personal	Significant emotional and mental health problems	Individual counseling and psychotropic medication if necessary
Attitudes/ orientation	Attitudes supportive of crime; poor attitude toward supervision	Learning to challenge criminal thoughts and replacing them with more constructive alternatives; accepting supervision and guidance

Note: LSI-R = Level of Service Inventory-Revised

The principal strength of the LSI-R is that as a result of being a risk/needs assessment instrument it addresses all eight components of the "central eight" risk/needs factors described at the beginning of this chapter. In addition, the LSI correlates well with another one of the broadband assessment procedures described in this chapter, namely the PICTS (Doležal & Mikšaj-Todorović, 2008). A further strength of the LSI-R is that it may be the strongest predictor of general recidivism of the four measures examined in this chapter and is comparable to the other three measures in predicting institutional adjustment and violent recidivism. The greatest weakness of the LSI-R is that while it covers a wide range of risk/needs factors it does not delve very deeply into any of these factors. Hence, the results one gets from the LSI-R may sometimes be superficial. As with the PCL-R, rater training is extremely important and as mentioned previously the reliability of the LSI-R drops in concert with rater inexperience. Overall, the LSI-R provides a broad evaluation of important risk/needs variables that does not go as deeply into specific areas as some of the other measures discussed in this section yet is capable of predicting institutional adjustment and recidivism on par with these other procedures. A strength the LSI-R shares with the LCSF, PCL-R, and PICTS is that it provides separate norms for males and females, an important consideration in conducting risk assessment (Austin, 2006).

Prediction-Oriented and Management-Oriented Risk Assessment

The four broadband clinical forensic assessment procedures described in this section correspond to different aspects of Heilbrun's (1997) prediction-oriented versus management-oriented risk assessment model. The goal of **prediction-oriented risk assessment**, according to Heilbrun, is to accurately predict the probability of a future event's occurrence. The goal of **management-oriented risk assessment**, by comparison, is to reduce the probability of a future event's occurrence. Prediction-oriented risk assessment relies on static and dynamic risk factors, is insensitive to changes in risk status, and is largely incapable of informing a program of intervention; management-oriented risk assessment relies exclusively on dynamic risk factors, is sensitive to changes in risk status, and is highly capable of informing a program of intervention. Heilbrun (1997) asserts that despite their differences, prediction-oriented and management-oriented risk assessment can complement one another. Given the prevalence of static items on the LCSF and PCL-R, these two broadband clinical forensic instruments would appear to fit best into a prediction-oriented risk assessment scheme. With many more dynamic than static items, the PICTS and LSI-R would seem to be better suited to management-oriented risk assessment. Hence, in working with a sex offender like Grace, the LCSF and PCL-R should probably be used primarily for risk identification, whereas the PICTS and LSI-R can provide information useful in developing a program of intervention or change. Of course, narrowband clinical forensic measures designed specifically for sex offender risk assessment can make for an even more comprehensive evaluation.

Narrowband Clinical Forensic Assessment Instruments

There are times when a clinician may want to include a narrowband clinical forensic assessment procedure in the forensic test battery to answer more specific questions. By their very nature, these narrowband instruments do not measure constructs, though they can be helpful in assessing risk and needs factors in specific situations. This is because they are based on the most salient predictors of a particular criminal outcome and normally take only a short period of time to complete. Cut scores on risk measures represent practical demarcations rather than true taxonic boundaries based on research showing that risk measures, like broadband clinical forensic assessment measures, are assessing dimensional constructs (see Walters, Knight, & Thornton, 2009). Three areas of adult clinical forensic practice in which valid narrowband clinical forensic assessment have been developed are covered in this section: general violence, domestic violence, and sexual violence.

General Violence

The **Violence Risk Appraisal Guide** (VRAG) (Webster, Harris, Rice, Cormier, & Quinsey, 1994) is a 12-item rating scale created to assess violent offense recidivism. Each item on the VRAG is weighted based on its empirical relationship to violent recidivism in a 7-year follow-up of 618 male criminal offenders and forensic patients and in a 10-year follow-up of a recalibration sample of 800 male criminal offenders and forensic patients (Harris, Rice, & Quinsey, 1993; Quinsey, Harris, Rice, & Cormier, 1998). The total VRAG score (range = −26 to +38) is used to assign individuals to one of nine risk categories. One of the most heavily weighted items on the VRAG is psychopathy as measured by the PCL-R. In a test of the VRAG's incremental validity, the VRAG failed to predict violence after controlling for the PCL-R (Edens, Skeem, & Douglas, 2006). Results from a recently published study on recidivism were more encouraging. In that study, the VRAG successfully predicted recidivism for violent and acquisitive crimes in both male and female offenders (Coid et al., 2009). The VRAG and the next procedure to be discussed (HCR-20) continue to be the two most popular procedures for assessing violence risk (Conroy & Murrie, 2007).

The **Historical-Clinical-Risk Management** (HCR-20) risk measure (Webster, Douglas, Eaves, & Hart, 1997) is a 20-item rating procedure composed of three scales: Historical (10 items), Clinical (5 items), and Risk (5 items). The 10 Historical items are static risk factors selected for their ability to predict aggression, whereas the 10 Clinical and Risk items are dynamic risk factors that also predict aggression but unlike the Historical items are also subject to change. Each item on the HCR-20 is scored on a 3-point scale: 2 = item is definitely present; 1 = item is possibly present; 0 = item is not present based on available information. The HCR-20 yields a total score and individual scores for the three scales. Structured professional judgment is used to assign examinees to high, moderate, and low risk categories. There are no standard cutoff scores for these categories, and the rater is encouraged to exercise clinical judgment in assigning examinees to categories. Interrater reliability has been found to range from poor to very good on the individual items and from fair to good on the total and scale scores (Douglas, Yeomans, & Boer, 2005). Like the VRAG, the HCR-20 is as effective in predicting recidivism in female offenders as it is in male offenders (Coid et al., 2009) and unlike the VRAG, the HCR-20 has been found to possess incremental validity relative to the PCL-R (Douglas et al., 2005; McDermott, Edens, Quanbeck, Busse, & Scott, 2008).

Domestic Violence

The **Spousal Assault Risk Assessment Guide** (SARA) (Kropp, Hart, Webster, & Eaves, 1994) is composed of 20 risk factors divided into two parts: Part 1 (general violence, 10 items) and Part 2 (spousal violence, 10 items). The 10 spousal violence items are past physical assault, past sexual assault or sexual jealousy, past use of a weapon or credible threats of death, recent escalation in frequency or severity of assault, past violation of "no contact" orders, extreme minimization or denial of spousal assault history, attitudes that support or condone spousal assault, severe or sexual assault (most recent incident), use of weapons or credible threats of death (most recent incident), and violation of "no contact" order (most recent incident). Items are rated on a 3-point scale (0 = absent, 1 = possibly or partially present, 2 = present) and "critical" items are identified. From these ratings, three scores are calculated: a total score (range = 0 to 40), the number of items rated present (i.e., 2 vs. 0 or 1; range = 0 to 20), and the number of critical items (range = 0 to 20). Subscores are then calculated from items found in Parts 1 and 2 of the SARA. All scores possess good internal consistency and interrater reliability and correlate significantly with the PCL:SV. However, only Part 1 (general violence) correlates with the VRAG and only Part 2 (spousal violence) consistently differentiates between recidivists and nonrecidivists (Kropp & Hart, 2000).

Sexual Violence

The **Minnesota Sex Offender Screening Tool-Revised** (MnSOST-R) (Epperson et al., 1998) is a 16-item rating scale composed of 12 historical items and four institutional adjustment items designed to assess extrafamilial sexual offending. Each item on the MnSOST-R is weighted according to its association with sexual reoffending in the normative sample. When these items are added together, they form a total score that can range from –14 to +30. Scores on the MnSOST-R are sometimes grouped into three categories: low risk (total score ≤ 3), moderate risk (total score 4–7), and high risk (total score ≥ 8). Research indicates that the MnSOST-R possesses adequate to good interrater reliability and correlates reasonably well with recidivism (Langton, Barbaree, Harkins, Peacock, & Arenovich, 2008). The total MnSOST-R score achieved a mean Cohen's d effect size of 0.76 in a recent meta-analysis of sexual recidivism studies (Hanson & Morton-Bourgon, 2009). Minimum levels for small, moderate, and large effect sizes using Cohen's d are .20, .50, and .80, respectively (Cohen, 1988).

The **Static-99** (Hanson & Thornton, 2000) is the risk assessment procedure most often used in civil commitment hearings on sex offenders in the United States and has also been found to be effective in predicting sexual recidivism in Denmark (Bengtson & Långström, 2007), Switzerland (Endrass, Urbaniok, Held, Vetter, & Rossegger, 2009), and New Zealand (Skelton, Riley, Wales, & Vess, 2006). Incorporating 10 nonredundant and static-historical items from the Rapid Risk Assessment for Sexual Offense Recidivism (RRASOR) (Hanson, 1997) and Thornton's Structured Actuarial Clinical Judgment-Minimum (SACJ-Min) (Grubin, 1998), the Static-99 generates a total score with a range of 0 to 12 that can be used to assign individuals to one of four risk categories: low risk (0–1), low–moderate risk (2–3), high–moderate risk (4–5), and high risk (6–12). The Static-99 is composed of two factors: a four-item sexual deviance factor and a six-item antisocial factor (Roberts, Doren, & Thornton, 2002; Walters, Deming, & Elliott, 2009). In the Hanson and Morton-Bourgon (2009) meta-analysis, the Static–99 obtained a mean Cohen's d of 0.67 as a predictor of sexual recidivism and a mean Cohen's d of 0.57 as a predictor of violent recidivism.

Clinical Forensic Evaluation of Grace

Grace was evaluated with four broadband clinical forensic assessment instruments (LCSF, PICTS, PCL-R, LSI-R:SV)—all of which have separate norms for males and females—and one narrowband clinical forensic assessment instrument (Static-99). It should be noted that the Static-99 does not have separate norms for males and females but in the handful of studies conducted on female sex offenders women have achieved rates of recidivism that are significantly lower than the rates traditionally observed in men (Cortoni & Hanson, 2005). Although the applicability of the Static-99 to female sex offenders has not yet been empirically demonstrated, it is nonetheless used by some jurisdictions to assess female sex offenders because of a lack of viable alternatives (Turner, Miller, & Henderson, 2008). The first question the current evaluation is designed to answer is the probability that Grace will engage in sexual and violent offending upon her release from prison. The second question this evaluation is designed to answer is whether Grace can be certified as a sexually dangerous predator and civilly committed upon completion of her sentence for sexual assault. The third question this evaluation is designed to answer is what strengths and weaknesses does Grace possess that can be included in a program of change. Grace's test results are reproduced in Table 4.6.

Table 4.6   Grace's Lifestyle Criminality Screening Form, Psychological Inventory of Criminal Thinking Styles, Psychopathy Checklist-Revised, Level of Service Inventory-Revised: Screening Version, and Static-99 Results

Lifestyle Criminality Screening Form (LCSF)	
Overall Involvement	
Total score	7 (24th percentile)
Risk level	Moderate
Factor Scores	
Violation (V) factor score	4
Impulse (I) factor score	2
V-I index	4:2
Subsection Scores	
Irresponsibility	2
Self-indulgence	1
Interpersonal intrusiveness	2
Social rule breaking	2

Psychological Inventory of Criminal Thinking Styles (PICTS)	
Higher-Order Factor	
General Criminal Thinking (GCT)	55
Composite Scales	
Proactive Criminal Thinking (P)	61
Reactive Criminal Thinking (R)	49
Thinking Style Scales	
Mollification (Mo)	48
Cutoff (Co)	46
Entitlement (En)	64
Power Orientation (Po)	48
Sentimentality (Sn)	56
Superoptimism (So)	55
Cognitive Indolence (Ci)	56
Discontinuity (Ds)	57
Psychopathy Checklist-Revised	
Total Score	21 (53rd percentile)
Factor 1 Score (Interpersonal/Affective)	14 (67th percentile)
Factor 2 Score (Social Deviance)	5 (39th percentile)
Facet 1 Score (Interpersonal)	8 (72nd percentile)
Facet 2 Score (Affective)	6 (58th percentile)
Facet 3 Score (Lifestyle)	4 (43rd percentile)
Facet 4 Score (Antisocial)	1 (37th percentile)
Level of Service Inventory-Revised: Screening Version	
LSI-R:SV Total Score	1 (42nd percentile)
LSI-R:SV Risk/Needs Category	Low
Static-99	
Total Score	4
Risk Level	Moderate-High
Sexual Deviance Factor	1
Antisocial Factor	3

Note: LCSF scores are raw scores (female norms), PICTS scores are T-scores (female norms), PCL-R scores are raw and percentile scores (female norms), LSI-R:SV scores are raw and percentile scores (female norms), and the Static-99 scores are raw scores.

Construct Assessment

P is a prominent feature of a PICTS profile that is for the most part flat and unremarkable. Overall criminal thinking is only slightly above average (GCT = 55), but the proactive–reactive split (T-score difference of 12) is significant and both P (P = 61) and a sense of privilege (En = 64) are moderately elevated. The other noteworthy feature of this profile from a construct assessment point of view is the PCL-R Factor 1–Factor 2 split, a consequence of Grace's maximum elevation on the interpersonal facet (72nd percentile). Taken as a whole, these findings denote the presence of an antisocial–narcissistic pattern where manipulation, scheming, and a strong sense of entitlement/privilege predominate. Although the Static-99 is not normally employed for construct assessment purposes, a 3:1 ratio of antisocial to sexual deviance scores also supports the notion that Grace's sexual acting out is more a function of her antisocial–narcissistic personality than it is a function of powerful sexual impulses and fantasies.

Risk Assessment

Overall risk of general and sexual violence is moderate as measured by the LCSF and Static-99, respectively. A total score of 4 on the Static-99 is associated with a 26% rate of sexual recidivism within 5 years, a 31% rate of sexual recidivism within 10 years, and a 36% rate of recidivism within 15 years in male sex offenders (Harris, Phenix, Hanson, & Thornton, 2003). The 3:1 ratio of antisocial to sexual deviance scores places Grace at the lower end of the moderate range of sexual recidivism risk, but the possibility that she actively seeks positions in close proximity to children (Sunday school teacher) places her at the upper end of the moderate range. If, in fact, Grace deliberately took the position of Sunday school teacher to gain access to potential victims (a possibility consistent with her high PICTS P score) rather than an impulsive decision based on opportunity and other situational factors, I would be inclined to move her risk of sexual recidivism up to the moderate–high range. According to the results of the LSI-R:SV, there are no obvious areas of need deficiency requiring attention, although her maximum score on Facet 1 (interpersonal) of the PCL-R indicates a need for honesty and truthfulness.

Overall Impression

Grace demonstrates a personality disorder of moderately high severity and presents moderate risk of future violent and sexual recidivism. Unfortunately, her risk cannot be reduced by addressing need deficits covered by the LSI-R:SV (interpersonal, psychological, substance misuse) because she does not appear to suffer from deficits in any of these areas. The odds are high that she will continue to commit property crimes. Whether she returns to sexual offending will depend largely on her level of sexual deviance. The Static-99 results suggest that deviant sexuality and deviant sexual fantasies are minimally responsible for her criminal conduct, but this may simply be because she is young and has never been caught for prior sexual offending or paraphilic behavior. It is also possible that the Static-99 is not valid for use with female sex offenders. We could learn a great deal about Grace's level of sexual deviance and be in a better position to answer the question of whether she is a dangerous sexual predator if we could determine whether she deliberately took the job as a Sunday school teacher to gain access to potential sexual victims.

Conclusion

The four broadband measures examined in this chapter, the LCSF, PCL-R, PICTS, and LSI-R, appear to satisfy the Daubert criteria for reliability and relevance. In addition, each taps a different one of the "big four" risk/needs factors identified in meta-analytic studies on disciplinary adjustment, violence, and recidivism prediction. Nevertheless, each is better suited for some purposes than others. The LCSF, for instance, would be a good choice as an initial screening measure but would be useless in evaluating change as a consequence of program involvement. The PCL-R would not make a very good screening device because of the amount of time it takes to administer, score, and interpret, but it could be a useful adjunct in a court or parole situation where future dangerousness is the primary question. The PICTS can be useful as both a screening device and measure of therapeutic change but may be less useful in evaluating an individual's readiness for parole given the fact that it relies exclusively on offender self-report. The LSI-R would appear to be particularly effective in release planning and in developing a program of parole/probation supervision but may be less helpful in shedding light on personality and cognitive factors important in understanding individual offenders than either the PCL-R or PICTS.

A competent clinical forensic assessment requires an evaluation of relevant constructs, risks, and needs. Broadband forensic assessment procedures like the PCL-R and PICTS can be used for construct assessment or risk assessment but their utility in identifying risk and needs factors is limited. Other broadband forensic assessment procedures like the LCSF and LSI-R do a better job of identifying risk and needs factors but should be supplemented by narrowband procedures when addressing issues of general violence, domestic violence, and sexual violence. The Static-99, for instance, supplied potentially valuable information on Grace beyond what the four broadband procedures were capable of providing. Differentiating between the antisocial and sexual deviance components of sexual offending is critical when conducting a clinical forensic assessment of someone with a sex offending history. In applying the Static-99 to Grace, it was shown that the antisocial component may be more prominent than the sexual deviance component. This information is vital in assessing her odds of reoffending sexually upon her release from prison. The continued viability of clinical forensic assessment depends on our ability to balance the strengths and weaknesses of broadband assessment procedures and add relevant and reliable narrowband procedures to the test battery when necessary.

Key Terms and Concepts

Clinical Forensic Assessment

Construct Assessment

Daubert Criteria

Dynamic Needs

Historical-Clinical-Risk Management

Level of Service Inventory-Revised

Lifestyle Criminality
Screening Form

Management-Oriented Risk Assessment

Minnesota Sex Offender
Screening Tool-Revised

Prediction-Oriented Risk
Assessment

Psychological Inventory of
Criminal Thinking Styles

Psychopathy Checklist-Revised

Risk Assessment

Risk Factors

Spousal Assault Risk
Assessment Guide

Static-99

Violence Risk Appraisal Guide

5

Development or Propensity

The Criminal Lifestyle in an Etiological Context

Experience is the name people give to their mistakes.

Oscar Wilde (1854–1900)

Born Under a Bad Sign

Jerry is a 31-year-old single white male serving a 12-year sentence for possessing and manufacturing methamphetamine. He was raised in a broken home, the youngest of three children. His biological father was in and out of jail and was never involved in Jerry's life. Jerry describes his mother as a good person who was overwhelmed by the responsibility of raising three active boys on her own. Jerry's criminal career began at age 5 when he and his brothers began breaking into neighbors' homes. The usual scenario was for the two brothers to lift Jerry up on their shoulders and squeeze him through a kitchen or bathroom window. Once inside, Jerry would let his brothers in the house by unlocking the front door. When he was 7 years old, Jerry was arrested for breaking into his next-door neighbor's house and remanded to the custody of his mother. His two brothers were not so fortunate; instead of being sent home, they were sent to reform school. It was around this time that

Jerry's stepfather entered the picture. A motorcycle gang member who sold marijuana and methamphetamine around the neighborhood, Jerry's stepfather was a bad influence from day one. He recruited the boy into his drug business and would pay him anywhere from $20 to $60 a day to deliver drugs in the neighborhood on his bicycle. Jerry was caught by the police at age 11 when he was hit by a car during one of his deliveries. This incident landed Jerry in reform school for 6 months.

Much of Jerry's adolescence was spent in group homes and juvenile detention facilities. His adjustment was poor, largely because of his use of alcohol and drugs. He began drinking alcohol and smoking cigarettes at age 8; graduated to huffing paint, gasoline, and glue around age 9; and was smoking marijuana at age 10. When he was 11 years old, Jerry observed his stepfather and several of his stepfather's motorcycle friends injecting cocaine and methamphetamine. Jerry watched with fascination as his stepfather injected the drug into his arm and eventually convinced his stepfather to show him how to use a needle to shoot drugs. From this point forward, Jerry was hooked on the drug lifestyle. He would use whatever drugs were available to him, but he preferred cocaine and methamphetamine. To support his growing drug habit, he began selling drugs other than marijuana. By mid-adolescence he was no longer delivering drugs for his stepfather but purchasing, packaging, and selling drugs as part of a budding criminal enterprise. Emancipated from the juvenile justice system at age 18, Jerry took his budding criminal enterprise and turned it into a full-time business. He went from selling drugs he bought from others to manufacturing his own drugs. It was not long before he had gained a countywide reputation as someone who was adept at using common household products and over-the-counter pharmaceuticals to make methamphetamine.

Jerry's drug history is matched only by his extensive criminal record. In his 31 years, Jerry has been arrested 18 different times, the first arrest coming at age 7. He has eight adult convictions and is serving his second adult incarceration. Jerry's total score on the Lifestyle Criminality Screening Form (LCSF) places him at the 96th percentile, and his criminality is marked by both impulsive acting out and the violation of others' rights (see Table 5.1). Unlike the LCSF results recorded by Pete, Rick, and Will (see Chapter 3), however, Jerry's scores on the LCSF reflect a tendency toward impulsive acting out in the form of irresponsibility and self-indulgence. Much of this relates back to his use of drugs. Although many offenders abuse drugs, Jerry was heavily involved in the drug lifestyle from an early age. In fact, his case illustrates how the drug and criminal lifestyles can coexist, interact, and empower one another. Table 5.1 also lists Jerry's Psychological Inventory of Criminal Thinking Styles (PICTS) scores. He demonstrates a clear commitment and identification with the criminal lifestyle through his thinking (General Criminal Thinking [GCT] score = 69) and elevates seven of the eight PICTS thinking style scales. The only area of criminal thinking Jerry does not endorse is mollification (Mo), suggesting that he is not one to blame outside circumstances for his past criminal exploits. Although he may be more prone to Proactive Criminal Thinking (P) than Reactive Criminal Thinking (R) (P > R by 10 T-score points), both composite scales are elevated. Hence, Jerry can be scheming and purposeful at one moment and have his attention diverted by events going on around him the next. He is most likely to have his attention diverted when drinking or using drugs.

Table 5.1   Jerry's Lifestyle Criminality Screening Form and Psychological Inventory of Criminal Thinking Styles Results

Lifestyle Criminality Screening Form (LCSF)	
Overall Involvement	
Total score	15 (96th percentile)
Risk level	High
Factor Scores	
Violation (V) factor score	5
Impulse (I) factor score	7
V-I index	5:7
Subsection Scores	
Irresponsibility	5
Self-indulgence	5
Interpersonal intrusiveness	1
Social rule breaking	4
Psychological Inventory of Criminal Thinking Styles (PICTS)	
Higher-Order Factor	
General Criminal Thinking (GCT)	69

(Continued)

(Continued)

Composite Scales	
Proactive Criminal Thinking (P)	74
Reactive Criminal Thinking (R)	64
Thinking Style Scales	
Mollification (Mo)	53
Cutoff (Co)	69
Entitlement (En)	66
Power Orientation (Po)	62
Sentimentality (Sn)	68
Superoptimism (So)	71
Cognitive Indolence (Ci)	68
Discontinuity (Ds)	62

Note: LCSF scores are raw scores, and PICTS scores are T-scored.

Development Versus Propensity in Explaining Crime

Two general categories of theory have been offered as explanations for the type of habitual or career criminal behavior displayed by Jerry: (1) developmental theories and (2) propensity theories. Whereas developmental theories use life experiences and trajectories of behavior to explain crime, propensity theories view crime as a consequence of stable individual-level pathological characteristics (DeLisi, 2005). In this section, we will explore two developmental theories and two propensity theories of habitual criminality.

Moffitt's Developmental Taxonomy

Terrie Moffitt (1993) has proposed a **developmental taxonomy** in which delinquency is held to follow one of two distinct trajectories: (1) the **life-course-persistent** (LCP) trajectory and (2) the **adolescence-limited** (AL) trajectory. The LCP trajectory, with onset in childhood or early adolescence and termination in mid-adulthood, is characterized by early environmental deprivations, deficits in verbal and executive functioning, and problematic social relationships. The AL trajectory, by contrast, usually begins and ends in adolescence and is characterized by fewer environmental deprivations, better verbal and executive functioning, and more positive social relationships than the LCP trajectory. Whereas LCP delinquency is characterized by early pathology in many areas of functioning, AL delinquency is often considered a normative reaction to the social pressures, increased responsibilities, and identity strivings of adolescence. Moffitt (1993) held that AL delinquents often learn the techniques and attitudes of crime by observing, imitating, and modeling the behavior of LCP delinquents through a process of social mimicry. The budding AL delinquent sees the autonomy the LCP delinquent achieves through crime and seeks to emulate some of these actions, although the delinquency observed in the AL trajectory tends to be less violent than the delinquency observed in the LCP trajectory.

In light of the severe psychopathology and harsh environmental conditions that give rise to the LCP trajectory, LCP delinquency is relatively rare. Researchers have determined that the rate of LCP delinquency in the general adolescent population is somewhere between 3% and 16% (Chung, Hill, Hawkins, Gilchrist, & Nagin, 2002; Fergusson, Horwood, & Nagin, 2000; Maughan, Pickles, Rowe, Costello, & Angold, 2000; Nagin, Farrington, & Moffitt, 1995; Raine et al., 2005; Tremblay et al., 2004; Wiesner & Capaldi, 2003). Because AL delinquency is considered a normative reaction to the stress, strain, and increased expectations and responsibilities of adolescence, AL delinquency is 5 to 15 times more common than LCP delinquency, with prevalences of 50% and higher (Moffitt, 2007). Based on these numbers, it is estimated that nondelinquents constitute 30% to 47% of adolescent samples. Intervention and prevention programs, according to Moffitt and her colleagues, need to be geared toward the LCP child and adolescent rather than the AL adolescent. The delinquency of the AL individual is typically less severe and nearly always less chronic than the delinquency of the LCP individual. The problem is that the neuropsychological deficits and early environmental conditions responsible for LCP are difficult to prevent and once in place virtually impossible to change.

Research has confirmed fundamental aspects of Moffitt's (1993) theory. Studies indicate that LCP delinquents accrue significantly more neuropsychological risk factors (delayed motor development, difficult temperament, low verbal intelligence and executive function deficits) and early environmental risk factors (poor parenting, peer rejection, low socioeconomic status) than AL delinquents (Jeglum-Bartusch, Lynam, Moffitt, & Silva, 1997; Moffitt & Caspi, 2001; Moffitt, Lynam, & Silva,

1994). Additional research indicates that the criminogenic effect is strongest when neuropsychological risk factors interact with familial (Arseneault, Tremblay, Boulerice, & Saucier, 2002; Tibbetts & Piquero, 1999) and extrafamilial (Lynam et al., 2000; Turner, Hartman, & Bishop, 2007) environmental risk factors. Consistent with Moffitt's (1993) theory, LCP delinquency starts earlier and ends later than AL delinquency (Ge, Donnellan, & Wenk, 2001; Moffitt, Caspi, Harrington, & Milne, 2002; Piquero, Brame, & Lynam, 2004) and LCP delinquency is characterized by poorer adult outcomes than AL delinquency, from domestic violence to health problems (Fergusson, Horwood, & Ridder, 2005; Mazerolle & Maahs, 2002; Moffitt et al., 2002; Piquero, Daigle, Gibson, Piquero, & Tibbetts, 2007). On the other hand, there is no support for Moffitt's (1993) contention that LCP and AL are conceptually distinct categories of behavior (Walters, 2011a).

Sampson and Laub's Age-Graded Theory of Informal Social Control

Robert Sampson and John Laub (1993) have formulated an **age-graded theory of informal social control** to explain persistent criminality. Whereas the police, courts, and criminal justice system exercise formal social control, one's family, friends, work, and school are sources of informal social control. Sampson and Laub (1993) theorized that people accumulate social capital through informal social control networks and that those with low social capital are more likely to follow a trajectory of crime than those with high social capital. Intrinsic to Sampson and Laub's (1993) model, however, is the idea that prosocial bonds can help move a person from a criminal trajectory to a noncriminal trajectory. A good marriage, a new child, or a fulfilling job are all capable of encouraging desistance from crime (Adler, 1993; Graham & Bowling, 1995; Laub, Nagin, & Sampson, 1998). Research indicates that young adults with a history of juvenile delinquency who end up in good marriages are more likely to desist from crime than young adults with a history of juvenile delinquency who are single or who end up in bad marriages (Simons, Wu, Conger, & Lorenz, 1994). In a reanalysis of Sheldon and Eleanor Glueck's (1950) *Unraveling Juvenile Delinquency* data, Laub and Sampson (1988) found that maternal supervision, parental discipline, and emotional attachment to parents had a more salient effect on future delinquency than social class and, in fact, mediated the effect of social class on future delinquency.

Sampson and Laub (1993) do not deny the importance of individual differences and early childhood experiences in delinquency initiation but believe that proximal events in a person's life wield a more powerful influence over delinquency than distal events. Adolescent and adult experiences, therefore, can have a profound facilitative or deterrent effect on criminal trajectories. According to Sampson and Laub (1993), criminality is characterized by both continuity and change. Continuity is a function of individual differences in temperament and intelligence, early childhood experiences within the home, and something Sampson and Laub (1993) referred to as "cumulative disadvantage." What Sampson and Laub mean by **cumulative disadvantage** is that serious delinquency can lead to such consequences as incarceration and labeling that then "knife off" opportunities for the development of corrective social bonds (marriage, school, occupation, military) and increase a person's chances of committing future crime. Change occurs as a result of life-course alterations in social bonds. Another unique feature of this theory is the role agency and choice play in desistance from crime. Sampson and Laub (2005) contended that offenders are active participants in the process that gives rise to desistance from crime and that along with social bonds or lack of social bonds choice factors help explain the age at which offenders finally exit crime.

Sampson and Laub's (1993) age-graded theory of informal social control has received a fair amount of attention from researchers. In one study, Mason and Windle (2002) uncovered support for Sampson and Laub's notion of cumulative disadvantage as an explanation for the continuity of crime. In two other studies, Doherty (2006) and Eggleston (2006) determined that informal social bonds predicted desistance independent of a person's level of self-control, a concept central to another criminological theory examined in this chapter, Gottfredson and Hirschi's (1990) general theory of crime. Whereas Sampson and Laub stress indirect sources of social control (attachments) in explaining desistance from crime, Gottfredson and Hirschi emphasize age as the principal cause of desistance in people previously involved in crime. Both indirect social control (job security) and formal criminal justice processing were found to predict desistance from crime in a group of sex offenders (Kruttschnitt, Uggen, & Shelton, 2000). Changing peer relationships are another important correlate of crime desistance, and several studies have shown that marriage can promote prosociality by reducing, and in some cases eliminating, time spent with antisocial peers (Sampson, Laub, & Wimer, 2006; Warr, 1998). Finally, there is support for Sampson and Laub's (1993) contention that the use of alcohol (Laub & Sampson, 2003) and illegal drugs (Schroeder, Giordano, & Cernkovich, 2007) loosens the social bonds that facilitate desistance from crime.

Hare's Psychopathy Construct

Robert Hare (1996, 1998) has spent the better part of a career constructing a theory of **psychopathy** based on the pioneering work of psychiatrist
Hervey Cleckley. In his book *The Mask of Sanity*, Cleckley (1941/1976)
listed 16 traits of the psychopathic personality. These traits included (1) superficial charm and average or above average intelligence, (2) absence of delu-
sions, (3) low anxiety, (4) unreliability and irresponsibility, (5) pathological
lying, (6) lack of remorse, (7) insufficiently motivated antisocial behavior,
(8) poor judgment and failure to learn from experience, (9) pathological egocen-
tricity, (10) poverty of feeling and affect, (11) poor insight, (12) ingratitude
toward others, (13) obnoxious behavior with and sometimes without drink,
(14) frequent suicide threats that are rarely carried out, (15) impersonal
sexual life, and (16) failure to follow a life plan. Hare used these traits to
develop a 22-item rating scale for psychopathy known as the **Psychopathy
Checklist** (PCL) (Hare, 1980), which was subsequently reduced to 20 items
and relabeled the Hare Psychopathy Checklist-Revised (PCL-R) (Hare,
2003). The PCL-R is scored using a semistructured interview and a review
of available records and takes approximately 2 hours to complete. Each item
is scored on a 3-point scale (0 = not present, 1 = may apply or applies to
some extent, 2 = definitely applies) and the total score can range from 0 to
40. Hare (1991) originally proposed a score of 30 as a cutoff for psychopathy, although scores ranging from 25 to 33 have been proposed as cutoffs
(Simourd & Hoge, 2000).

Hare (1996) speculated that psychopathy is caused by superficial linguistic processing that interferes with a person's ability to learn from punishment
and conditioning. However, his theory of psychopathy lags behind his methodology (PCL-R). The PCL-R has become popular with forensic and correctional psychologists. Research indicates that the PCL-R, particularly the
behavioral–antisocial portion of the scale, is capable of predicting general
recidivism, violent recidivism, and institutional infractions (Leistico, Salekin,
DeCoster, & Rogers, 2008; Walters, 2003b, 2006c). The PCL-R is also the
most commonly used criterion measure of psychopathy in basic research on
the epidemiology, etiology, and treatment of psychopathic personality disorders. Clinically, the PCL-R is often used to assess risk and treatment amena-
bility. Concerns have been raised, however, as to the appropriateness of the
PCL-R for more specific clinical questions like future dangerousness in death
penalty cases and sexual predator determinations in civil commitment pro-
ceedings for convicted sex offenders (Edens & Petrila, 2006). Hare (1998)
placed the prevalence of psychopathy in the general population at 1% and
in prison populations at 15% to 25%. Owing to the fact that two to three

times as many offenders satisfy the criteria for antisocial personality disorder (ASPD) as satisfy the criteria for psychopathy, Hare (1996) concluded that psychopathy is the more useful and discriminating of the two diagnoses. This is an empirical question that requires further study.

Controversy surrounds the factor structure of the PCL-R. Initially, Hare and his colleagues found evidence of two factors (Hare, 1991; Harpur, Hakstian, & Hare, 1988; Harpur, Hare, & Hakstian, 1989). The first factor (Factor 1) covers the interpersonal and affective aspects of psychopathy and has been labeled "selfish, callous, and remorseless use of others." The second factor (Factor 2) covers the impulsive and antisocial aspects of psychopathy and has been labeled "chronically unstable and antisocial lifestyle." A study by Cooke and Michie (2001), however, revealed the presence of a three-factor structure for the PCL-R: arrogant and deceitful interpersonal style (Factor 1) and deficient affective experience (Factor 2) from the original Factor 1 and impulsive and irresponsible behavioral style (Factor 3) from the original Factor 2. Hare and Neumann (2006) added a fourth factor, antisocial behavior, to the three-factor model to create a four-factor model of the PCL-R. The controversy over whether the PCL-R is made up of three or four factors is intensified by research indicating that Factor 4 (antisocial behavior) is superior to the first three factors in predicting criminal justice outcomes like institutional adjustment and recidivism (Walters & Heilbrun, 2010; Walters, Knight, Grann, & Dahle, 2008; Walters, Wilson, & Glover, 2011). Hence, if the best predictor of criminal justice outcomes is not even part of the psychopathy construct, as Cooke and his colleagues contend (Cooke, Michie, & Skeem, 2007; Skeem & Cooke, 2010), then this brings into serious question the relevance of the psychopathy construct in general and the PCL-R in particular to crime.

Gottfredson and Hirschi's General Theory of Crime

Michael Gottfredson and Travis Hirschi (1990) offered a propensity theory of habitual criminality based on low self-control, which they refer to as the **general theory of crime**. The **self-control** construct is composed of six interrelated personality dimensions: (1) diligence, (2) prudence, (3) sensitivity to the needs of others, (4) high-level cognitive functioning, (5) delay of gratification, and (6) anger control. According to Gottfredson and Hirschi's (1990) general theory of crime, low self-control has its origins in weak parental socialization whereby parents fail to monitor, supervise, and discipline their children and therefore fail to teach their children self-control. By the time a child is 8 to 10 years old, low self-control has become a relatively stable trait that can lead to a lifetime of impulsivity, irresponsibility, and antisocial behavior. Those with low self-control "pursue short-term, immediate pleasure" irrespective of the long-term consequences of these actions and are more apt to pursue criminal opportunities than those with high self-control (Gottfredson & Hirschi, 1990, p. 93). Desistance occurs because absolute self-control improves with age and the aging process makes it progressively more difficult for the individual to participate in formal criminal activity because of decreased physical stamina and reduced opportunities for crime. Relative self-control (level of self-control compared to other individuals of the same age), on the other hand, does not change, so individual differences in self-control endure over time. Gottfredson and Hirschi (1990) considered self-control impervious to the effects of adolescent and adult interventions, although they are more optimistic about interventions taking place in childhood. All manner of crime, according to Gottfredson and Hirschi (1990)—from impulsive street crimes to highly sophisticated white-collar crimes—is a consequence of low self-control.

Gottfredson and Hirschi's (1990) general theory of crime, perhaps because of its simplicity and ease of operationality, has generated an impressive body of research in the past 2 decades. In a 21-study meta-analysis of the self-control construct, Pratt and Cullen (2000) recorded an overall effect size (r) of .20, which was one of the largest effect sizes obtained in the study. However, when the stability, resiliency, exclusivity, universality, and versatility postulates of the general theory have been evaluated the results have only been partially supportive of Gottfredson and Hirschi's (1990) theorem. Arneklev, Cochran, and Gainey (1998) observed stability in self-control measures administered to college students 4 months apart, but Turner and Piquero (2002) found only modest stability in a national probability sample tested over a longer period of time. Mitchell and MacKenzie (2006), by comparison, found no evidence of absolute or relative stability when self-control was measured 6 months apart. Hay and Forrest (2006) observed reasonable stability in a majority of their participants but then witnessed substantial instability in both absolute and relative self-control in 16% of their sample. This 16% of the sample displayed either significant gains or significant declines in self-control, changes that occurred well past the age (10 years of age and younger) Gottfredson and Hirschi believe meaningful change takes place. Self-control is resilient to questionable correctional interventions like boot-camp programs (Mitchell & MacKenzie, 2006) but improves in concert with decreased recidivism for evidence-based cognitive and behavioral correctional programs (Andrews & Bonta, 2003).

Consistent with Gottfredson and Hirschi's (1990) general theory of crime, ineffective parenting is a robust correlate of both low self-control and crime (Gibbs, Giever, & Martin, 1998; Hay, 2004). The exclusivity postulate, however, in which parental socialization is held to be the sole source of self-control, is challenged by research showing that genetic factors (Wright & Beaver, 2005), prenatal injury (McCartan & Gunnison, 2007), school socialization (Turner, Piquero, & Pratt, 2005), and neighborhood context (Pratt, Turner, & Piquero, 2004) all affect self-control independent of parental socialization. Gottfredson and Hirschi's (1990) universality postulate holds that all crime is a function of low self-control. Low self-control has been found to correlate with such varied offenses as animal abuse (Arluke, Levin, Luke, & Ascione, 1999), digital piracy (Higgins, Fell, & Wilson, 2006), domestic violence (Chapple & Hope, 2003), employee theft (Langton, Piquero, & Hollinger, 2006), fraud (Grasmick, Tittle, Bursick, & Arneklev, 1993), and shoplifting (Deng, 1995), although its applicability to white-collar crime has been challenged (Benson & Moore, 1992; Walters & Geyer, 2004). Ganon and Donegan (2006) obtained evidence of versatility in the self-reported backgrounds of college students who acknowledged engaging in insurance fraud (i.e., high levels of excessive drinking, problem gambling, license suspensions, and lying on resumes) but contrary to Gottfredson and Hirschi's (1990) prediction, these students did not demonstrate significantly lower self-control than students who denied engaging in insurance fraud. A number of other studies support Gottfredson and Hirschi's (1990) versatility postulate, making it one of the more consistently supported elements of their general theory of crime (Chapple & Hope, 2003; Piquero, Paternoster, Mazerolle, Brame, & Dean, 1999; Xiaogang & Lening, 1998).

Strengths and Weaknesses of the Four Models

One of the principal strengths of Moffitt's (1993) developmental taxonomy is the assumption that a minority of offenders are responsible for a majority of crimes. The fact that a small portion of the criminal population is responsible for a lion's share of the crimes committed by the population has been so consistently documented as to become almost axiomatic (Figgie Corporation, 1988; Hamparian, Schuster, Dinitz, & Conrad, 1978; Shannon, 1982; Vaughn & DeLisi, 2008; Wolfgang, Figlio, & Sellin, 1972). Such individuals' criminal careers normally begin earlier, end later, and include more violence than the careers of less prolific criminals, all of which are captured in Moffitt's notion of the LCP offender. A weakness of Moffitt's theory is that it considers only two crime trajectories (LCP, AL) whereas mixture modeling analyses conducted on nine different samples from four different countries indicate the presence of as many as four separate crime trajectories (Broidy et al., 2003; D'Unger, Land, McCall, & Nagin, 1998; Nagin et al., 1995; Nagin & Land, 1993).

Strengths of Sampson and Laub's (1993) age-graded developmental theory of crime include the ability to accommodate more than two crime trajectories, consideration of informal social control influences, and an emphasis on choice and dynamic change. A comprehensive theory of criminal behavior needs to address the issue of change and the dynamic nature of Sampson and Laub's theory provides an avenue by which change can be studied, analyzed, and encouraged. A weakness of Sampson and Laub's theory is that much of the foundational research for the theory is based on reanalyses of Glueck and Glueck's (1950) *Unraveling Juvenile Delinquency* sample. Not only did Glueck and Glueck oversample serious offenders but the cohort was formed in the late 1920s and official crime measures (arrest records) were utilized, thus raising the possibility of cohort, generational, and method effects. In a study using self-report data collected on a less severe population sampled from a more recent cohort, Giordano, Cernkovich, and Rudolph (2002) failed to uncover a relationship between attachment to school, attachment to spouse, or job security and adult criminality in both male and female participants.

Hare's (1996, 1998) psychopathy construct also has a number of strengths. Chief among these is the methodological advances that have been achieved with the PCL-R. In addition, the psychopathy construct emphasizes the planned deceit and manipulativeness that plays such an important role in the criminal lifestyle. This is particularly true of the original Factor 1 items (conning, manipulative, charming, pathological lying) but is also frequently true of the total PCL-R score (Cornell et al., 1996; Woodworth & Porter, 2002). A limitation of Hare's model is that it is as weak on theory as it is strong on methodology. For Hare's psychopathy construct to become a true theory of crime, the role of Facet 4 (antisocial) of the PCL-R in psychopathy will need to be clarified and the linguistic processing and conditioning problems Hare believes cause psychopathy will need to be studied and developed further.

Like Hare's (1996, 1998) psychopathy model, Gottfredson and Hirschi's (1990) general theory of crime emphasized an individual's propensity for crime. Unlike Hare's psychopathy model, Gottfredson and Hirschi postulate an environmentally mediated predisposition to low self-control as the cause of crime rather than a biologically mediated predisposition to psychopathy. Whereas Hare's model emphasizes proactive or planned criminality, Gottfredson and Hirschi's general theory emphasizes reactive or impulsive criminality. Together these two dimensions of criminality form a comprehensive theory; alone they provide only a partial explanation of criminal propensity. Hence, Gottfredson and Hirschi's exclusive focus on reactive criminality, despite assertions that they have discovered a general theory of crime, is a major weakness of the theory. In addition, Gottfredson and Hirschi have been criticized by Akers (1991) for circularity in the sense that the predictor (low self-control) may simply be another term for the criterion (crime). Developing clearly distinct predictor and criterion measures is there-fore vital for further development of Gottfredson and Hirschi's theory.

A Lifestyle Theory of Crime

DeLisi (2005) classified Walters's (1990) lifestyle model as a propensity theory of career criminality. The lifestyle theory of crime, however, is more accurately described as a mixed or integrated theory in which both develop-mental and propensity factors are represented. With an emphasis on early onset and associated risk factors (Moffitt), dynamic interaction and change (Sampson & Laub), proactive criminality (Hare), and reactive criminality (Gottfredson & Hirschi), the lifestyle model seeks to provide a comprehen-sive theory of crime development and etiology. According to lifestyle theory, development of a criminal lifestyle can be divided into four phases: (1) the initiation (precriminal) phase, (2) the transitional (early criminal) phase, (3) the maintenance (advanced criminal) phase, and (4) the burnout and maturity phase. All of the major influences and factors that contribute to the rise and fall of a criminal lifestyle as well as desistance from the lifestyle are contained in these four phases. First, however, we discuss two important precursors to a criminal lifestyle.

Precursors to a Criminal Lifestyle

Even before a person enters the initial phase of a criminal lifestyle, his or her thinking and behavior have been shaped by early interactions and expe-riences with the environment that make it more or less likely that he or she will eventually enter a criminal lifestyle. A **template** of sorts is created via the child's early interactions with the wider social environment, an environment that includes cultural and subcultural factors, peer and school influences, and the current family context. Growing up in a culture that emphasizes material gain over prosocial values, an environment saturated with antiso-cial peers, and a family that provides little in the way of consistent emotional support can create a template more conducive to crime than growing up in a subculture that emphasizes prosocial values over material gain, an environ-ment where the individual is surrounded by conventional role models, and a family that provides ample amounts of emotional support. The child can then put this template into action before engaging in his or her first official act of delinquency or crime in a **trial run.** Blaming a sibling for breaking your mother's prized vase when you, in fact, broke the vase could be considered a trial run for mollification. Grabbing a toy out of another child's hands could serve as a trial run for interpersonal intrusiveness. A template and the ability to practice elements of this template in various trial runs act as precursors to a criminal lifestyle and illustrate the dimensional nature of criminal thinking and behavior (i.e., everyone is represented at some point along the continuum).

Phase I: Initiation

Each phase of a criminal lifestyle is a function of **incentive, opportunity, and choice.** Incentive can be traced back to the primordial condition of existential fear, opportunity constitutes the genetic and learning factors that either increase or decrease a person's risk for future criminal involvement, and choice is the decision-making apparatus that leads to actual criminal behavior. **Lifestyle initiation,** the first phase of a developing criminal lifestyle, is characterized by experimentation and exploration of lifestyle practices and themes. Although an earlier age of onset in antisocial behavior is a risk factor for future crime as an adult, most children who engage in antisocial behavior do not go on to become adult criminals (Natsuaki, Ge, & Wenk, 2008). Accordingly, the majority of people who enter the initial phase of a criminal lifestyle do not move on to the next phase. This section features the motivating influence of existential fear and how genetic, learning, and choice factors help shape a criminal lifestyle.

Incentive: Existential Fear

The motivational component of lifestyle theory rests on four fundamental assumptions originally outlined in Walters (2000a). Assumption number one is that personal advantage (the organism's ability to survive) is on par with survival fitness (the organism's ability to pass its genetic material onto future generations) in motivating behavior. Assumption number two is that all living organisms possess a life instinct, the goal of which is to preserve the organism by supporting its survival. The third assumption upon which the lifestyle theory of motivation is based is that the "reward systems" of the brain, the dopamine-rich pathways of the mesolimbic system and the opiate-rich pathways of the medial forebrain bundle, make it possible for the organism to associate the life instinct with specific survival-supporting behaviors. Whereas the first two assumptions extend to all organisms, the third assumption only extends to organisms with brains capable of generating a reinforcing response (i.e., vertebrates). The fourth assumption upon which the lifestyle theory of motivation rests is that the environment is continually in motion and thus presents a challenge or threat to the organism's life instinct, thereby encouraging the development of adaptive strategies designed to protect and advance the organism's survival.

Existential fear is confined to humans who are at least 18 to 24 months old, the age at which human children show initial signs of distinguishing between themselves and the surrounding environment (Lewis & Brooks-Gunn, 1979). Those who are capable of differentiating between themselves and the external environment are capable of experiencing existential fear. Existential fear is made up of two principal elements: (1) a fear of nonbeing or nonexistence borne of the realization that everything that lives will eventually die (Tillich, 1952) and (2) a sense of separation and alienation from the environment (subject–object duality) made possible by human self-awareness (Boss, 1963). What ultimately molds existential fear into a unique expression of a person's current existential condition is how it interacts with three areas of life experience: (1) affiliation, (2) control/predictability, and (3) status. Someone with worries in the affiliation realm may channel their existential fear into concern over possible social rejection, abandonment, or nonacceptance. Someone with concerns of a control/predictability nature may fear loss of control, uncertainty, or decision making. In someone searching for status, existential fear may be experienced as a fear of anonymity, failure, or success.

Lifestyle theory seeks to understand how people perceive, process, and manage threats to their survival. Preponent cues are environmental stimuli the organism is biologically prepared to respond to with fear or withdrawal (Seligman, 1971). The baring of teeth by a wild animal, the slither of a snake through high grass, or the change in pressure on the skin as a spider walks across the back of one's neck are all examples of prepotent stimuli capable of eliciting a fear response. Although in vivo therapeutic techniques based on learning and conditioning principles are highly efficacious in the treatment of many forms of anxiety disorder, particularly simple phobias (Choy, Fyer, & Lipsitz, 2007), research indicates that nonassociative or Darwinian variables are more intimately involved in the formation of fears and phobias than are associative or conditioning variables (Menzies & Clarke, 1995). Compared to simple organisms, which rely on a narrow range of innate mechanisms to combat threats to survival, complex organisms such as humans can override and alter their genetic programming with learned responses, some of which are coded as cognitive schemes. Humans and primates, unlike lower organisms, can become desensitized to prepotent cues and sensitized to nonprepotent cues via learning and symbolic thought.

Once a threat is perceived and before it can be managed, it must be effectively processed. Threat processing can take one of three forms. At its simplest level, a threat is processed as survival strain, which can be defined as automatic movement toward nourishing stimuli and away from noxious stimuli. A flower growing toward sunlight would be an example of the former, and a hand reflexively removed from a hot stove would be an example of the latter. A more advanced level of threat processing is available to organisms with a central nervous system. Through activation of the autonomic "fight or flight" response, an organism with a central nervous system is capable of processing threats as primal fear. In the wake of a challenge to an organism's immediate survival, autonomic activity increases and the organism prepares for action. Existential fear is the third and most advanced form of threat processing. Whereas survival strain and primal fear involve direct threats to an organism's survival, existential fear constitutes a symbolic threat to the organism's psychological survival made possible by the human organism's ability to associate certain thoughts and behaviors with activation of the reward systems of the brain. Humans are capable of processing threat at all three levels but must be capable of perceiving themselves as separate from their environment before processing a threat as existential fear.

In managing a threat to their survival, organisms make use of both defensive and constructive strategies. Whereas **defensive strategies** are designed to eliminate or neutralize an existing threat, **constructive strategies** are designed to prevent a future threat from surfacing. Common defensive strategies in response to survival strain and primal fear are approach/withdrawal, aggression, immobilization, and appeasement (Marks, 1987). Common constructive strategies in response to survival strain and primal fear are affiliation, control/predictability, and status seeking (Walters, 2000a). Defensive and constructive survival strategies in the face of existential fear are more cognitive than behavioral in that the threat is more symbolic and less immediate than the threats processed as survival strain or primal fear. As a group, constructive and defensive threat management strategies give rise to global styles of threat management. The first global style is despair whereby the organism is overwhelmed by environmental change. In humans who process a threat as existential fear, this first style of threat management is characterized by marked imbalance between construction and defense and between **accommodation** (creating a new scheme to account for environmental information) and **assimilation** (incorporating environmental information into an existing scheme) (Piaget, 1963), with construction and accommodation predominating. The second global style of threat management is patterning whereby the organism reduces sensitivity to environmental change and establishes a cognitive pattern of defense over construction and assimilation over accommodation. The third and final global style of threat management is adaptation. Adaptation is marked by a dynamic balance between the defensive and constructive behavioral strategies and the assimilating and accommodating cognitive strategies.

I have been approached by colleagues who have expressed interest in many aspects of lifestyle theory but who find existential fear too amorphous to grasp and study. Although existential fear, like evolutionary theory, cannot be tested directly, there are tests that can and must be done to assess, validate, and refine this construct. Existential fear is the motivating or driving force behind lifestyle development and provides an incentive for lifestyle behavior. People enter the initial phase of a criminal lifestyle, in part, because they believe that this lifestyle will provide them with something they believe has been missing from their lives, whether the missing ingredient is excitement, power, freedom, or respect. It is not until sometime later that they realize the promises made by a criminal lifestyle are illusory and short-lived. After all, how much excitement, power, freedom, and respect can be found in jail or prison? During the early phases of a criminal lifestyle, however, the promise of social acceptance (affiliation), power and control (predictability), and social respect (status) are realized to some extent by those who engage in various forms of criminal behavior and this serves as motivation to enter into lifestyle activities. Based on research indicating that criminality is often associated with low anxiety or fearlessness (Newman & Schmitt, 1998), a weak bond between existential fear and physical survival can leave one vulnerable to the promise of a criminal lifestyle. The fearlessness hypothesis is discussed further in Chapter 8 of this text.

Opportunity: Genetics and Learning

Existential fear may provide the incentive for lifestyle initiation, but criminal opportunity and choice must also be in place before a criminal lifestyle can be initiated. Opportunity factors increase or decrease risk rather than determine behavior and so no single factor or set of factors is responsible for a criminal lifestyle. Instead, it is the accrual of multiple risk factors that contributes to a person's position on the dimensions of a criminal lifestyle. One opportunity factor is temperament. There is a significant genetic component to some dimensions of temperament (Isen, Baker, Raine, & Bezdjian, 2009), which may be why a small but consistent relationship has been observed between crime and various genetic indices (Rhee & Waldman, 2002; Walters, 1992). Lifestyle theory divides temperament into five dimensions: (1) sociability, (2) activity level, (3) emotionality, (4) novelty seeking, and (5) information processing speed. Children high in sociability, activity level, and negative emotionality and low in novelty seeking are said to be at risk for future antisocial behavior (Walters, 2000a). Environmental stress and strain is a second opportunity factor relevant to crime. Stress increases a person's odds of entering a criminal lifestyle by reducing rational thinking and opportunities for prosocial alternatives (Agnew, 2006). Socialization likewise plays an important role in initiating a criminal lifestyle. Either strong socialization to criminal definitions of behavior (antisocial peers, violent media) or weak socialization to noncriminal definitions of behavior (prosocial peers, noncriminal parents) can lead to the initial phase of a criminal lifestyle (Simons, Simons, & Conger, 2004). Availability is a fourth opportunity factor capable of increasing future risk of experimenting with a criminal lifestyle (DiCataldo & Everett, 2008).

Interactions between different opportunity factors may play a particularly salient role in initiating a criminal lifestyle. DeLisi, Beaver, Vaughn, and Wright (2009), for instance, found evidence of a gene x environment interaction between a polymorphism in a dopamine receptor gene (DRD2) and having a criminal biological father in a group of African American girls. Whereas the DRD2 polymorphism and criminal biological father failed to predict subsequent delinquency and crime, the interaction between the DRD2 polymorphism and criminal biological father was significant. In another study, the well-documented relationship between substance abuse and serious delinquency was found to be moderated by such potentially important opportunity factors as parental attitudes, exposure to delinquent peers, and gender (Kuhns, 2005). Whether opportunity factors combine in an additive fashion or interact with one another, they are an important source of influence in the initiation of a criminal lifestyle.

Choice

Lifestyle theory is not deterministic in nature. Although incentive drives behavior and opportunity shapes it, the individual still makes choices. Even in the face of strong incentive, difficult temperament, and high levels of antisocial socialization, an individual can choose to do something other than crime. The decision-making process that gives rise to choice can be divided into two stages: (1) the generation stage and (2) the evaluation stage. Whereas the generation stage is concerned with the creation of multiple choice options, the evaluation stage is designed to appraise the choice options identified during the generation stage. People who fail to generate a sufficient number of alternative solutions to a problem are just as handicapped as people who cannot accurately assess the costs, benefits, and probabilities of various options. Developmental and experiential factors both play a role in the choices we make. With experience and brain maturation, we are in a better position to consider the likely consequences of our actions and use this in our overall analysis of options. Crime often begins before the person's brain has fully matured and the person has been exposed to a wide array of life experience. Hence, options that require less work and promise larger or more immediate rewards are often favored over options that require more work and offer smaller or delayed rewards (Horner & Day, 1991). Criminality often begins in adolescence when an individual's choice and decision-making skills are nonoptimal and enmeshment in a criminal lifestyle inhibits these skills further. Consequently, one focus of intervention is improving the individual's problem-solving skills.

Each of the four models described in the first part of this chapter highlights one or more of the content features that contribute to the initiation of a criminal lifestyle. Temperament, on the one hand, is relevant to both Moffitt's (1993) developmental taxonomy and Hare's (1996) psychopathy construct. Sampson and Laub's (1993) age-graded theory and Gottfredson and Hirschi's (1990) general theory of crime, on the other hand, highlight socialization influences: Sampson and Laub emphasizing the informal prosocial influences that contribute to desistance and Gottfredson and Hirschi the antisocial parental influences that inhibit the formation of self-control and ultimately lead to crime. Stress plays a peripheral role in Sampson and Laub's theory, whereas availability and choice are central to both Sampson and Laub's age-graded theory of informal social control and Gottfredson and Hirschi's general theory of crime. The initiation phase of a criminal lifestyle is characterized by an interaction of incentive (existential fear), opportunity, and choice and the surfacing of preliminary patterns of antisocial behavior. The extent to which these initial patterns become habitual and internalized through repetition, reinforcement, and ritualization is the degree to which they serve as the foundation for the second (transitional) phase of a criminal lifestyle.

Phase II: Transition

The **transitional phase** of a criminal lifestyle is marked by a growing commitment to a criminal or antisocial pattern. Although there is no age range for this or any other phase of the criminal lifestyle, the transitional phase most often starts in late adolescence or early adulthood. Like a young person embarking on a career, the transitional phase involves a decision to devote oneself to the lifestyle. Devotion to the pattern grows over the course of the transitional phase and becomes maximal during the third or **maintenance phase**. The number of people dropping out of a criminal lifestyle during this second phase is less than the number dropping out during the first phase but more than the number dropping out during the third phase. In other words, desistance during the transitional phase is not the norm but it is far from rare. According to Sampson and Laub (1993), desistance is encouraged by early adult life changes (job stability, marriage, military service) and while a substantial slice of individuals desist as a consequence of job stability or marriage, many more transition into the maintenance phase.

Incentive: Fear of Lost Benefits

The transitional phase of a criminal lifestyle is characterized by a growing commitment to the criminal lifestyle and a dawning realization that crime pays. Experimentation during the lifestyle's initiation phase exposed the individual to the material and psychological benefits of crime and antisocial behavior. Existential fear promotes a transition in the criminal lifestyle by creating a fear of losing the material and psychological (affiliation, control, status) benefits of crime. Existential fear, as expressed in a fear of losing the benefits of crime first realized during the initial phase of the lifestyle, is the driving force behind the transition from crime experimentation to criminal lifestyle commitment. This incentive then interacts with certain opportunity and choice factors to give rise to the second or transitional phase of a criminal lifestyle, which is characterized by increased internalization of lifestyle goals, values, and beliefs.

Opportunity: Schematic Subnetworks

As the criminal lifestyle becomes more internalized, the opportunity factors, which were largely behavioral during the initial phase, become more cognitive. Lifestyle theory, as was previously mentioned in Chapter 2 of this book, holds to a hierarchical view of criminal cognition with belief systems at the top of the hierarchy, individual criminal thoughts at the bottom of the hierarchy, and several levels of **schematic subnetworks** sandwiched in between. The six schematic subnetworks central to lifestyle theory are (1) attributions, (2) outcome expectancies, (3) efficacy expectancies, (4) goals, (5) values, and (6) thinking styles. During the transitional phase of a criminal lifestyle, bifurcation often occurs in people's attributions for their own and others' negative behavior. Whereas their own problematic behavior may be attributed to external, global, unstable, and uncontrollable factors ("I don't know why I do what I do"; "It wasn't my fault"), other people's problematic behavior is attributed to internal, specific, stable, and controllable factors ("He's an asshole"; "She got what she deserved"). Self-serving bias, which is present in many walks of life (Miller & Ross, 1975), in extreme cases can lead to hostile attribution biases whereby ambiguous behaviors displayed by others are interpreted as deliberate slights or signs of disrespect (Matthews & Norris, 2002). Hostile attribution biases have the greatest likelihood of surfacing in a cognitive system that is high in reactive criminality (Smithmyer, Hubbard, & Simons, 2000; Walters, 2007c).

Outcome and efficacy expectancies also change over the course of the transitional phase. Outcome expectancies for crime become progressively more positive and progressively less negative during the transitional phase of a criminal lifestyle and the specific types of positive outcomes the person anticipates receiving from crime (power, respect, excitement, freedom) can give rise to specific criminal actions. Efficacy expectancies also change during the transitional phase such that the individual becomes increasingly more confident in his or her ability to carry out crime and increasingly less confident in his or her ability to live a conventional lifestyle. The goals a person pursues during the transitional phase of a criminal lifestyle become increasingly more short-term and his/her values and priorities gravitate toward the visceral (hedonistic) value cluster and away from the social, work, and intellectual value clusters. Finally, criminal thinking styles begin to take root during the transitional phase of a criminal lifestyle as a means of protecting, justifying, and promoting lifestyle behavior. The degree to which proactive and reactive criminality drive the lifestyle also becomes more evident during the transitional phase, with mollification (Mo), entitlement (En), power orientation (Po), and super-optimism (So) supporting proactive criminality and cutoff (Co), cognitive indolence (Ci), and discontinuity (Ds) supporting reactive criminality.

Choice

The decision-making process may narrow as the individual moves through the transitional phase and begins to consider fewer and fewer options other than crime. Walters (1990) speculated that problems are more likely to surface in the generation of options rather than in the evaluation of options during the transitional phase of a criminal lifestyle. This, of course, assumes that the individual possessed adequate problem-solving skills to being with. In many cases, especially in those individuals classified by Moffitt (1993) as early onset LCP offenders, early rule breaking interfered with personal and social skill development and the individual never possessed adequate problem-solving skills from the start. However, in those individuals who possessed adequate problem-solving skills prior to the onset of the transitional phase, generation stage skills (producing options and alternatives) are usually more seriously affected than evaluation stage skills (exploring the advantages and disadvantages of each option).

The transitional phase relates only weakly to the four developmental or propensity models discussed earlier in this chapter. Of the four models, Sampson and Laub's (1993) age-graded theory of informal social control and Gottfredson and Hirschi's (1990) general theory of crime probably have the most to contribute to our understanding of the transitional phase of criminal lifestyle development. Increased opportunities for crime and decreased opportunities for conventional behavior correspond reasonably well to the lack of informal social control mechanisms central to Sampson and Laub's age-graded theory and the emphasis Gottfredson and Hirschi (1990) place on opportunity and choice. Other models, such as Bandura's (1986) social cognitive theory (attributions, outcome expectancies, efficacy expectancies, goals), Yochelson and Samenow's (1976) criminal personality (thinking styles) and Cornish and Clarke's (1986) rational choice model (decision making), are more in line with elements of the transitional phase of criminal lifestyle development than the four developmental or propensity models reviewed at the beginning of this chapter.

Phase III: Maintenance

The constructive and defensive coping strategies described in an earlier section of this chapter serve as precursors of constructive and defensive cognition. According to lifestyle theory, people construct their own reality and then they go about defending this reality. During the transitional phase of a criminal lifestyle, the individual constructs belief systems designed to support the lifestyle. Defending these belief systems and one's continued involvement in a criminal lifestyle is the purpose of the lifestyle's third or maintenance phase. During the maintenance phase, the individual becomes fully committed to the criminal lifestyle, sees few viable alternatives to crime, and comes to rely on the criminal thinking patterns to make sense of the world. Because the level of commitment is so high during the maintenance phase, only a small portion of people voluntarily exit the lifestyle at this juncture. Involuntary exit from the lifestyle via incarceration or death and temporary suspension of lifestyle activities during imprisonment are more common, however. For some, incarceration is a stimulus for change; for others, incarceration temporarily arrests the lifestyle; and for still others, incarceration neither arrests nor slows the lifestyle.

Incentive: Fear of Change

Why do people who are unhappy with their lives not change? Many do but many more do not, and much of this can be attributed to a **fear of change**, which is, in effect, a fear of the unknown (Carleton, Sharpe, & Asmundson, 2007) or a fear of fear (Williams, Chambless, & Ahrens, 1997).

As frightening as a person's situation may become, change is even scarier. In the eyes of many individuals, continuation of the pattern is preferable to the uncertainty of change. Whereas existential fear is channeled into a fear of losing the potential benefits of crime during the transitional phase of a criminal lifestyle, it is expressed as a fear of losing something one has become accustomed to during the maintenance phase. In the maintenance phase of a criminal lifestyle, the threats that stir fear converge around loss of the individual's lifestyle-based worldview and social relationships (Sable, 1989); past, present, and future views and sense of power and control (Castelnuovo-Tedesco, 1989); and self-view and long-standing criminal identity (Bugental & Bugental, 1984). Loss of any one of these realized benefits of crime may be interpreted as symbolic death by someone who has committed him- or herself to a criminal lifestyle (Walters, 2000a).

Opportunity: Psychological Inertia

According to Sir Isaac Newton an object at rest will remain at rest, and an object in motion will remain in motion unless acted upon by an outside force. This first law of motion, also known as Newton's law of inertia, illustrates how opportunity perpetuates the lifestyle during the maintenance phase. Once a criminal lifestyle has been set into motion, it will continue to function and maintain itself unless acted upon by an outside force, in this case, change. There are several aspects of the maintenance phase that support **psychological inertia** (Walters, 2000a). First, there is attribution through self-labeling. Labeling oneself a criminal, bank robber, or drug dealer can perpetuate a criminal lifestyle by shaping one's self-view, shutting off avenues of change, and creating a self-fulfilling prophecy. Low self-efficacy for conventional behavior leads to atrophy of conventional skills for individuals who once possessed such skills and prevents the development of conventional skills in individuals who never possessed these skills in the first place. Enabling behavior on the part of friends and family members can also lead to psychological inertia such that the individual does not feel the need to develop or use responsibility and personal coping skills. Learning and conditioning contribute to psychological inertia and the maintenance phase of a criminal lifestyle by reinforcing, routinizing, and ritualizing current lifestyle patterns. Unless there is something standing in its way, the lifestyle will continue to operate, if for no other reason than psychological inertia.

Choice

There is a tendency on the part of many individuals functioning in the maintenance phase of a criminal lifestyle to act as if they do not have a choice. During the maintenance phase, a fair number of individuals may comment that they feel "stuck" in the lifestyle with no apparent way out. This is understandable given the fact that during the maintenance phase the driven quality of a criminal lifestyle is maximal, the person's evaluative skills are often as weak as his or her generational skills, and many options have been knifed off (Sampson & Laub, 1993) by the individual's near-exclusive involvement in and commitment to lifestyle activities. The cumulative disadvantage described in the Sampson and Laub (1993) age-graded theory of informal social control, the continuity of life-course antisocial behavior mentioned in Moffitt's (1993) developmental taxonomy of antisocial behavior, the stability of the psychopathy–violent criminality relationship emphasized in Hare's (Gretton, Hare, & Catchpole, 2004) psychopathic model of crime, and the immutability of low self-control that Gottfredson and Hirschi (1990) reference in their general theory of crime all reflect aspects of the maintenance phase of criminal lifestyle development.

Phase IV: Burnout and Maturity

The fourth and final phase of a criminal lifestyle is **burnout** and **maturity**. Burnout is marked by a decrease in the physical pleasure a person derives from crime as well as the reduced physical strength and stamina people experience as they age. Maturity is a psychological process marked by a rising interest in goals and activities incongruent with crime. Physical burnout is more prevalent and reliable than psychological maturity to the extent that it occurs in the vast majority of cases, usually sometime during the 4th or 5th decades of life (Massoglia & Uggen, 2007). Psychological maturity is less frequent than burnout, can occur at any age, and may not occur at all in a significant portion of cases. Hirschi and Gottfredson (1983) call the age–crime relationship one of the brute facts of criminology, and longitudinal research on crime trajectories indicates that most offenders demonstrate declining patterns of offending beginning in their late 20s to early 30s and that very few offenders are criminally active after age 40 (Ezell & Cohen, 2005; Massoglia & Uggen, 2007). Whereas the shift from the maintenance phase of a criminal lifestyle to burnout and maturity can be abrupt, in most cases it is a gradual and uneven process that requires months, and in some cases, years to enact (Le Blanc & Fréchette, 1989).

Incentive: Fear of Death, Disability, and Incarceration

By the time an offender enters the burnout/maturity phase of a criminal lifestyle, existential fear has come full circle. The innate incentive designed to protect the physical survival of the organism became linked to psychological survival of the lifestyle during the transitional and maintenance phases and in the process paradoxically put the individual's physical survival in jeopardy for the sake of the lifestyle. During the burnout/maturity phase, existential fear is once again positioned to serve physical survival. It is during the burnout/maturity phase that many offenders develop a growing fear of incarceration (Ayers et al., 1999). Whereas before, the individual may have viewed incarceration as an occupational hazard or as an opportunity to gain street credibility, now incarceration is viewed as a burden and an embarrassment (Irwin, 1970). The fear of incarceration has the greatest probability of encouraging desistance when accompanied by a fear of death, serious injury, or lifestyle-related disability (Cusson & Pinsonneault, 1986). The fear of dying in prison is a particularly salient incentive for desistance.

Opportunity: Approach and Avoidance

The opportunity (risk and protective) factors involved in burnout and maturity are of two types: (1) approach factors and (2) avoidance factors. Opportunity factors that support burnout and maturity by encouraging the individual to approach goals, activities, and outcomes incompatible with crime include marriage and parenthood (Irwin, 1970; Laub et al., 1998), a reliable social support network of noncriminal friends and family members (Adler, 1993; Clark, 1992; Hughes, 1998), meaningful employment (Graham & Bowling, 1995), and participation in noncriminal extravocational and extradomestic activities (Adler, 1993). Opportunity factors that support burnout and maturity by encouraging the individual to avoid goals, activities, and outcomes compatible with crime include the accumulated negative effects of crime and incarceration (Cusson & Pinsonneault, 1986), decreased preoccupation with material success (Shover, 1996), abandonment of old criminal associations and friendships (Sommers, Baskin, & Fagan, 1994), a growing awareness of the futility of crime (Cusson & Pinsonneault, 1986; Shover, 1996), and reduced positive outcome expectancies and attenuated efficacy expectancies for crime (Ayers et al., 1999; Shover, 1996). These opportunity factors interact with one another to reduce the risk of future criminal involvement and increase the probability that the individual will embrace a noncriminal way of life.

Choice

Desisting from crime is as much a matter of decision making as it is a matter of changing incentives and opportunities. In addition, choice plays just as big a role in exiting crime as it does in entering crime. As the negative effects of crime accumulate even someone with weak problem-solving skills can see that the costs of crime outweigh the benefits. Crime may pay during the early phases of the lifestyle but by the time the individual enters the burnout and maturity phase the cost of crime nearly always outweighs its benefits. Age facilitates burnout and maturity to the extent that it buttresses the individual's problem-solving skills (both the generation and evaluation of options improve with age) (Amirkhan & Auyeung, 2007) and reduces the perceived benefits of crime. With the cost–benefit balance shifting in a direction favorable to desistance, the individual arrives at the decision to exit the criminal lifestyle (Sommers et al., 1994). This is often a series of decisions rather than a single decision, and there may be several lapses and backtracks before the decision is eventually implemented. In some cases, the individual never desists, but this is relatively rare in individuals over the age of 40. Even the highly recidivistic sample of early-onset offenders included in the Glueck and Glueck (1950) study was relatively free of crime after age 50 (Sampson & Laub, 2003; see Figure 5.1).

Figure 5.1   Proportion of Participants Arrested by Age

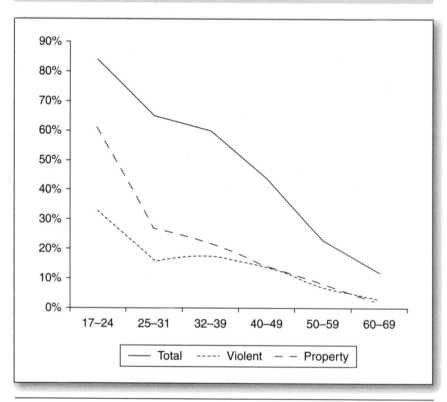

Source: Sampson & Laub (2003) reanalysis of Glueck & Glueck (1950)

Of the four developmental and propensity models described at the beginning of this chapter, Sampson and Laub's (1993) age-graded theory of informal social control does the best job of explaining burnout and maturity. The notion that family attachments and new responsibilities bring reductions in crime lies at the heart of the burnout and maturity phase. Moffitt's (1993) views on the AL pattern also fit well with the notion that the criminal lifestyle is self-limiting. Her contention that LCP offenders, if they desist at all, do not do so until mid-to-late adulthood, however, is inconsistent with lifestyle theory's position that all offenders eventually burn out and the vast majority mature sufficiently to exit the lifestyle. Gottfredson and Hirschi (1990) asserted that the age–crime relationship is invariant across race, gender, culture, and a host of other variables and that while people's absolute level of criminal propensity may decline, there is no change in relative criminal propensity as people age. In other words, those who commit the most crime during early adolescence will also commit the most crime during middle adulthood. Unfortunately, they provide no real explanation for the age-based drop in crime except to say that the organism grows weaker and has fewer opportunities for crime with age. Hare and his associates (Hare, McPherson, & Forth, 1988) also acknowledged that a good portion of the criminal behavior committed by the psychopathic offender also declines after age 40, but like Gottfredson and Hirschi (1990) they offered little in the way of a satisfactory explanation for this phenomenon.

Jerry Revisited: A Developmental Analysis

Jerry entered the initiation phase of a criminal lifestyle at age 5 when he and his brothers started breaking into neighbors' homes and committing various other forms of vandalism. He was socialized into the criminal lifestyle by his brothers and stepfather, who provided Jerry with a template of thoughts and behaviors that helped facilitate his initiation into a criminal lifestyle. From an early age, Jerry made the choice to commit crime, but he did not appreciate the ramifications of his choice. He has spent the better part of his life, however, paying for his bad decisions. Availability was another factor contributing to Jerry's initiation into the criminal lifestyle. He lived in an environment ripe with criminal opportunities, from his brothers' antisocial adventures to his stepfather's drug-dealing business. Genetically based temperamental factors may also have contributed to Jerry's entrance into a criminal lifestyle as evidenced by a history of criminality in several biological relatives (natural father, brothers) and his impulsive and hyperactive behavior during early childhood.

The principal objective of the transitional phase of a criminal lifestyle is the internalization of lifestyle attitudes, goals, and values. Jerry's entrance into the transitional phase began when he was 9 or 10 years old and was aided by a growing fear that he was missing out on the lifestyle (e.g., asking his stepfather to show him how to shoot drugs) and development of strong positive outcome (power, excitement, freedom) and efficacy ("I'm good at making meth") expectancies for crime. Around this time, Jerry's thinking began to change, and he started believing that he was entitled to the fruits of his criminal activity (En) and was so good at crime that he would never get caught (So). His ability to use crime and intimidation to get what he wanted from others soon became a dominant force in his life and led to the proactively oriented thinking that would later play a major role in his adult criminal behavior.

Jerry apparently entered the maintenance phase of a criminal lifestyle in his late teens. Although this is earlier than most offenders, it is consistent with his early entrance into the initiation and transitional phases. Fear of change is clearly present in his thinking, even today. On more than one occasion he has expressed ambivalence about change: "What if I change and I don't like it?" At this point in time, he still views change as a potential waste of time and a very scary prospect. Self-labeling ("I accept the fact that I am a criminal, and I'm not sure that will ever change"), self-efficacy for crime ("I am very good at making meth"), and enabling ("Throughout my life my mom has always been there to bail me out of trouble") are also prominent. Psychological inertia clearly governs Jerry's current thinking and behavior. He has been in the maintenance phase for so long (12 years) that the lifestyle seems to be on automatic pilot. This suggests that change is an active process and if one does nothing the lifestyle will continue if for no other reason than psychological inertia.

At age 31, Jerry remains in the maintenance phase of a criminal lifestyle. Many of the behavioral aspects of the criminal lifestyle are currently arrested because Jerry is in prison, but the cognitive aspects continue to operate. Before Jerry can enter the burnout and maturity phase of the criminal lifestyle, his fear of the negative consequences of this lifestyle (death, disability, incarceration) must surpass his fear of change, negative outcome expectancies for crime must eclipse positive outcome expectancies for crime, efficacy expectancies for noncrime must exceed efficacy expectancies for crime, and the accumulated perceived negative effects of the lifestyle must outweigh the accumulated perceived positive effects. The desistance that often comes as a result of a person's entrance into the burnout and maturity phase of a criminal lifestyle will be discussed further in Chapter 7 of this text.

Conclusion

Rather than applying a propensity approach to habitual criminality, the lifestyle model integrates aspects of propensity and development in the formation of a comprehensive theory of the criminal lifestyle. It does so by incorporating incentive (motivation), opportunity (genetic and environmental risk/protective factors), and choice (decision making) into a single model. Incentive derives from existential fear. As the individual proceeds through the various phases of a criminal lifestyle, existential fear is transformed from a concern for physical survival to a concern for psychological survival and back again. What begins as a concern for physical survival mutates into a concern for psychological survival and continuation of the lifestyle during the transitional phase of a criminal lifestyle. The paradox is that the concern for psychological survival and continuation of the lifestyle places one's physical survival at risk. Desistance requires that existential fear convert back to a concern for physical survival. Opportunity factors instrumental in the formation of a criminal lifestyle are largely behavioral at first but become increasingly more cognitive over time. In other words, a person starts acting like a criminal before he or she starts thinking like one. Interventions for the criminal lifestyle, however, target criminal cognition first and criminal behavior second based on the theory that a change in thinking precedes a change in behavior. Hence, treatment of a criminal lifestyle proceeds in a manner opposite to how the lifestyle develops. Two of the propensity and developmental theories profiled at the beginning of this chapter (Moffitt, Hare) make short shrift of choice, but the other two theories (Sampson & Laub, Gottfredson & Hirschi) consider choice an important piece of the crime puzzle. In line with the latter two theories, choice serves as a linchpin, along with incentive and opportunity, in lifestyle theory's developmental model of criminal behavior.

Key Terms and Concepts

Accommodation

Adolescence-Limited

Age-Graded Theory of Informal Social Control

Assimilation

Burnout

Choice

Constructive Strategies

Cumulative Disadvantage

Defensive Strategies

Developmental Taxonomy

Existential Fear

Fear of Change

General Theory of Crime

Incentive

Life-Course-Persistent

Lifestyle Initiation

Maintenance Phase

Maturity

Opportunity

Psychological Inertia

Psychopathy

Psychopathy Checklist

Schematic Subnetworks

Self-Control

Template

Transitional Phase

Trial Run

6

Phenomenology

The Criminal Lifestyle in a Subjective Context

The greatest way to live with honor in this world is to be what we pretend to be.

Socrates (469 BC–399 BC)

Married to the Mob

Roger is a 37-year-old white male serving a 32-year sentence for gun possession, robbery, and murder. The older of two children, Roger bounced from home to home during his formative years. His parents divorced when he was a year old, and he first went to live with his mother in several lower socioeconomic homes in and around New York City. When he was 6 years old, he was sent to live with an affluent aunt in Tennessee. He also spent several years living with his father and on one occasion lived with his maternal grandparents. Roger acknowledged that abuse was common in both parental homes and that when he started running away on a regular basis he was sent to a foster home. Roger left home for good at the age of 16. To support himself, he burglarized homes and businesses. Crime was nothing new for Roger, who starting at age 11, served as a "lookout" for several criminals who worked in his father's machine shop and made extra money stealing car bumpers. A number of these individuals were associated with organized crime. In adolescence, Roger came to the attention of several organized crime families. One of these families eventually "adopted" him and made him a close associate. Through his interactions with members of organized crime, Roger achieved a sense of acceptance, belonging, and stability that had been missing from his family life up until that point. He responded with undying loyalty and conformance to their standards (e.g., avoidance of all drug use and obedience to all orders).

Roger is friendly, likable, and engaging. His social skills allow him to manipulate others, but not all of his relationships are superficial or exploitive. He has been married for 12 years and has a 12-year-old son who is very important to him. His father-in-law is a reputed member of an organized crime family and a "man's man," according to Roger. Although Roger never graduated from high school, his IQ is well above average. The reason he did not complete high school was that he was incarcerated at age 16. He received his GED while in prison and took several college courses as well. Given that he has spent only about 24 months in the community since the age of 16, his work record is spotty. In fact, most of the job skills he picked up while in prison were criminal (i.e., bookmaking, auto theft). Roger's first three documented arrests occurred when he was 16: two for burglary and one for criminal tres-passing. He spent 1 year in jail as a result of these offenses. He then spent time in state prison between the ages of 17 and 20, followed by new state sentences of 4 years and 5 years between the ages of 21 and 25 and between the ages of 25 and 30, respectively. Roger has been incarcerated in federal prison since age 31 for the instant offense. His ability to abide by the rules of prison is no better than his ability to abide by the rules of society. In the past 5 years, he has received four disciplinary reports—three for fighting.

A review of Roger's Lifestyle Criminality Screening Form (LCSF) profile (Table 6.1) indicates significant involvement in a criminal lifestyle (total raw score = 10) and a tendency to be involved in criminal activities that violate the rights of others rather than criminal activities that stem from impulsiveness and irresponsibility (V > I). Roger has no compunction against committing intrusive crimes, and despite a total LCSF score at the lower boundary of the high risk range, he is at elevated risk for engaging in violent criminality. The Psychological Inventory of Criminal Thinking Styles (PICTS) results are unremarkable for the most part and a little surprising. The General Criminal Thinking (GCT) score is barely signifi-cant (T-score of 51), there is no elevation or difference between the

Proactive Criminal Thinking (P) and Reactive Criminal Thinking (R) composite scores, and most of the thinking style scales are below average (T-score < 50). Roger's elevated scores on the power orientation (Po) and superoptimism (So) scales, however, are worthy of note. I would argue that much of Roger's criminality is socialized antisocial behavior in which he demonstrates high socialization to a deviant subculture (i.e., the mob) instead of low socialization to the larger culture. Hence, he gains both a sense of control (Po) and invincibility (So) from his associations with others in this deviant subculture. In other words, the harm Roger inflicts is less an attempt to impose his will on others and more a manifestation of his higher loyalties to a deviant subculture that preys on others.

Table 6.1 Roger's Lifestyle Criminality Screening Form and Psychological Inventory of Criminal Thinking Styles Results

Lifestyle Criminality Screening Form (LCSF)	
Overall Involvement	
Total score	10 (64th percentile)
Risk level	High
Factor Scores	
Violation (V) factor score	6
Impulse (I) factor score	1
V-I index	6:1
Subsection Scores	
Irresponsibility	2
Self-indulgence	1
Interpersonal intrusiveness	4
Social rule breaking	3
Psychological Inventory of Criminal Thinking Styles (PICTS)	
Higher-Order Factor	
General Criminal Thinking (GCT)	51

(Continued)

(Continued)

Composite Scales	
Proactive Criminal Thinking (P)	50
Reactive Criminal Thinking (R)	48
Thinking Style Scales	
Mollification (Mo)	48
Cutoff (Co)	40
Entitlement (En)	41
Power Orientation (Po)	60
Sentimentality (Sn)	49
Superoptimism (So)	61
Cognitive Indolence (Ci)	58
Discontinuity (Ds)	48

Note: LCSF scores are raw scores, and PICTS scores are T-scores.

Phenomenology

Phenomenology was introduced into philosophy in the early 20th century by the German philosopher, Edmund Husserl (1859–1938). Such major existential thinkers as Martin Heidegger (1889–1976), Jean-Paul Sartre (1905–1980), and Maurice Merleau-Ponty (1908–1961) expounded on Husserl's original work to make phenomenology a major force in both philosophy and psychology. It is important to understand, however, that phenomenology is both a school of thought and a research methodology. The school of thought that is phenomenology concerns itself with understanding social and psychological phenomena from the perspective or internal frame of reference of the individual experiencing the event or events in question (Gubrium & Holstein, 2000). With respect to a criminal lifestyle, then, the school of phenomenology is interested in how someone in the lifestyle experiences the thoughts, feelings, and actions that contribute to the lifestyle. It is the lived experience of people involved in a particular activity that drives phenomenology and attracts the interest of the phenomenologist (Greene, 1997).

Phenomenology is also an investigative method. The phenomenological method is a process by which the unique personal experiences of the research participants are explored in detail (Groenewald, 2004). As a method of research, phenomenology requires a **qualitative** approach and design. Husserl used the term **epoché** to describe the suspension of judgment that occurs when all questions of truth and reality are bracketed out and the observer focuses on the speaker's **subjective experience** (Bentz & Shapiro, 1998). **Bracketing** (setting aside the researcher's assumptions) was used in interviews with Roger, who was presented with 10 open-ended questions (see Table 6.2) designed to illuminate his experiences in the criminal lifestyle and his attitudes toward the lifestyle, himself, and society. Phenomenological interviews are frequently audiotaped, but audiotaping was not used in this case because it is against prison policy to tape-record inmates. Attempts were made, however, to present Roger's narrative as close to verbatim as possible, with minimal interpretation by me, the observer. In addition, Roger reviewed the chapter for accuracy prior to publication.

Table 6.2   Ten Guiding Questions

Q1. Tell me about your life before crime.
Q2. Describe your initiation into crime.
Q3. Discuss how you became committed to a criminal lifestyle.
Q4. What do you think you learned from prison?
Q5. What factors encourage or facilitate your continued involvement in a criminal lifestyle?
Q6. What factors discourage or hinder your continued involvement in a criminal lifestyle?
Q7. Relate to me your view of society (its people, policies, and institutions).
Q8. How do you rate yourself on the (eight) thinking styles and (four) behavioral styles of a criminal lifestyle?
Q9. If you were to abandon the lifestyle today, what would you miss most?
Q10. How do you see your future?

Responses to the Ten Questions

Q1. Tell Me About Your Life Before Crime.

Roger characterized his early home life as "chaotic." He states, "My mother and father separated when I was 1 [and after the separation] I went to live with my mother. . . . My mother had mental problems, and she would pick guys who would beat her up. I remember this one time when this particularly brutal guy beat her with a two-by-four. She went to the hospital and me and my brother went to a foster home." When his mother got out of the hospital, the family went to live in a women's shelter on the outskirts of the ghetto. Roger recalls being put down and teased by kids from the projects because living in the women's shelter was considered worse than living in the projects. "When I was 6, my father arranged for me to live with a rich aunt and her husband in Tennessee." This opened Roger up to a whole new life of "private schools, manners, regimentation, and Sunday brunches," but there was something that did not change. The aunt's husband was as brutal as the men his mother lived with, and there were allegations of sexually inappropriate behavior on the part of the aunt: "She would exercise nude in front of us." Roger responded by running away from home just a few months before his 10th birthday. After running away from his aunt's house, he spent the next year living with his maternal grandmother, followed by a 2-year stint with his father, a year with his mother, and then back again to his father's house at age 14.

Teachers informed Roger's father that Roger had leadership skills and that many of the other children in school looked up to him. Unfortunately, Roger did not always lead his classmates in a positive direction. "I was a little ring leader. It never occurred to me that I was short because I never see people that way. . . . You know, what they're wearing, how you look, or how tall you are . . . none of that's important." In describing what is important to him, Roger relates that "I look into people's souls. I see people for what they are rather than for what they pretend to be." He attributes his ability to "read" subtle emotional signals from others to the physical abuse he suffered as a child: "It makes you more sensitive to people's moods and facial expressions." Being more intelligent and articulate than most of his classmates, Roger would often stand up for them in arguments with teachers. "The teachers would get mad at me and tell me to stop acting like the other kids' lawyer." Roger reports that his father would always make him find answers to his questions and that this "made me think for myself. I therefore could argue better than most other kids and sometimes better than the teachers." His rebelliousness toward authority and his success in arguing eventually got to the point where school officials gave Roger's father an ultimatum when Roger was in the ninth grade: "Either take him out of school for the rest of the year or he will be expelled."

Roger's rebelliousness was not restricted to school and started long before he set foot in a classroom. A variety of authority figures felt the sting of his antiauthoritarian attitude and rapidly became targets of his animosity. He describes a wooded area near his home where he and his friends would build forts, play war, and explore nature. Several years after they discovered the area, the local government started using it as a dump for large slabs of concrete, wood deposits, and other waste materials from construction sites. "My friends and I were like eco-terrorists—you know, ELF [Earth Liberation Front] and such—long before eco-terrorism was popular. We would pour sand in the gas tanks of the trucks and tractors so that they wouldn't start. . . . We'd throw bottles at the workers. One time I got onto a crane and nearly drove it into the ocean." To Roger and his friends, it was wrong that the city was using their forest as a dump and they responded by "taking matters into our own hands." Roger has done that for most of his life, but unlike many offenders he does not complain about the consequences of his actions or the bad breaks he has had in life. Despite the unhealthy life circumstances under which he was raised, Roger does not blame his parents. "I would tell you stories and you would blame my parents, but I never did. That's too easy. Things are more complicated than that."

According to Roger, "authority figures have to prove themselves before I will listen. What right do they have to tell me what to do, anyway . . . what books to read, what subjects to study, what information is important and what information isn't important." Roger notes that he first developed a negative attitude toward authority when he was 4 years old and would observe some of the men in his mother's life beat her up and abuse him and his brother. As a child, Roger was curious and filled with questions. When he started getting answers that didn't make sense to him he grew cynical and rebellious. "I am skeptical of most authority figures because they lack honesty and integrity." Referencing the "eight billion dollars people spend on their pets each year" and comparing this to the horrid way animals in factory farms (e.g., pigs, cows, chickens) are treated even before they are slaughtered to make food for humans, Roger highlights society's hypocrisy. Noncriminals are not "morally superior to criminals," says Roger; they are just afraid of external sanctions (e.g., punishment, prison). "I can't be controlled in that way. I don't fear pain, prison, or death," he retorts. "You can't punish me. You have to show me the error of my ways." When authorities were about to place him in a special school because of his history of frequent school moves, he warned them "I assimilate to any situation and I will become just like those kids in the special school." Nobody listened.

Q2. Describe Your Initiation Into Crime.

"My father had a machine shop, and after work he would go to his girlfriend's house. Some of the guys who worked at the shop would take my father's car after work and drive it around the city looking for Cadillac bumpers to steal." While these adults were under a Cadillac, surreptitiously removing the bumper, 11-year-old Roger would be sitting in the front seat of his father's car acting as a lookout. "I would beep the horn if anyone was walking up or down the street." Roger reasons, "I wasn't acceptable to society, but I was acceptable to these criminals." Because he had a track record of frequent school changes, he was sent to a special school for troublesome children when he was 14 years old. "Kids would be fighting in the halls and selling drugs right there on school grounds, just like out of a movie or something." For Roger, it became a school for crime. At his new school, he learned new ways to profit from crime. The profit for him, however, was more emotional than material. "It wasn't for money. It was to show you that I was smarter than you." Early on, he took an idealistic approach to crime: "I never messed with civilians, only businesses," but his idealism soon faded, in part because of his growing disillusionment with the morality of everyday people.

One of the first crimes Roger committed by himself was burglary of a business. "The holy grail for the kids at school was robbing a bicycle store, but I did them one better—I robbed a gun store. I went to the public library and took out books on spies and other stuff and used this [information] to crack the gun store." He disconnected the alarm by cutting the phone lines and then cut the sheet metal that held the two locks. "The locks fell to the ground, and I just left them there so that there would be no mystery how I did it." This illustrates that even as a teenager Roger sought to show up the police and thumb his nose at authority at every opportunity. A year later, he was arrested for the first time. After his third arrest in several months, he was sent to an adult jail for 12 months at the age of 16. "I didn't realize they could put you in an adult jail when you were 16. I thought you had to be 18." He admits, however, that knowing this ahead of time would not have changed the path he was on. When he went to the mostly black jail, he was surprised to see that it was populated by many of the same kids he went to school with at the special school. "Back then, when a white kid went to jail he could expect to get beaten up and have his property taken from him. For me, however, it was no big deal because everyone knew me." He adds that going to jail opened him up to an entirely new society, people whose entire existence was based on doing crime, day in and day out. "I romanticized the lifestyle and took to it like a duck to water."

"I wasn't born bad. I don't think anyone is, but I'm in prison and that needs to be explained. I explain it as something I learned and something I chose to do. Life is what you make it." What, however, would possess someone to voluntarily assume the villain role? In other words, "Why would you want to be the bad guy? The way I look at it, good people are good because of external authority not because of internal authority. They aren't honestly moralistic because they only do good for fear of the consequences should they do bad." Roger has struggled with his decision to enter into a life of crime. He resolves the struggle, in part, by rationalizing his actions and finding a higher moral purpose for his behavior. "I was above people morally because I chose to do what I did, not because I was afraid of the government or afraid of God. . . . If I don't hurt you it's not because I'm afraid of being punished for it but because I don't think it's right to hurt you." In his mind, he is on higher moral ground because he is honest about his desire to live a criminal lifestyle and tries to avoid harming civilians not because he is afraid of going to jail if he does so but because it conflicts with his internalized moral code.

Roger freely admits that he "chose crime with the full knowledge of the consequences," including the possibility of going to jail. He admires and to some extent identifies with people like John Dillinger and Edward Teach (Blackbeard the Pirate). "I can relate to those guys. They chose their path [in life]. John Dillinger chose to be John Dillinger. Blackbeard chose to be Blackbeard. They made a conscious decision not to be a stooge or pay homage to the queen. They chose to be the bad guy. Set out to be the villain. I can respect that." He then goes on to assert that we do ourselves a disservice by labeling John Dillinger or Blackbeard evil rather than trying to understand their behavior. "If you dismiss Blackbeard as a monster, you miss the opportunity to understand him, why he did what he did. Something happened in his life that disillusioned him. Keep in mind, this guy (Blackbeard) was dining with mayors and governors in America. He was accepted by certain members of our [colonial] government. John Dillinger was a smart guy, not some cold-blooded killer. . . . What this shows is that we cannot just accept everything we are told. You must look deeper into the subject." I took Roger's advice and looked deeper into the subject of Blackbeard and discovered that despite his frightening reputation there are no verified accounts of Blackbeard ever killing anyone (Konstam, 2006).

Q3. Discuss How You Became Committed to a Criminal Lifestyle.

At the age of 15, Roger made the transition into a criminal lifestyle. He initially viewed crime as an outlet for his high energy, but it was the perceived benefits of crime that drew him into the lifestyle. Roger maintains that before he turned 15 he was not hyperactive because he was involved in both physically (i.e., mountain climbing, hiking, playing sports) and mentally (i.e., playing chess, reading an hour or more a day) challenging tasks that channeled his energy into productive activities. When he was 15, however, something happened that made him feel the need to channel his energy into crime. He admits "that if I had put the amount of energy I spent on crime into business or some other legitimate pursuit I would be a very successful person today." Instead he sits in a prison cell, away from his family and disillusioned with his chosen lifestyle. "When I first started out in crime, I met guys (older criminals) who were more protective and helpful than any person I had ever met. They were like warriors. They would jump into a situation if you were getting beat up or in a jam. You strive to be like these guys. You think these are the guys you might eventually work for or even kill for and that they came up like you. They earned their bones, so to speak. This is the impression we are given, but as you go through the ranks you begin to realize that a lot of them aren't like you." Just like the kings in days of old "the ruling class [of criminals] is born into it, a lot of them got there because of their fathers or their uncles, by manipulating situations, or by dumb luck. As soon as they get arrested, they flip [cooperate with the authorities]."

The first crimes Roger committed with any degree of regularity were "smash and grab" robberies. Roger and two or three friends in what were known as "crash crews" would smash through the glass counter and grab whatever they could get their hands on. They did this at jewelry stores, electronics stores, and even a comic book store: "I once stole 4,000 comic books" he states, proudly adding that he "read every last one of them." Roger attributes his choice of "smash and grab" robberies to two factors. "When you're a kid and don't have any technical skills, that ["smash and grab" robbery] was the path of least resistance. It was easy, and you got better at it over time." In addition, "this is a high adrenalin type of crime. I didn't get high on drugs, but it was a real rush seeing those flashing red lights in the rearview mirror. I've been in seven car chases in my life. It's a major rush. . . . It can be dangerous though. Dangerous to you and dangerous to others. Luckily all my chases occurred early in the morning, 2 or 3 o'clock, and no civilians were ever hurt." Going to prison at age 16 only refined his criminal skills and increased his criminal contacts. He began a lifelong association with members of organized crime and moved into such mob-run activities as numbers running, bookmaking, and managing joker poker machines. He also started doing freelance armed robberies. "This may sound strange, but I had never done armed robberies before and felt that I needed to round out my career, fatten up my résumé. I would plan things out, just like in the movies. Before the robbery, we would go to a theatrical supply store and get wigs and real neat disguises. I'd use guys from different boroughs who didn't know each other so that if they got caught they could not tell on anybody but me. Guys felt comfortable doing the robberies because I looked out for them."

From mid-adolescence to early adulthood, Roger's self-efficacy as a criminal grew, and his positive outcome expectancies for crime increased.

Every time he went to jail or prison, he added new skills and information to his repertoire. "I went to jail, and it was not as detrimental as it should have been. It didn't deter me because I already knew everybody there and was well taken care of." Prison, for Roger, was like a college for crime. "I spent a lot of time in jail picking people's brains. How did you get caught? What errors did you make? I developed rules to do crime by." For a time, the rules helped him get away with most of his crimes, but this didn't last. "Eventually you become lackadaisical and let your guard down. If you would only stick to the rules, you could be successful." The problem with street crime, however, is that street criminals measure success in the short-term rather than in the long-term. "It's like anything. You can develop a system [for crime]; it's just a matter of following the system. I had a system, but I didn't always follow it." Roger admits, "I liked the excitement, the adrenalin rush. Sometimes you can get so caught up in the excitement that you forget about your plan. That's when you make mistakes." He explains the process using a poker analogy. "I play poker. I go by the numbers. I grind it out. If I play poker, this way I am going to maximize my wins and minimize my losses, but playing good poker is boring. Sometimes you go tilt and start gambling. That's when you lose."

The progressive nature of a criminal lifestyle is not lost on Roger. "Everything was gradual. Little by little, I started breaking through my inhibitions. . . . There were certain things I couldn't do, but then you work your way up to them. You slowly become desensitized." Roger described a situation in state prison a number of years ago when he was having problems with another inmate. His father-in-law learned of the conflict and sent Roger some oil with instructions to heat it up and throw it in his antagonist's face. Roger responded that he would never throw hot oil into another person's face and that he would rather use his hands or a shank (homemade knife). However, 3 years later he ran into "a similar problem with another inmate and I didn't hesitate throwing hot oil in the guy's face." The progressive nature of the criminal lifestyle has made Roger realize that things can only get worse, not better. The more he invested in the criminal lifestyle, the more he realized the futility of crime. "I dedicated my life to this [criminal lifestyle], and I'm very bitter. It was too late in life when I realized that this thing [criminal lifestyle] is not what it seems and a lot of the people in it aren't what they pretend to be. I don't believe in the life anymore, but I still won't flip."

Q4. What Do You Think You Learned From Prison?

"What I like about jail, still like about jail, is that you can't hide . . . from yourself. . . . When you come here [to prison] you find out who you are. No glamour, no masks. Sometimes you find out things about yourself that you didn't know before. It strips you down. You are not your car. You are not your clothes. You are not your house. You are yourself. You are stripped of everything external and left with yourself. You can't fake it. You can't lie to yourself. Everything that defines you comes out." Roger states that because of prison, "I know who I am." He adds that "in society you are judged by how much you make and what you own, in prison you are judged by who you are." Roger observes that many of the people who are considered successful by society's materialistic standards are "morons who couldn't make it in prison. In prison, you are on equal footing with everybody else. It doesn't matter how much you had out there [in society]. In [prison], if you don't know who you are, you will soon find out and so will everybody else. You can learn a lot about yourself from prison—your strengths and weaknesses, what you can do and what you can't do." According to Roger, "it's the small things you do in prison that are important. The small details are what define you. How you handle food, are you stingy or are you generous? How you approach someone. Anybody can handle the big things, but it's how you handle the small things that defines you as a person."

As a consequence of daily exposure to the same group of people over an extended period of time, "the friendships you form in prison are closer than the friendships you have on the streets. You depend on each other, have each other's backs. If someone has a beef with you, they also have a beef with your friends." Roger theorizes that "prison is like a microcosm of the world. You have different groups that are like countries. Each group or tribe has its leaders, ambassadors, and warriors. I'm an ambassador myself who goes out and meets with the other groups. The way things operate in here are like how the world works. Wars, treaties, negotiations—it happens in prison just like it happens in the world, but instead of being between prison groups and tribes it's between countries and nations." Like anything else, a person must learn the rules, roles, and rituals that define his or her membership in a prison group: "Even the jungle has rules." Roger states that a lot of the rules and roles are learned through stories or oral tradition. "Someone might say 'when Charlie did so and so Harry backed him up' or 'when this guy said something disrespectful to Mel this is how we handled it.' If we are part of the same crew and you have a problem with a guy but are injured or scheduled for release in 2 weeks and I have 10 more years to do I am going to step up and handle the problem . . . in prison you learn a code of conduct, rules to live by."

Roger states that he learned the "code of conduct" from doing time in state prison. "A lot of my statements come from state prison, which can be brutal. There are clear-cut lines of behavior in state prison. A system is in place for both convicts and staff. The tribe, family will protect you, but you must be accepted into the group." Social affiliation means adopting the roles, rules, and rituals of the group. After you are accepted into the group, you can expect to be backed up if you run into a problem. "You fight for each other, and because of this you have to be careful what you do because this comes back on you and your brothers. You have to realize that you're not by yourself. You affect others in the group, tribe. Because of this, you have to be careful when making moves." Roger remarks that he once helped another inmate whom his friends had ostracized. This individual was having problems with a Hispanic group, and so Roger accompanied him to the prison yard, armed to the teeth with several homemade knives in case there was a problem. A few minutes later, several of Roger's friends showed up to provide support, but they made it clear that they were there for Roger and not for the other individual, whom they considered a "scumbag." It was then, Roger admits, that he learned the value of friendship in prison and the importance of not straining that friendship by making bad decisions.

Prison is also a "badge of honor" to those in the criminal lifestyle, says Roger. "If you want to be taken seriously as a criminal, you must do time. There is no way to get around it. When you're a bad guy, you get caught and you go to prison. It's just that simple." People who have never done time or who have never done "serious" time (at least a few years at a stretch) are either treated with suspicion or dismissed as fake gangsters and cardboard criminals. The suspicion comes from the fact that if you have never done serious time, one possibility is that you are working with the authorities. Dismissal comes from the fact that if you only commit low-risk crimes (e.g., loan sharking, numbers running) then you are not a serious criminal and undeserving of respect as a criminal. Nevertheless, these "bottom feeders," as Roger calls them, end up getting rich off the sweat of real criminals and don't have to pay the price of coming to prison for long stretches. Using an analogy from medieval times, Roger recalls the time when knights would go out to fight for the king, which in many cases meant expanding the kingdom. "Some of the knights would die in the process of getting more revenue and tax dollars for the kingdom. The cooks and bakers who didn't have the guts to go out and fight reaped the benefits that these warriors died for." He is quick to admit, however, that the choice made by the cooks and bakers of old and the "bottom feeders" of today is "the smart choice."

Q5. What Factors Encourage or Facilitate Your Continued Involvement in a Criminal Lifestyle?

To Roger, his father-in-law symbolizes values, beliefs, and an ideology that Roger has lived his life by but which he had trouble articulating until just recently. He met his father-in-law in prison before he met his wife, when his father-in-law was just a guy from the neighborhood whom everyone respected. Upon their release from prison, Roger began working for his future father-in-law as part of his father-in-law's **crew** (component of a larger criminal organization or family). "He was just an ideal of what I was looking to become. I used to think that a person like him could not exist. The fact that he did exist just amazed me. . . . He's a man's man, someone you can believe in." Roger openly acknowledges his love for his father-in-law: "the kind of love that men reserve for those of the same sex, not a fag thing. It's the kind of love you instill in someone you respect. You'll die for that person." Although Roger was unable to put into words exactly what it was about his father-in-law that attracted him, loyalty, leadership, and family bonding all appeared to be important. "Words escape the emotions I am trying to express. I made a conscious decision to not live for him but to live like him. That kept me in the lifestyle. When I came home [from prison] I started working for him; I was on his crew. When I met him, he was a soldier, not a wise guy, but he was working on becoming a wise guy . . . everyone respected him, he was a legend in my neighborhood. He believes in family, he's a family man."

It was his father-in-law who initially cemented Roger's commitment to the criminal lifestyle, and it is his father-in-law who continues to be his primary inspiration for remaining in the lifestyle. It wasn't so much the man, however, as what he symbolized to Roger. "He was an embodiment of an ideal. He was a physical manifestation of that ideal." Roger's relationship with his father-in-law also provided him with a doorway into organized crime. "That organizational structure, I took to it like a duck to water. It was justified. I never questioned anything. You follow what I'm saying. I believed so much in the people. I never asked any questions." The fact that he suspended his skepticism when he first entered the mob illustrates the hold organized crime had over Roger when he was a young man. Yet, that hold remained tied to his father-in-law. "If he [father-in-law] quit the mob and owned a deli, I would have been happy working for him, sweeping the floor." The love and admiration that Roger feels for his father-in-law is reminiscent of the love and admiration a son holds for his father. It could be stated without exaggeration that his father-in-law became the father figure and organized crime the family that were missing from Roger's early life, and he consequently formed a strong attachment and sense of obligation to both. Wives and girlfriends can also reinforce the lifestyle if, like Roger's wife, who according to Roger "grew up in [prison] visiting rooms," they accept certain fundamental tenets of the lifestyle (e.g., don't snitch).

The affection Roger felt for his father-in-law and the mob as he was constructing his criminal lifestyle was matched only by the repulsion he felt toward authority figures and the government. "Laws [are designed to] make people sheep and the government the shepherd. They are put into place for controlling purposes. It's actually quite clever." Roger maintains that from an early age he suspected something was wrong and that while he could not put his finger on the problem it fueled his antagonism toward authority. He knew it had something to do with hypocrisy, however. "Many people reap benefits they do not deserve." Roger referenced his comment by citing the work of Thomas Edison, who allegedly stole or bought many of his inventions from Nikola Tesla, Joseph Swan, and others. He adds that the only difference between pirates like William (Captain) Kidd and freebooters like Sir Francis Drake was that pirates refused to share their booty with the king and were consequently reviled instead of beloved. Even the Iran-Contra affair makes its way into Roger's diatribe: "The government brings drugs into the country but the individual who sells drugs on the street corner is a scumbag. We have lost focus on the real problem. The wolves have pulled the wool over our eyes. Every time I feel bad about being a criminal, being in pain, and wondering if I should have been a normal citizen, working 9-to-5, I think about these things. And it keeps me warm at night. It justifies my actions. I have no problem with my situation. I am an enemy of the state. I am happy being an enemy of the state."

Being a criminal is a "badge of honor" to people like Roger and as we saw previously, going to jail and prison is part and parcel of the lifestyle. Roger relates the story of a 60-year-old "wise guy" who was approached by the government to turn informant. "This guy was told he would be getting at least 20 years and probably wouldn't make it home. He responded that he has to shave every morning, meaning he has to look at himself in the mirror every day and live with what he has done. He didn't take the deal, and he did the entire 20 years." Continuing in the lifestyle means continuing to go to jail and prison, a fact Roger knows all too well. "They want, need a guy like me to go to jail and become a criminal. I am not part of their system. I don't fit in. I'm not a worker bee. If you let me and guys like me in society and we proliferate, guess what happens? We become a group, a force to be reckoned with. We become a revolutionary group. We become the ruling class. So they take guys like me and put us in prison and we become better criminals. That's part of the system." Roger acknowledges that given modern technology revolution would be futile, and so he remains content to continue playing the role of criminal. "The government controls people through drugs and television . . . movies and television are the best leash and chain ever invented. Things can be happening, but then the *Sopranos* or *American Idol* comes on and everybody has to get in front of the TV." Because he doesn't use drugs and rarely watches television, "the government controls me by keeping me locked up."

Q6. What Factors Discourage or Hinder Your Continued Involvement in a Criminal Lifestyle?

"Every time I get released, I hit the street running, except this last time. My wife and my kid should have been enough motivation to quit the lifestyle. I worked a legitimate job . . . construction . . . lugging concrete. I busted my ass." Despite his good intentions, Roger lasted less than 3 months on the job and from there jumped right back into the lifestyle. "A man given the choice between responsibility and pride is going to choose pride every time, especially if the responsibility makes you feel less than a man." During the brief period in which he worked a legitimate job, Roger felt "like a fish out of water." He adds that living a legitimate lifestyle made him "feel like an alien," and he longed for the comfort of the criminal lifestyle. "It [a legitimate life] takes you out of your comfort zone. I never got comfortable in that situation. I didn't know how to handle it." Roger would go around asking people he knew in legitimate jobs how they handled certain situations and tried to imitate them but it was to no avail; he couldn't shake the feeling that something was missing from his life. Still, he felt bad for his wife and child: "If you're going to have a wife, you have to live a certain way. Having a wife and kid gave me a sense of civility but I'm not civil and I could never be a civilian." In his words, "I fled from responsibility."

As much as it might hurt his wife and child, Roger felt as if he needed to return to the criminal lifestyle—not so much because of what it offered but because of how "vulnerable" he felt without it. Being away from the lifestyle "injured my pride in the sense that I had set myself apart from society. That's why I never ratted. It was too much like giving in to the enemy. I don't work a regular job, I don't pay taxes, I get my income from the land, hunting and gathering, so to speak. Now I'm in trouble, and I'm going to call the police? It's like an atheist who goes through life preaching against God and the first time he finds himself in trouble pulls out the rosary beads and starts praying." Much of this relates to image, something of great importance to Roger. "I'm short, I ain't no big fuckin' guy, but I walked through prisons and I'm respected. What do you think the key to that was? It was because of the persona I projected. It showed that I was willing to go the extra step, had nothing to lose, and would take it to the next level." Roger goes on to state that "we live in a visual world" and cites research noting the presence of a positive correlation between a man's height and his salary. He then goes on to state that "in jail I have a reputation. In society I don't have that status and there is no legitimate way to get that status, except for being a criminal."

The draw of a legitimate lifestyle was not enough to discourage or hinder Roger from crime: "The perks of society . . . weren't enough for me to change what I was or do something different. My conflicting dilemma is that I know what I am, I am comfortable with what I am, but I wish I could have been someone other than who I am." Fear is also not enough to dissuade Roger from crime: "I pride myself in not feeling fear. There is something missing in me. I'm attracted to high-intensity situations . . . running on pure adrenalin . . . without fear." Perhaps disillusionment with the lifestyle or remorse for actions committed over the course of the lifestyle would be more effective in discouraging and hindering Roger from continued involvement in a criminal lifestyle. He admits that he is "disillusioned" with the lifestyle and that except for a few individuals like his father-in-law people in the lifestyle are not what they seem. Many, in fact, have become government informants and "snitches." "All of my heroes are wearing wires," he laments. "I spent too long following the same dream. It didn't exist. You can't go back and recapture the past. It's over." Quoting from the movie *Carlito's Way*, Roger observes that "criminals don't get rehabilitated. They just run out of steam." Remorse could also potentially play a role in hindering Roger's continued involvement in a criminal lifestyle. "My regrets are not what I did but what I didn't do . . . taking care of my wife, my child, and my parents." Roger may never become an upstanding citizen but neither is he destined to commit crime for the rest of his life unless he convinces himself that this is his fate.

Q7. Relate to Me Your View of Society (Its People, Policies, and Institutions).

As you might expect, Roger holds an antagonistic view of conventional society ("I'm disillusioned with the lifestyle, but I am also disillusioned with the world in general") although like many offenders his antagonism is far from absolute. "My best friend's father worked for the railroad for 25 years. He had a house, brought up his kids, went to work, never abandoned his family. His wife left him for a short period, his son went to prison, but he never forgot his values. He was a working Joe, and I always admired him. I admired him because he believed in what he did . . . what's important is being true to yourself. I respect people who believe in what they do." Roger adopts a similar view of priests. "I don't believe in God or that Jesus walked on water. I believe in priests. Priests and monks give their lives for something . . . sacrifice for what they believe in. I may not believe in what they believe in, but I respect them for believing in something." Roger has very little respect for those who are not "true to themselves. Take President Obama for example. Being president of the United States has got to be one of the greatest jobs in the world. Yet he can't be himself or say what he wants to say. He is a politician, and he can't say this because it will offend this group and he can't say that because it'll offend some other group." Roger goes on to say, "I never wanted to live that way. I don't do anything halfway. I went full throttle into the lifestyle. If I had gone off and got a regular job and then failed at that job I would have felt ashamed not because I failed but because I was not being true to myself."

Although Roger may respect certain individual citizens, he has little respect for those in law enforcement. "I understand the need for law and for cops to enforce the law. The problem you get into is bigger than you and me. It's a corrupt system. We [meaning society] are enforcing laws we have no business enforcing. You start out with a noble purpose, but once you start enforcing laws just for the sake of controlling people, keeping people in line, and justifying certain kinds of behavior you have corrupted your reason for being here. You look at the New York constitution, and it says you can't have gambling. It's bad for you . . . pictures of Mayor LaGuardia breaking up gambling machines . . . but then 20 years later we have a state lottery. They put people in jail for consensual crimes: prostitution, using drugs. At the Republican National Convention, they truck in hookers by the droves. It's something we look past. Over here it is illegal. Over there it is legal. It depends on who is doing it." He goes on to state that "these laws were invented to keep people under their thumb. They have to lock up the Martha Stewarts, the G. Gordon Liddys, and the rap stars to keep people in line and remind them that it can happen to anyone."

Roger believes the police and courts are instrumental in maintaining the hypocrisy and corruptness of the legal system. "I was arrested for burglary when I was 16. This was my first arrest, and I felt highly remorseful for what I did. Who knows how it might have turned out . . . I am a sucker for a rational argument. If someone had sat me down and explained things to me, maybe I would have taken the hook. But when I arrived at the station this detective walks up to me and with me sitting in a chair says 'you are going to tell me everything you know' as he repeatedly slaps me across the face. I remember this icy feeling came over my head. All emotion drained from me, and right then and there they became my enemies. I had nothing to say to them. In an instant, I went from an innocent kid to a hardened criminal. Then they put me in jail with adult criminals." Describing a scene from the movie *The Departed*, Roger relates that when police go to a psychologist after killing a suspect in the line of duty, they act remorseful. "Just like they said in the movie, they *want* to use their gun. That's why they sign up in the first place. You follow what I'm saying? That scene, that's why I am what I am!" In a later interview, Roger comments "you get a very cynical view of the criminal justice system once you become part of the system. The prosecutor's job is to make a case, not right or wrong. If they don't prosecute and make cases, they won't have a job. They can't afford to make moral decisions. I don't like it, but I understand it."

Roger is smart enough to realize that with technology there is no way a person can get away with street crime for any appreciable length of time. I therefore asked him why he engaged in behavior that was destined to fail. His response was that "a man does not fight for victory alone." He then used a scene from the movie *Lord of the Rings* to illustrate his point. "When the group is going up against insurmountable odds, this one guy asks the king why they are attacking the fort when they know they can't win. The king replies, 'We can't win, but we will meet them in battle nonetheless.' This is what we have to do. People sacrifice for the good of the clan, the tribe." Later in the interview, Roger states "I love technology, I don't want to go back to the stone ages. If I had been born 200 years ago, I would have been a good citizen. This [the United States] was a country that really made money. England and France got rich by plundering and taking over other countries, but the United States became great by developing its raw materials. Now all we have are paper pushers and Wall Street stooges . . . other countries, like Japan, have taken our technology and run with it. Innovation is no longer rewarded. . . . Bill Gates is another Thomas Edison . . . [he] gets his ideas from others." Roger ended this portion of the interview by stating, "I don't get hung up on money . . . I just care about honor," and to his way of thinking there is no honor in hypocrisy.

Q8. How Do You Rate Yourself on the (Eight) Thinking Styles and (Four) Behavioral Styles of a Criminal Lifestyle?

I thought it would be interesting to get Roger's take on the eight thinking styles and four behavioral styles of a criminal lifestyle as they relate to his own thinking and behavior. Whereas he achieved only an average score on the PICTS sentimentality (Sn) scale, Roger identified Sn as his most prominent thinking style. "I always romanticize what I do. In the beginning, it was a Robin Hood kind of thing—striking out against the system, sticking it to the man, glorifying your actions. I didn't set out to be the bad guy, the black sheep of the family . . . [but] set out with good intentions." Mixing Sn and mollification (Mo) he asserts that "as long as I stuck to business, didn't take anyone's personal money, didn't hurt any civilians," it was okay. In some respects, he pictured himself a high-minded revolutionary "striking out against the capitalistic system." At another level, however, he realized that his motives were not pure: "If I had been raised in a communist country, then I would have fought with my capitalist brothers against that system. . . . It all comes down to hyperbole." It is likely that Sn was strong during the early phases of his lifestyle but was also nurtured by his interactions with others both inside and outside the lifestyle: "My father-in-law would always say that even though we were the bad guys, we were the good bad guys . . . [straight] people like criminals, they live vicariously through them."

Roger also believes that power orientation (Po) has played a significant role in his criminal lifestyle, although not as strong a role as Sn. "I don't know if it's an oxymoron or just a contradiction, but here you are fighting against the power structure and you are seeking power yourself. You devote your life to being against authority. Yet the crimes you commit are geared toward power. What's power? It's not that I'm seeking to control people. I want to be respected. In order to obtain that goal (respect), I have to get violent. I had to go from nonviolent crime to shooting people. I live in the criminal world. The money I make is from crime. If someone tries to shake me down or take what I have, I can't go to the police, to the authorities. You have to adopt a violent lifestyle to deter people from taking things from you. So therefore, you start out with this antiauthority, antipower kick and you realize you have to have some power yourself to live unmolested and in relative freedom. It's ironic, a catch-22." Roger acknowledges that Po is vital to survival in a correctional environment: "In prison, people understand violence. That's the way disputes are settled and order is maintained." Power to Roger is a means to an end; the end in this case is surviving in a criminal lifestyle. Roger's penchant for instrumental aggression suggests a proactive pattern of criminality even though his PICTS proactive composite is only two points higher than his PICTS reactive composite.

There are several thinking styles that Roger believes do not relate to him. "I definitely wasn't into entitlement. I definitely wasn't into mollification. I made it a point not to blame things on others. . . . It all goes back to my father. He was always saying, since I was 12, to accept the consequences of your actions. He would say 'take responsibility for the consequences of your actions. Don't blame others for the things that you do.' I took that to heart." Even though superoptimism (So) was the highest elevated thinking style scale on the PICTS, Roger doesn't believe that it played much of a role in his lifestyle. "I was never superoptimistic because I never believed I was going to get away with anything. I never had Captain Kirk [from *Star Trek*] superoptimism . . . the belief that I could never lose. . . . I remember one time when my friend and I were doing a burglary, and we said we hoped that if we were caught that we could at least be celled together, . . . superoptimism was burned out of me early in life. . . . I was never a rose-colored glasses kind of guy, the glass was always half empty." Despite the wild life he has led, Roger insists that superoptimism was never part of that life. "You've heard of

Murphy's law, well here's Roger's law, 'if nothing can go wrong, it will.' I clipped this guy in a hotel room. There was no evidence, no DNA, no witnesses, yet 4 days later I have the state homicide police following me." Apparently, the victim had told his girlfriend where he was going and who he was going with (Roger), and she relayed this information to the police who then made Roger their prime suspect—further evidence, in his mind, that if nothing can go wrong it will.

Of the four behavioral styles that define a criminal lifestyle, Roger considers interpersonal intrusiveness and social rule breaking to be more indicative of his lifestyle than irresponsibility and self-indulgence. In our discussions, he focused heavily on social rule breaking. "When I was on the streets, I would commit at least one felony a day. I don't mean a burglary a day, but some form of criminal activity . . . meeting with other convicted felons . . . conspiring about future crimes. . . . Every day I was pursuing the criminal thing. Every day I was doing something illegal. It's almost subconscious with me. I do it without thinking about it. I try to break the rules. See this thing Doc [pointing to the glass mug in his hand which is technically contraband], my case in point. I'll sit there, this raging thing inside me against authority. These rules are ridiculous. There are so many of them." Roger also acknowledges a great deal of interpersonal intrusiveness but only with other criminals. "I'm antisocial, but I'm also very social sensitive. I walk gently around citizens. If I ever hurt civilians, it bothers me." Within the lifestyle, however, interpersonal intrusiveness was something Roger engaged in on a daily basis. "Power is simply imposing your will on someone else. In order not to have people impose their will on you, you must impose your will on them—a preemptive strike so to speak. In this lifestyle, the only way to survive is to impose your will on others in the lifestyle. I learned that from an early age . . . you have to be violent, even excessively violent, to survive the lifestyle."

Q9. If You Were to Abandon the Lifestyle Today, What Would You Miss Most?

Roger responded in two ways to my question about what he would miss most about the lifestyle if he were to abandon it right now. He states that if he were to abandon the criminal lifestyle he would lose his sense of identity but that he would also be better off and happier. "The only thing I would miss if I left the lifestyle is who I am. It [the lifestyle] is how I carry myself. I would not know who I was. I would not know how to float. Without the lifestyle, you wouldn't know Roger. Who I am flows from the criminal lifestyle. If I had grown up as a citizen, maybe I would have been as charismatic and funny as I am now, but I wouldn't be the same person." Much of one's identity, Roger insists, is based on the fact that "we live in a visual society—a society where things seem better than they really are. I don't have the social trappings that society requires. What I do have is the way I carry myself, the way I am, the respect I get from people. . . . I'm an average guy, but I've been around wise guys, millionaires, people in high places, people with much more social standing than me. Yet I am treated as an equal. I'm on equal ground with everyone. . . . I would miss that equality in my standing. That's what I like about jail. We are all the same, nobody has more [material things] than the next guy." The gist of Roger's belief is that he gains his identity and status from his involvement in a criminal lifestyle and that without this involvement he would be like "a ship without a rudder." In effect, the lifestyle gives him a sense of direction. Lifestyle theory holds that purpose and meaning are essential in the development and eventual abandonment of a criminal lifestyle; Roger's beliefs in this area clearly support this particular postulate of lifestyle theory.

Despite losing his sense of identity with abandonment of a criminal lifestyle, Roger also believes that he would be happier and better off had he never been involved in the lifestyle. "I know this sounds contradictory, but there is a part of me that wishes I was never in the lifestyle . . . like a failed actor who says they wished they'd never gotten involved in Hollywood . . . that they failed in Hollywood. . . . In my case, it would be more accurate to say that Hollywood failed the actor." Roger then goes on to describe how he believes the lifestyle failed him. "Every gangster wants to be a standup guy. I stood up in the face of relentless pursuit by the government. I was relentlessly pursued by the government. They [the government] took my lawyer from me. They approached my lawyer three times to ask if I would flip on my father-in-law. When that didn't happen, they went to the judge to get her [Roger's lawyer] taken off the case. They gave me another lawyer. I told him [the new lawyer] to tell the U.S. attorney that they could give me 10,000 years or the death penalty, and I'm still not going to say anything. They originally threatened to go for the death penalty . . . but I knew . . . they never give the death penalty to someone for killing another criminal. Even when they did go for the death penalty, I didn't flip." Roger then compares his own refusal to cooperate with the authorities in the face of heavy pressure with how some in the higher echelons of organized crime have handled similar pressure. "They go down like a house of cards . . . a domino effect. The top guy goes down and everyone else follows . . . some guys you never would have guessed . . . but when they were tested they failed the test." He concludes by stating, "My world is collapsing around me" but adds "I can look at myself in the mirror . . . I am content with my 32 years."

Q10. How Do You See Your Future?

When asked about his future, Roger's initial response was that his future is set for the next 2 decades. "I'm in here for 22 more years. That's my future. Some people can't see beyond 2 months, let alone 22 years . . . the routine . . . hamburgers on Thursdays [referring to the prison menu]. . . . I don't want to be negative and say my life is over. . . . To answer your question, as far as society goes, I don't have much to contribute. One thing I am going to do is spend the next 22 years trying to keep my family together. I'm lucky to have a close-knit family. All of the stuff I do on top [referring to making gifts in the institution hobby craft shop] is for my family. To keep them happy." Although he has no regrets for the lifestyle he has led, Roger admits that living in prison for the next 22 years has its downside. "We're social beings. We want to be around people. Autonomy is bullshit. Everyone wants to be part of a particular group, the human race. The cost is putting up with little things, normal human foibles and weaknesses. . . . Ninety percent of your peers don't understand what you're saying. You can make a clever joke, and they just have this blank stare on their face. They just don't get it . . . there are a few people who do understand, and they're like gems—someone you can actually have a meaningful conversation with." Another common trait of those with whom he lives in prison that is irritating to Roger is gossip. "Gossip is so demeaning, but it's necessary; it's ingrained in your head [referring to evolutionary views on social ostracism]. Some of the guys I live with are like old washerwomen . . . and half the time they'll rant and rave about things they themselves do, being oblivious to the contradiction."

When I asked Roger to speculate on his future after prison he replied, "Obviously, the criminal lifestyle is over. It is definitely a young person's game. I don't think most criminals get rehabilitated. They just get burned out. You don't have the energy it takes [to commit crime]." In discussing future employment opportunities, Roger remarked that "ideally . . . I have a friend who is a coffee salesman. I keep saying I'm going to get a coffee shop and get free coffee from [my friend]. It's realistic in the sense that I have done it before. You can put together a nice coffee shop with $15,000. I've done it before. I'm not living in Disneyland [like many inmates]. I'm looking at a plausible scenario. The secret to a good restaurant is . . . food is definitely important, but the most important thing is ambience, and I'm personable. I would have people who would come regularly to my coffee shop and discuss things with me every day. I had regular customers." On the topic of future family relationships, Roger continues to do what he can to maintain his marital relationship but realizes a lot can happen in 22 years. He sometimes jokes with his friends that "today is my future girlfriend's birthday." When his friends ask him how he knows this, he replies, "Because she was just born today. She'll be 22 when I get out." On a more serious note, he states, "I will try to stitch together what relationship is left with my kid. He'll be in his thirties when I get out. If I'm a grandfather, maybe I can make a go of being a good granddad," with the implication that like his own father, he has not been much of a father to his child.

In closing out the interview, Roger speaks about his future with respect to human nature, violence, and societal attitudes toward crime. "Anybody can kill. I'm the same Roger I was before I did that [committed murder]. . . . Violence is part of our nature. There was a Stephen King novel where they found something in the water that calmed people down . . . when they put it [the chemical] into the worldwide water supply people began to die, they gave up. People just lost their will to live." Roger surmises that "all of us have a Timothy McVeigh in us. The fact that we don't go around bombing buildings makes us civilized. . . . By having wars [society] gives young men the opportunity to play with guns and get their aggression out. . . . I don't like to kill animals, but I sometimes eat meat. We are meat eaters. . . . Do you think a lion is going to hell for killing a zebra? I don't think you are going to hell for killing another person. If you take killing away, you are denying what we are. You have to take the good with the bad." Roger goes on to state that "society believes people who do crime are evil. You get this stigma. You commit a crime and become less of a person. You are an outcast. They [people in society] act as if they were incapable of such an act, but everybody can have a bad day and end up with a felony. Look at Martha Stewart. Martha Stewart wasn't doing anything 80% of her detractors were doing. You want to know what I think? [I think] people don't go to jail, don't get ostracized or slandered for what they did . . . but because they got caught. Once you're caught you're reviled. You're a barbarian. You can be forgiven for everything but getting caught."

Conclusion

My objective in writing this chapter is to provide the reader with a glimpse into the subjective world of a habitual criminal. I have tried to minimize my own input and opinions and maximize, as much as possible, the individual's personal view of himself, the world, and the lifestyle that he leads.

I will, nonetheless, offer several general observations before concluding this chapter. Roger is brighter and more articulate than most inmates and comes across as a kind of self-styled convict philosopher. Nevertheless, he raises questions and issues germane to offenders of all intellectual and academic persuasions. First, Roger believes he was justified in his actions and offers no excuses for his past criminal conduct, except, of course, in the end when he adopts the common offender ploy of "the only difference between you and me is that I got caught." Second, Roger is rather idealistic in his view of the world and uses examples of societal hypocrisy as stepping-stones to crime. Therefore, while neither Roger nor the PICTS identified mollification as a major facet of his thinking, mollification does appear to have played a role in both initiating and maintaining his lifestyle. Third, Roger's criminal history clearly demonstrates how he was enticed by the expanding benefits and opportunities offered by crime and as he got more involved in crime his access to legitimate opportunities gradually declined. Fourth, Roger identifies strongly with the criminal lifestyle as evidenced by the fact his criminal identity was the one thing he would miss if he were to abandon the criminal lifestyle. Finally, Roger concurs with the PICTS that power orientation is a major component of his criminal thinking but disagrees with how the PICTS rates him on sentimentality and superoptimism. I believe the disagreement on sentimentality is a case of the PICTS failing to detect aspects of sentimentality that are present in Roger's thinking. The disagreement between Roger and the PICTS on superoptimism, however, may be more a consequence of Roger's mistaken belief that superoptimism is a general belief in complete and total invulnerability when in fact it is a more specific belief about one's current ability to avoid the negative consequences of circumscribed lifestyle behavior. Subjective analysis of offender self-report would appear to have a great deal to offer a general theory of criminal behavior and may be a rich source of hypotheses on the etiology, development, assessment, and alteration of a criminal lifestyle.

Key Terms and Concepts

Bracketing

Crew

Epoché

Phenomenology

Qualitative

Subjective Experience

7

Intervention

The Criminal Lifestyle
in a Programmatic Context

A man who has committed a mistake and doesn't correct it is committing another mistake.

Confucius (551 BC–479 BC)

The Boxer

Angel is a 29-year-old divorced Hispanic male serving an 8-year sentence for assaulting a police officer. Angel grew up, the fifth of six children, in a working-class home environment. An average student, Angel graduated from high school and stayed out of serious trouble with the law until age 20. Much of his early life, however, was spent serving as a punching bag for his father and four older brothers. He responded by learning to box and picking fights with peers. Although he was never suspended from school, violence became a way of life for him: He was a target of violence at home and a perpetrator of violence outside the home. When he was 12 years old, Angel began boxing at a local gym and was considered good enough to enter the Golden Gloves competition. He also boxed semiprofessionally for a brief period in late adolescence and early adulthood. A budding career as a boxer, however, did not prevent him from experimenting with crime. Angel's first arrest came a month before his 20th birthday when he assaulted his boxing manager while drunk. Over the next 2 years, he was arrested three more times—once for trespassing, once for drug possession, and once for public intoxication. Angel's first incarceration came at the age of 23, and he spent the next 3 years in a state penitentiary serving a 3- to 6-year sentence for robbery and assault. After his release from prison, he spent the next 18 months in the community before committing the instant offense and coming to federal prison.

Angel has an extensive family history of alcoholism and substance misuse. He states that both his father and paternal grandfather were heavy drinkers who died in their late 40s/early 50s from causes directly and indirectly related to their chronic misuse of alcohol. All four brothers also have had serious problems with alcohol, and his younger sister has been hospitalized for substance abuse on three separate occasions. Angel himself has a history of alcohol and cocaine abuse. He reports that he started drinking heavily around age 19 and attributes his current incarceration to his involvement with crack cocaine. A review of Angel's substance abuse history indicates that he has all the earmarks of *Type II or male-limited alcoholism,* a pattern of moderately severe alcohol abuse characterized by early onset (before age 25), antisocial and impulsive behavior, stimulant and other drug abuse, and severe alcoholism in paternal biological relatives, especially the father (Cloninger & Sigvardsson, 1996). Angel married at age 21, and his wife divorced him while he was in state prison. The marriage produced one child, and Angel has one other child from an on-again, off-again relationship he had with his manager's daughter. Angel has failed to provide financial support for either child and was in arrears for unpaid child support, even while he was in the community working full-time. Besides boxing semiprofessionally, Angel has worked on and off as a roofer.

Angel obtained a total raw score of 11 on the Lifestyle Criminality Screening Form (LCSF) (see Table 7.1) and displays a fair balance between the LCSF violence and impulse factors (V-I index = 5:6). Besides earning a moderate score on the interpersonal intrusiveness section of the LCSF (3), Angel achieved a very high score on the self-indulgence section of the LCSF (5), reflecting his tendency to pursue instant gratification through alcohol and drug use, sex, and perhaps gambling. The LCSF results denote significant behavioral involvement in a criminal lifestyle. Cognitive commitment and identification with the lifestyle are evident on the Psychological Inventory of Criminal Thinking Styles (PICTS), where Angel earned a General Criminal Thinking (GCT) score of 61. Angel's score on the PICTS Reactive Criminal Thinking (R) composite exceeded his score on the PICTS

Proactive Criminal Thinking (P) composite by nearly 20 T-score points. This suggests a pattern of impulsivity, hostile attribution biases, and reactive aggression. The pattern of individual PICTS thinking style scores recorded by Angel insinuate that he seeks power and control over others (power orientation, or Po), perhaps as a way of compensating for his lack of control over his own emotions (cutoff, or Co) and thinking (discontinuity, or Ds). Administration of the Antisocial Personality Disorder section of the *Structured Clinical Interview for DSM-IV Axis II Personality Disorders (SCID-II)* (First, Gibbon, Spitzer, Williams, & Benjamin, 1997) revealed that Angel satisfies the *DSM-IV* criteria for antisocial personality disorder.

Table 7.1 Angel's Lifestyle Criminality Screening Form and Psychological Inventory of Criminal Thinking Styles Results

Lifestyle Criminality Screening Form (LCSF)	
Overall Involvement	
Total score	11 (73rd percentile)
Risk level	High
Factor Scores	
Violation (V) factor score	5
Impulse (I) factor score	6
V-I index	5:6
Subsection Scores	
Irresponsibility	1
Self-indulgence	5
Interpersonal intrusiveness	3
Social rule breaking	2
Psychological Inventory of Criminal Thinking Styles (PICTS)	
Higher-Order Factor	
General Criminal Thinking (GCT)	61
Composite Scales	
Proactive Criminal Thinking (P)	56
Reactive Criminal Thinking (R)	75

Thinking Style Scales	
Mollification (Mo)	38
Cutoff (Co)	76
Entitlement (En)	54
Power Orientation (Po)	75
Sentimentality (Sn)	44
Superoptimism (So)	49
Cognitive Indolence (Ci)	56
Discontinuity (Ds)	70

Note: LCSF scores are raw scores, and PICTS scores are T-scores.

Programmed Intervention

A book on the criminal lifestyle would be incomplete without a chapter on intervention, treatment, or what I call psychological programming. The goal of psychological programming is to promote change in offenders so that they are in a position to avoid the kinds of thoughts, decisions, and behaviors that pave the way to recidivism. Change, therefore, is the objective of programmed intervention. I prefer the term *programming* to *therapy* or *treatment* for two reasons. First, change is an active process that must be worked on to be achieved. Therapy and treatment, terms derived from a medical model of intervention, convey, at least to me, an impression that the individual suffers from a condition that requires intervention by an outside expert (therapist or doctor) who will then apply certain techniques and procedures designed to change the individual. I am opposed to this perspective on offender rehabilitation and adopt the view that change originates from within rather than from without and is an active rather than a passive process. Second, the change process can be stimulated by any number of programs, not just mental health interventions. Accordingly, I group psychological programming with other forms of change-promoting programming, whether these programs are educational, vocational, religious, or recreational in nature. It is the emphasis on changing old habits and patterns that identifies something as a programmed intervention. The purpose of the present chapter is to provide an overview of the construction, implementation, and evaluation of change-promoting programs for offenders, whether incarcerated in jail or prison or on parole or probation in the community.

One of the primary functions of a mental health professional or paraprofessional working in a correctional setting is providing psychological programming to the offender population. Boothby and Clements (2000)
determined that therapy was the second most common task performed by a
group of 830 state and federal correctional psychologists—the first most
common task being administrative duties (see Figure 7.1). Whereas the psychologists participating in this survey estimated that they spend 26% of their
time doing therapy, they indicated that they would prefer spending at least
a third of their time on this activity. Alternately, compared to spending an
average of 30% of their time on administrative tasks, these psychologists
said that they would prefer spending about 18% of their time performing
administrative duties. It is anticipated that the mental health paraprofession-
als working under the psychologists participating in the Boothby and
Clements (2000) study probably spent the majority of their time doing
therapy, which is why so much of the psychologists' time was devoted to
administrative tasks. There are several reasons, however, why doctoral-level
psychologists should not be removed from the therapy equation. First, many
psychologists have a great deal to offer offenders in terms of therapeutic
expertise and second, in order to be effective supervisors of paraprofessional
therapists psychologists should themselves be well schooled and practiced in
the art of therapy. The present chapter begins with a brief review of the unassisted change construct, continues with a synopsis of the history and current
status of the "nothing works" argument against correctional programming,
and ends with an overview of psychological programming (assisted change)
in correctional settings broken down into three parts: (1) finding a philosophy of intervention, (2) implementing a program of intervention, and (3) evaluating a program of intervention.

Unassisted Change

Before moving into a discussion of programmatic or **assisted change**, it is
imperative that we consider the notion of **unassisted change**. The majority of individuals who desist from substance abuse desist on their own,
without professional help (McMurran, 1994). It seems likely that the
same is true of those who desist from crime. A 3-year follow-up of
272,111 inmates released from state prison in 1994 revealed that 67.5%
were rearrested and 51.8% were reincarcerated within 3 years of their
release (Langan & Levin, 2002). To the extent that most released offenders who are not rearrested or reincarcerated within 2 or 3 years will
never be rearrested or reincarcerated (Forst, Rhodes, Dimm, Gelman, &

Figure 7.1   Percentage of Time Spent in Job-Related Activities by
830 Correctional Psychologists

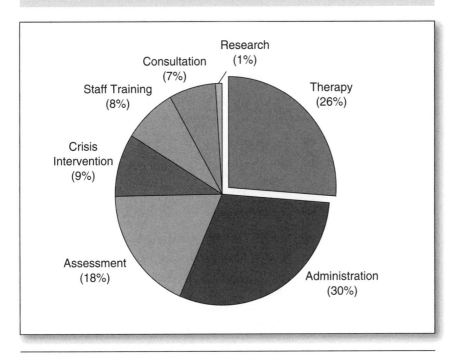

Source: Boothby & Clements (2000).

Mullin, 1983; Hoffman & Stone-Meierhoefer, 1980), we can assume that
a large minority of released offenders desist from serious crime; to the
extent that only one in eight state prisoners are in mental health treatment or therapy (Beck & Maruschak, 2001), we can assume that unassisted change was the primary means by which many of these individuals
desisted from crime.

Fifteen individuals previously involved in a criminal lifestyle cited reduced
positive outcome expectancies for crime, an increased fear of incarceration,
a growing awareness of the futility of crime, and creation of a satisfying
relationship with a woman as central to their decision to desist from crime
without formal treatment (Irwin, 1970). A 10-year follow-up of 65 individuals who had been involved in drug dealing and smuggling on an international level revealed that 13 had given up crime completely (Adler, 1993).
The reasons given for unassisted change by this group of 13 ex-felons
included the return of previously held legitimate interests, application of

entrepreneurial skills developed from their involvement in the drug trade to legitimate activities, and formation of noncriminal interpersonal relationships. Decreased preoccupation with material success, appreciation of the futility of crime, and construction of a prosocial self-view were central to the decisions of 50 property offenders to abandon crime without assistance (Shover, 1996). Finally, a recent study on male property offenders, 23 of whom had managed to avoid reconviction over a 10-year period, revealed that self-efficacy for non-crime, regret for prior criminal behavior, and social bonding (marital and occupational attachments) were all instrumental in promoting unassisted change in these individuals (LeBel, Burnett, Maruna, & Bushway, 2008).

Unassisted change from a criminal lifestyle is real and powerful. We can take advantage of this fact by constructing assisted change programs that address the functions that seem to drive the unassisted change process. Based on research findings, several of which were reviewed in this section, it is postulated that unassisted change is a function of three factors: (1) changed involvements, (2) changed commitments, and (3) changed identifications. In other words, an offender's odds of desisting from a criminal lifestyle are enhanced when he or she stops associating with criminals and starts associating with and gaining support from noncriminals, replaces the short-term immediate gratification of crime with long-term goals and values incongruent with crime, and rejects a criminal identity in favor of a noncriminal identity. Before moving into a discussion of assisted change programs and strategies, it is imperative that we examine and discard old beliefs that stand in the way of effective programming, one of which is the **"nothing works"** argument.

The "Nothing Works" Controversy

In 1966, the New York State Governor's Committee on Criminal Offenders commissioned Douglas Lipton, Judith Wilks, and Robert Martinson to conduct a literature review of prison program efficacy. Nine years later, the results of the Lipton, Martinson, and Wilks (1975) review were made public. The firestorm of controversy that this paper created in the mid-1970s continues to this day. Reviewing studies on individual and group therapy, educational and vocational training, medical treatment, environmental manipulation, and parole/probation supervision, Lipton et al. (1975) concluded that there was no evidence that any one of these forms of intervention had an ameliorative effect on recidivism. A review or meta-analysis, however, is only as good as the studies it contains and the majority of studies included in the Lipton et al. (1975) review suffered from serious methodological flaws. Randomized control group designs were rare, follow-ups were nonuniform, and several studies did not even test for statistical significance when evaluating the results of an intervention (Bernstein, 1975). Essentially, Lipton et al. (1975) concluded that there was no evidence that any of the programs they evaluated successfully reduced recidivism, hence giving birth to the "nothing works" perspective on prison programming. Fortunately, this was not the last word on correctional intervention.

In a review of studies with experimental or quasi-experimental designs that reported the results of statistical analyses and included follow-ups of at least 6 months, Gendreau and Ross (1987) determined that psychological intervention was capable of reducing future criminality. They also discerned that better designed programs had a greater impact on recidivism than more poorly designed programs. Around the time of this review, there were several major meta-analyses being conducted on the offender rehabilitation literature (Davidson, Gottschalk, Gensheimer, & Mayer, 1984; Garrett, 1985; Izzo & Ross, 1990; Whitehead & Lab, 1989), the results of which seemed to corroborate the conclusions of Gendreau and Ross (1987) and the overall efficacy of psychological intervention with criminal offenders. The lone exception was a meta-analysis of juvenile correctional programs administered by Whitehead and Lab (1989) in which minimal support was found for the rehabilitation hypothesis and where more methodologically sound studies produced weaker results than less methodologically sound studies. Reanalyzing 45 of the 50 studies from the Whitehead and Lab (1989) meta-analysis and adding another 35 studies to the analysis, Andrews and colleagues (1990) determined that appropriate psychological services, as defined by the principles of risk, need, and responsivity, achieved a significant effect, whereas inappropriate psychological services and nonrehabilitative criminal sanctions failed to produce an effect (see Figure 7.2). Hence, programs must address offender risk, need, and responsivity to be effective, a topic covered in a later section of this chapter.

Finding a Philosophy

All program providers who intervene with offenders, whether or not they are aware of it, are guided by a philosophy of intervention of one sort or another. Four such philosophies are examined in this section: (1) conflict, (2) moral, (3) fulfillment, and (4) learning.

Figure 7.2   Effect Size Estimates for Criminal Sanctions, Inappropriate
Correctional Services, and Appropriate Correctional
Services

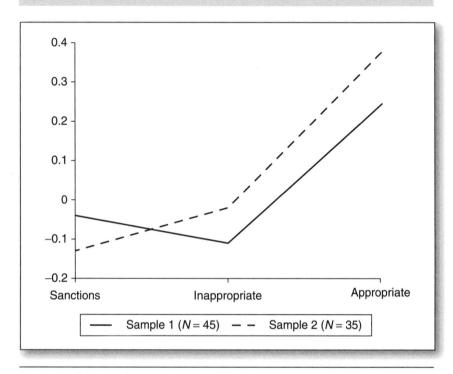

Source: Andrews et al. (1990)

The Conflict Philosophy

The **conflict philosophy** attributes crime to a conflict between basic
instinctual drives like sex, aggression, and greed and the social conventions
under which people must live. Psychoanalysis is a prime example of a system
of intervention founded on a philosophy of conflict. Because the conflicts in
psychoanalysis are often attributed to early life situations, the conflict position takes a strong historical focus such that a person's past is emphasized
and effort is directed at understanding the present in light of the past.
Conflict is resolved, according to advocates of the conflict position, when
pent-up emotion generated by the conflict is released (catharsis), the connection between past experiences and current problems is understood (interpretation), and unconscious drives are sublimated and channeled into socially
acceptable behavior.

The Moral Philosophy

To clinicians adopting a **moral philosophy** of intervention, crime is a consequence of moral lassitude and spiritual bankruptcy. Many faith-based programs and self-help initiatives like Alcoholics Anonymous and Narcotics Anonymous are grounded in a moral philosophy of intervention. Yochelson and Samenow's (1976) work on the criminal personality also derives from a moral philosophy. In the second volume of their three-volume treatise on the criminal personality, Yochelson and Samenow (1977) argued that criminal behavior can only be treated by addressing the thinking errors of criminals. However, the thrust of their intervention is to convince the person that he or she should abandon his or her criminal thinking and learn morality, a clear indication of Yochelson and Samenow's moral philosophical leanings. Intervention from a moral standpoint involves acknowledging one's moral failings (confrontation) and making amends for the negative consequences of prior criminality (atonement).

The Fulfillment Philosophy

The **fulfillment philosophy** holds that crime is a consequence of social situations and pressures that encourage people to abandon innate styles of positive interaction with the environment in favor of negative and self-defeating styles of environmental interaction. Fulfillment approaches assume the innate goodness of people and maintain that negative behaviors like crime are caused by parental and societal injunctions that run counter to the wisdom of the organism. Crime, rather than being seated in the individual, as it is assumed by those adopting a conflict or moral philosophy, is seated in the environment or in a person's relationship to the environment, according to advocates of the fulfillment model. Humanistic and existential therapies are grounded in a philosophy of fulfillment. The goals of intervention that guide someone operating out of the fulfillment philosophy are to affirm the person's humanity (valuation) and display respect for the wisdom of the organism by reflecting back the person's thoughts, feelings, and aspirations (empathy).

The Learning Philosophy

According to proponents of the **learning philosophy**, crime is the result of faulty learning acquired through conditioning (classical learning theory), reinforcement (operant learning theory), and observation (social learning theory). There is no such thing as a born criminal according to proponents of the learning philosophy; rather, the individual learns to engage in crime by associating positive outcomes with crime and negative outcomes with noncrime, receiving reinforcement for crime and punishment for noncrime, and being more exposed to the actions of criminals than to the actions of noncriminals. Behavioral and many cognitive approaches utilize a learning philosophy of intervention. Learning may be the most popular philosophy adopted by clinicians working with offenders as evidenced by the fact that the top three theoretical orientations utilized by the 830 correctional psychologists participating in the Boothby and Clements (2000) survey were cognitive, behavioral, and rational–emotive, respectively. Change, according to behavioral theorists, is realized by learning new behaviors (instruction) and being reinforced in the performance of these behaviors (rehearsal).

Instead of subscribing to a single philosophy of intervention, some mental health practitioners blend two or three philosophies together. Based on my training in graduate school and my 29 years of experience working with inmates, I have developed a learning philosophy of intervention that incorporates certain features of both the fulfillment and moral philosophies. For instance, I agree with the fulfillment position's emphasis on valuing the person but do not believe that people are necessarily born good. I also agree with Yochelson and Samenow's (1977) emphasis on choice, but I do not believe that offenders must be shamed into making better choices. Some theorists, like Hervey Cleckley and Robert Hare, are skeptical of change in certain categories of offender, in this case the psychopathic criminal. As such, they would have no philosophy of change because they do not believe that change is possible for the group of offenders with whom they work. Philosophies of intervention follow from a person's philosophy of life and should be articulated before undertaking the arduous and oftentimes frustrating task of trying to help offenders change.

Implementing the Program

Program implementation will be discussed in five parts. In the first part of this section, the decision to employ an individual versus group format when conducting an intervention is discussed. This will be followed by subsections describing the preconditions for change, the four phases of change, factors that need to be taken into account when matching offenders to interventions, and specific intervention strategies that can be used to promote change in criminal offenders.

Individual Versus Group Intervention

Individual and group modes of intervention have their advantages and disadvantages. One advantage of the individual format is the privacy/confidentiality it affords the client; additional advantages include depth of discussion, ability to focus on personal issues rather than group issues, and the flexibility individual counseling provides in terms of scheduling a meeting time (see Table 7.2). The disadvantages of individual counseling are the cost, the higher dropout rate compared to group counseling (Weyant, Dembo, & Ciarlo, 1981), and the prospect of an offender forming a transference-like dependency on the therapist. Scholars continue to debate whether group counseling is more cost-effective than individual counseling. While a recent review of the literature revealed that group counseling was more cost-effective than individual counseling in interventions for depression and childhood disorders, it failed to identify a meaningful difference in cost-effectiveness between individual and group counseling for substance dependence, anxiety, and social phobias (Tucker & Oei, 2007). Even so, group therapy is less expensive if not more cost-effective than individual counseling given that several individuals can be seen in a single session. In addition, the group format allows for social support, the modeling of positive behaviors, role-playing or behavioral rehearsal, the ability to gain a new perspective by watching how other people resolve personal problems, and learning by helping others. The disadvantages of group therapy include decreased privacy/confidentiality, the possibility of destructive feedback from other group members, the modeling of inappropriate behaviors, and a sense of being overwhelmed by others' problems. Taking into account the strengths and weaknesses of each format for the type of program one is proposing, the program provider selects an individual, group, or mixed format.

Preconditions for Change

Offenders fall at several different levels of change readiness, although one of the largest groupings is Prochaska and DiClemente's (1992) **precontemplation** stage in which the offender fails to entertain any serious thoughts of change. Through **motivational interviewing**, application of the stages of change model, and formation of a **shaman effect**, the program provider can help establish an atmosphere conducive to change.

Motivational Interviewing

In direct contrast to a trait view of motivation, Miller (1985) contended that motivation for change is a dynamic process that evolves as the helping relationship between the program provider and offender unfolds. Although the motivational interviewing approach that Miller introduced was originally designed to foster change in substance-abusing clients, many of whom

Table 7.2   Advantages and Disadvantages of Individual and Group
Programming Formats

Format	Advantages	Disadvantages
Individual	1. Privacy/confidentiality 2. Depth of analysis 3. Attention to personal issues 4. Flexible meeting times	1. Time intensive 2. Relatively high dropout rate 3. Dependency on therapist
Group	1. Cost-effectiveness 2. Social support 3. Modeling of appropriate behavior 4. Role-play/behavioral rehearsal 5. Gaining different perspective 6. Learning by teaching	1. Less privacy/confidentiality 2. Destructive group feedback 3. Modeling inappropriate behavior 4. Listening to others' problems

were initially resistant to change, the applicability of this approach to offender populations seems self-evident even though it remains largely untested (Walters, Clark, Gingerich, & Meltzer, 2007). Instead of directly confronting an offender about his or her negative behavior, those utilizing a motivational interviewing approach to intervention avoid arguing with the client, express empathy, roll with clients' natural resistance to change, supply the client with useful information, support self-efficacy, and develop discrepancies between a client's stated goals and what he or she is currently gaining from his or her actions (Miller & Rollnick, 2002). Motivational interviewing frequently serves as an adjunct to more intensive forms of cognitive or cognitive–behavioral intervention and can be particularly effective in establishing the preconditions for change.

Transtheoretical Model of Change

The **transtheoretical model** conceptualizes motivation for change as a process divided into several distinct but overlapping stages (Prochaska & DiClemente, 1992; Prochaska, DiClemente, & Norcross, 1992). The first stage of change in Prochaska and DiClemente's model is precontemplation, whereby the individual displays little or no desire for change. Bringing attention to the negative consequences of an offender's criminal behavior is one way of reaching offenders in the precontemplation stage. Precontemplation is followed by **contemplation,** in which the individual expresses ambivalence toward change. Exploring discrepancies between current behavior and personal goals and values is an effective strategy for use with offenders functioning at this stage of the change process (Miller & Rollnick, 2002). Preparation, the third stage of change in Prochaska and DiClemente's model, can best be managed by resisting the natural urge to move faster than the offender is ready or willing to move at the present time. The fourth or action stage of the change model entails making actual changes in behavior and is supported by interventions that provide new opportunities for learning and the development of self-efficacy. Maintenance is the fifth and final stage of Prochaska and DiClemente's transtheoretical model of change and involves sustaining and reinforcing changes acquired during the action phase. Social support and creation of a relapse prevention plan are useful interventions for offenders functioning at this stage of the change process. Given the frequency of relapse in both a drug and criminal lifestyle, it is often included as a sixth stage in many versions of the Prochaska–DiClemente model.

Shaman Effect

We all accept the fact that a placebo (an inert substance made to look like an active medication) can exert a powerful effect on behavior. However, we are less willing to acknowledge that a reduction in stress and hopelessness, as might occur following a visit to the office of a mental health practitioner, can produce a similar effect. The growth-promoting consequences of forming a working alliance or therapeutic bond with a therapist, counselor, or mental health professional come under the heading of the shaman effect. The **placebo effect** is said to be mediated by a release of **endorphin,** an endogenous opiate found in the brain (Levine, Gordon, & Fields, 1979). Some researchers believe that a helping relationship can foster a similar biochemical response (Shipley, 1988). One of the few things that therapists from different schools of thought generally agree on is that a good working relationship between the therapist and client is essential for change to occur. Interpersonal functioning and the development of a solid therapeutic bond have been shown to predict positive outcomes in substance abuse counseling (Valle, 1981), and there is no reason to suspect anything less in our work with criminal offenders. I would argue that one of the best ways to achieve a helping relationship is through development of a shaman effect (Walters, 2001), the five principal components of which are listed and defined in Table 7.3.

Table 7.3 Descriptions of the Five Components of the Shaman Effect

Component	Description
Sensitivity	Reassurance is gained from believing that the program provider understands one's inner world by way of empathy, interpretation, or successful prediction.
Ritual	Regularity and predictability of sessions, the provision of a safe environment, and the presence of a competent program provider promote empowerment in inmates.
Metaphor	Concretizing abstract concepts capitalizes on the healing power of rhetoric and creates a shared meaning between the program provider and inmate that can help forge a therapeutic bond between the two.
Dialectics	Formation of counter-myths to dysfunctional myths in order to create more adaptive personal myths is given by way of the thesis–antithesis–synthesis process.
Attribution triad	Self-inference is characterized by (1) belief in the necessity of change (responsibility), (2) belief in the possibility of change (hope), and (3) belief in one's ability to effect change (confidence).

Phases of Change

The four phases of lifestyle change parallel the four phases of lifestyle development. The first three phases have the same names as the first three phases of lifestyle development: (1) initiation, (2) transition, and (3) maintenance. Instead of burnout/maturity, however, the fourth phase of lifestyle change is called the change phase. Before discussing the four **phases of change**, it is important to understand the respective roles of behavior and cognition in the change process. In Chapter 5, I indicated that a person starts acting like a criminal before he or she starts thinking like one. The sequence is reversed with change; an individual must stop thinking like a criminal before he or she stops acting like one. The reason for this is simple. In the course of its development, a criminal lifestyle accumulates cognitive factors (expectancies, attributions, and thinking styles) that support its emerging behavioral patterns. These cognitive factors, like the walls of a castle, serve to protect and defend the lifestyle. If change is to occur, the wall must come down. As a result, criminal cognition must be confronted before meaningful change can occur in criminal behavior.

Initiation Phase

The initiation phase of lifestyle change involves committing oneself to change. Such commitment often begins with a crisis. A crisis can be defined as one's perception that the lifestyle is no longer delivering on its promises or that the dissatisfying aspects of the lifestyle outweigh the satisfying aspects. We normally think of a crisis as a monumental negative event, but a crisis can be either positive (e.g., birth of a child) or negative (e.g., loss of freedom), monumental (e.g., getting shot by the police) or relatively minor (e.g., buildup of many "small" hassles associated with the lifestyle). The criminal lifestyle is marked by many crises, most of which eventually resolve and do not result in meaningful change. For a crisis to lead to significant change it must be accompanied by a public pronouncement of change and one of the five components of the shaman effect (i.e., the attribution triad).

A public pronouncement of change means sharing with another person or a group of people one's desire for change. Tice (1992) found that making a commitment in front of what the individual believed was an audience, even though the audience was actually imaginary, led to greater change in the individual's self-view than commitments made in the absence of an audience. A change plan (Walters, 1998) completed by the client and shared with the therapist meets the requirements of a public pronouncement of change. The commitment initiated by a public pronouncement of change can be solidified by participating in actions consistent with the pronouncement (Kiesler, 1971) and adopting the three attitudes of the attribution triad—(1) belief in the necessity of change, (2) belief in the possibility of change, and (3) belief in one's ability to effect change.

Transitional Phase

Whereas the initiation phase of change is primarily emotional/motivational in nature, the transitional phase of change is primarily cognitive. The overriding objective of the transitional phase of change is to develop the expectancies and skills required to transition into a way of life incompatible with crime. For change to occur, positive outcome expectancies for crime (excitement, power, and respect) must be replaced by negative outcome expectancies for crime (loss of family, friends, and freedom). Walters (2004) reported that negative outcome expectancies for crime rose over the course of a brief psychoeducational intervention. Efficacy expectancies must also change during the transitional phase such that efficacy expectancies for crime weaken and efficacy expectancies for noncrime strengthen. Self-efficacy and hope appear to have a significant facilitative effect on long-term desistance in released offenders provided the individuals are not saddled with too many social problems and deficits (Burnett & Maruna, 2004).

Skill development is another major feature of the transitional phase of lifestyle change. Condition-based skills are designed to promote change by teaching offenders how to manage their emotions (affect regulation), avoid lifestyle-supporting cues (cue management), reduce opportunities for life-style enactment (access reduction), avoid lifestyle-supporting social relationships (interpersonal change), and overcome fear of change (fear management). Choice-based skills promote change by increasing options (brainstorming, social skills training) and teaching the individual how to properly evaluate and implement these options (interpersonal problem solving). Cognition-centered skills are used to challenge lifestyle-supporting beliefs (criminal thinking styles) and develop cognitive complexity and critical reasoning skills that can be used to combat the criminal lifestyle.

Maintenance Phase

In contrast to the emotional/motivation emphasis of the initiation phase and the cognitive emphasis of the transitional phase, the maintenance phase of change is primarily behavioral in nature. This just said, it is important to understand that motivation, cognition, and behavior are impossible to disentangle completely and that all phases of development and change involve some combination of motivation, cognition, and behavior. Hence, during the early phases of an intervention behavioral change may lead to cognitive change, as documented by research on cognitive dissonance (Festinger, 1957), just as cognitive change can facilitate behavioral change during the later phases of an intervention, as documented by research on identity change (Vignoles, Manzi, Regalia, Jemmolo, & Scabini, 2008). There are, nevertheless, differences in emphasis between the four phases and the focus of the maintenance phase of lifestyle change is on behavior. The maintenance phase of change also borrows from research on unassisted change in the sense that behavioral changes in involvement, commitment, and identification guide assisted-change interventions taking place during this phase.

Change Phase

The change phase of the four-phase model of change proposed by lifestyle theory is based on the belief—intrinsic to lifestyle theory—that because the world never stops changing the individual must continue to change and adapt as new situations arise. According to this view, change is a process rather than a destination. In many instances, the criminal lifestyle begins as an adaptation to adverse life circumstances but over time patterning sets in and the person becomes increasingly less adaptive as he or she becomes increasingly more dependent on the lifestyle to cope with the problems of everyday living. This is another way of saying that today's adaptation can become tomorrow's lifestyle if ongoing change is not incorporated into one's change plan. Hence, the current model emphasizes that change is an ongoing process that must be nurtured to prevent the criminal lifestyle from resurfacing.

Matching Offenders to Interventions

The **Risk-Need-Responsivity** (RNR) (Andrews & Bonta, 2003) model of offender rehabilitation is rapidly becoming a standard approach in the correctional and forensic psychology fields, in part because it provides a means by which offenders can be matched to interventions. The risk principle of the RNR model holds that static risk factors capable of predicting institutional adjustment and recidivism should be considered when assigning offenders to interventions. The "Big Four" risk factors described in Chapter 4 of this book (i.e., history of antisocial behavior, antisocial personality pattern, antisocial cognition, and antisocial associates) can be used to assess risk level. Individuals with an extensive history of antisocial behavior, clear evidence of antisocial personality traits, strong antisocial cognition, and many antisocial associates are at considerably higher risk for future institutional adjustment problems and recidivism and should benefit more from intervention than individuals with no prior arrests, no evidence of antisocial personality traits, weak antisocial cognition, and few antisocial associates. Research indicates that programs targeting high-risk offenders generally produce better results than programs furnishing high- and low-risk offenders with the same level of intervention (French & Gendreau, 2006).

Criminogenic needs are dynamic factors capable of reducing an offender's odds of future institutional disciplinary adjustment problems and recidivism by increasing his or her adaptive resources. Andrews and Bonta (2003) highlighted six criminogenic needs as vital to a person's ability to avoid future criminal opportunities. These include (1) developing better self-control, (2) creating a sense of community, (3) developing prosocial values, (4) seeking prosocial associations, (5) reconnecting to family support systems, and (6) becoming involved in substance abuse treatment. Matching offenders to interventions through a consideration of criminogenic needs indicates that some interventions do a better job than other interventions in addressing the individual needs of specific offenders. In most cases, an intervention designed to create a sense of community or reconnect the individual to a family support system will differ from an intervention designed to enhance self-control or develop prosocial values. What effective interventions share in common, however, is their ability to address criminogenic needs with behavioral, cognitive–behavioral, social learning, and other evidence-based strategies rather than relying on untested techniques and procedures (Andrews & Bonta, 2003).

The third principle of the RNR model, responsivity, maintains that an intervention will be most effective when tailored to the individual needs, learning style, motivation, and belief systems of the offender to whom it is applied (Taxman, Shepardson, & Byrne, 2004). An offender with an active learning style, for instance, may do better in a group where self-exploration is emphasized and the therapist is less active, whereas an offender with a passive learning style may benefit more from a highly structured group intervention where the therapist assumes a more active role. In the previous section, we discussed how an offender's current level of motivation can be used to match the offender to a particular intervention style or strategy. An intervention may also need to be varied depending upon whether the offender's criminal thinking is more proactive or reactive. Whereas proactive criminal thinking requires an intervention that engages the offender in an evaluation of the costs and benefits of crime and the illusory nature of many of his or her criminal outcome expectancies, reactive criminal thinking requires a skill-based approach designed to teach offenders how to more effectively cope with stress, disappointment, and angry feelings.

A risk and needs assessment was conducted on Angel based on the risk, need, and responsivity principles advanced by Andrews and Bonta (2003). Three of the four risk factors (antisocial behavior, antisocial personality pattern, and antisocial cognition) are relevant to Angel's case, with fighting (antisocial behavior), impulsiveness (antisocial personality disorder [ASPD]), and the thinking styles of Co, Po, and Ds (antisocial cognition) being particularly salient targets for intervention. Three of the six need factors (self-control, reconnecting to family support systems, and substance abuse treatment) are also vital to Angel's change plan. In that Angel's criminal thinking is more reactive than proactive, the responsivity principle dictates that Angel will benefit more from skills-based programming than from evaluative/expectancy programming. Accordingly, Angel should be enrolled in skills-based interventions (anger or stress management, social-communication skills development, basic education) designed to curb aggression, increase self-control, manage reactive criminal thinking, reduce hostile attribution biases, and increase drug knowledge. Finally, Angel's change plan should focus on emotional and cognitive goals initially but become increasingly more behavioral over time.

Specific Intervention Strategies

Previously, in the section on finding a philosophy of intervention, eight different intervention strategies were mentioned, two for each philosophy. In this section, we examine each of these strategies in light of what they can contribute to a comprehensive program of change for incarcerated and non-incarcerated offenders. The eight strategies to be discussed in this section are (1) catharsis, (2) interpretation, (3) confrontation, (4) atonement, (5) valuation, (6) empathy, (7) instruction, and (8) rehearsal.

Catharsis

The release of pent-up emotion can be a highly reinforcing experience— so reinforcing, in fact, that it can be used to create a shaman effect. Affording offenders the opportunity to "vent" their feelings or talk about their situations can go a long way toward alleviating negative effects, particularly frustration, and in the process foster development of a strong therapeutic alliance (Bohart & Tallman, 1999). Whereas catharsis derives from the psychodynamic tradition it can be a useful technique regardless of the philosophy of intervention the program provider chooses to adopt. Granting offenders permission to express their opinions and views without having to worry about being chastised for their remarks can be a freeing experience capable of reaping huge dividends once the program provider moves beyond the formation of a therapeutic alliance to asking the offender to begin the difficult and demanding task of self-confrontation.

Interpretation

In addition to emphasizing catharsis, the conflict philosophy of psychodynamic models also emphasizes interpretation. Psychodynamic therapists engage in interpretation as a way of overcoming the unconscious conflicts believed to be at the root of criminal behavior. In effect, the psychodynamic therapist slowly and tactfully uncovers the offender's inner conflicts. Most practitioners enlist some form of interpretation in their work with offenders, regardless of the intervention philosophy they follow. Moral models utilize a form of interpretation whereby the moral limitations held to support criminal behavior are uncovered. Fulfillment models use interpretation to expose the social conditions alleged to be responsible for criminal behavior. Learning models employ interpretation for the purpose of identifying and challenging irrational beliefs and self-defeating cognitions. Interpretation is where the program provider explains the offender to himself or herself. Because getting to know oneself can sometimes be a threatening—even frightening—experience, the program provider must know when and how to engage in the process of interpretation.

Confrontation

Research in the substance abuse field has consistently shown that direct confrontation of a client is often counterproductive to the extent that it makes the client more defensive and resistant to change (Miller, Benefield, & Tonigan, 1993). Therefore, rather than directly confronting the individual's lifestyle, as is commonly done by practitioners affiliated with the moral philosophy of intervention, it may be more efficacious to encourage clients to engage in the process of **self-confrontation.** The key is getting someone who is resistant to change and strongly opposed to examining his or her contributions to a problem to commence with self-confrontation. One of the advantages of using a group format with incarcerated offenders is that offenders are often more willing to listen to a peer who has lived the lifestyle than to an outsider, as the program provider is likely to be perceived. With development of a shaman effect, the program provider may be granted some leeway in confronting criminal attitudes and beliefs, although these confrontations should be indirect rather than direct and rest on motivational interviewing principles (e.g., creating discrepancies, pointing out inconsistencies, rolling with the resistance) rather than moral principles.

Atonement

Moral models of intervention require that clients atone for their past mistakes. One of the 12 steps of Alcoholics Anonymous is to make amends for harm done to others. Yochelson and Samenow (1977) likewise call upon criminals to atone for prior moral mistakes. The goal of atonement, irrespective of the model used, is for offenders to realize the destructive nature of their past criminal actions and commit themselves to more constructive future behavior. How this is accomplished will, of course, depend on the offender, the situation, and the program provider's philosophy of intervention. Atonement to a conflict theorist means coming to terms with the dynamic roots of one's criminality and replacing socially destructive patterns with socially constructive patterns. To theorists operating out of a fulfillment philosophy, atonement means accepting the wisdom of the organism and rejecting the destructive scripts instilled by parents and other representatives of society. Learning theorists probably view atonement as the extinction of previously learned criminal patterns of behavior and the establishment of new noncriminal patterns of behavior.

Valuation

There is now evidence that some individuals begin to engage in crime and delinquency because they lack confidence in their own ability to get their needs met without assistance from a criminal lifestyle (Carroll, Houghton, Wood, Perkins, & Bower, 2007). One way to boost confidence is to provide offenders with skills; another way is to validate their existence. Although valuation derives from a fulfillment philosophy of intervention, it is relevant to our work with offenders regardless of the philosophy we choose to adopt. Treating offenders with respect should be something to which all program providers aspire. Valuation does not mean catering to unreasonable demands; what it does mean is valuing the offender as a unique human being capable of change. The derogatory terms and labels that are often attached to offenders reinforce their negative self-views and quickly become self-fulfilling prophecies. Through valuation one achieves insight in the conflict model, spirituality in the moral model, and generalization in the learning model—all worthwhile goals.

Empathy

One of the first skills counselors in training are taught is empathy (Clark, 2007). This is because empathy is a highly trainable skill that often serves as the foundation for other therapeutic skills. Accordingly, empathy is vital to the formation of a strong therapeutic alliance. From the standpoint of the program provider, empathy is the ability to understand the emotional elements of a client's communication and then reflect this understanding back to the client (Clark, 2007). As was previously mentioned, empathy serves as the foundation for many other therapeutic skills, including those that have been discussed previously in this section. Through empathy, offenders gain a sense of relief from being understood (catharsis), a different perspective on themselves (interpretation), a view of themselves as worthwhile (valuation), an awareness of how destructive their lifestyle has been (atonement), and an ability to challenge the beliefs and assumptions upon which a criminal lifestyle is based (confrontation). Needless to say, empathy is an important therapeutic skill for a mental health practitioner working with offenders to possess.

Instruction

Those who follow a learning philosophy of intervention assume that people engage in criminal behavior because of faulty learning and that crime can be controlled by instructing offenders in prosocial forms of behavior. If this assumption is true then a major aspect of working with incarcerated offenders is extinguishing criminal patterns of behavior and instructing them in the formation of prosocial patterns of behavior. Even if this assumption turns out to be false, education and instruction can effectively alleviate many of the problems confronting incarcerated and nonincarcerated offenders by furnishing them with job and educational skills and teaching them social and coping skills. Job and educational skills can improve an offender's employment opportunities, whereas social and coping skills can improve an offender's ability to manage the problems of everyday living. Conflict theorists emphasize introspection, moral theorists contrition, and fulfillment theorists independence—all three of which rely on instruction and education.

Rehearsal

Another therapeutic technique borrowed from the learning tradition is behavioral rehearsal. It has been my experience that many offenders respond favorably to active forms of intervention like role-playing and behavioral rehearsal. Research indicates that role-playing and behavioral rehearsal can improve job performance (Taylor, Russ-Eft, & Chan, 2005). While these techniques may also be effective in reducing institutional disciplinary problems and recidivism, there are no empirical data currently available to test this assumption. Encouraging offenders to learn through instruction and observation, having them rehearse and practice the behaviors, and placing them in real-life situations where they can successfully enact and be reinforced for engaging in the behavior are ideal ways of expanding an offender's behavioral repertoire and boosting his or her confidence. Behavioral rehearsal and role-playing are not restricted to the learning tradition; they are also used by practitioners from the conflict (transference), moral (moral inventory), and fulfillment (empty chair) traditions.

The four core elements of change proposed by the lifestyle model of change—(1) responsibility, (2) confidence, (3) meaning, and (4) community (Walters, 2002)—are represented in the eight techniques described in the present section. Responsibility entails assuming accountability for one's actions and appreciating the role choice plays in one's life. Accordingly, the two intervention strategies described in this section with the greatest likelihood of instilling a sense of responsibility in an offender are confrontation and atonement. Confidence is a belief in oneself and one's ability to handle future temptation, frustration, and disappointment. Social learning theorists refer to confidence as self-efficacy. Of the eight therapeutic strategies discussed in this section, instruction and rehearsal would seem to have the most to offer offenders interested in improving their confidence or self-efficacy. Meaning can be defined as viewing oneself and the world in a different light; oftentimes the self-view becomes less restrictive and the worldview becomes more benevolent. Catharsis and interpretation are two ways by which meaning can be achieved. Finally, community is an awareness of one's connection to people and events outside oneself as manifest by the view that what we do affects not only ourselves but everyone around us. Valuation and empathy are two avenues through which community is realized.

Angel participated in group sessions as part of the institutional drug program and the Lifestyle Change Program (LCP) (Walters, 1999, 2005d). The emphasis of the drug program is on instruction, whereas the LCP uses different intervention strategies at different points in the change process. Initially, the LCP focuses on instruction, catharsis, empathy, and valuation with basic education and development of a shaman effect being particularly prominent. Interpretation, confrontation, atonement, and rehearsal, however, become increasingly more important as the LCP moves into its advanced and relapse prevention phases. Angel programmed for a little over a year, enrolling in the institutional drug program and several classes (groups) of the LCP and participating in a handful of individual sessions. In that time, he demonstrated improved discipline in the form of a reduction in the average number of disciplinary reports received annually (1.1 pretreatment versus 0.4 posttreatment) and did not receive a single "shot" or disciplinary report for fighting in the four years since he graduated from the LCP (compared to two "shots" for fighting prior to entering the LCP). Angel's postprison adjustment cannot be determined at this time because he still has several months left to serve before he is released back to the community.

Evaluating the Outcome

Once a philosophy of intervention has been selected and a program of intervention has been implemented, the next step is to evaluate the program's ability to improve disciplinary adjustment in prison and retard recidivism upon release from custody. Long gone are the days when program administrators simply assumed that an intervention worked. Now an intervention must be verified through research and classified as an **evidence-based practice** or empirically supported treatment (EST) (Chambless & Ollendick, 2001). This section will begin with conceptual, sampling, practical, and measurement issues that need to be taken into account when evaluating correctional intervention programs and end with a brief description of one of these programs, the LCP (Walters, 1999, 2005d).

Conceptual Issues

More effective programs are generally more clearly conceptualized than less effective programs (Gendreau & Ross, 1987). Many of the programs evaluated in the Lipton et al. (1975) review lacked a solid theoretical rationale, which may explain why these authors failed to uncover evidence of an effect in their review of the correctional rehabilitation literature. It has also been noted that programs with a behavioral or cognitive–behavioral emphasis generally achieve better outcomes than nonbehavioral programs (French & Gendreau, 2006). This may be because behavioral and cognitive–behavioral programs are usually more clearly conceptualized than nonbehavioral programs or it may be because behavioral and cognitive–behavioral interventions do a better job of addressing the underlying issues associated with criminal behavior. Either way, behavioral and cognitive–behavioral interventions have earned EST status in the corrections field.

Sampling Issues

Control and randomization are the sine qua non of scientific research. Unfortunately, it is not always possible to randomly assign participants to conditions when conducting therapy research in prison for both practical and ethical reasons. Even when randomization is not feasible, a control group should be identified. Many of the studies reviewed by Lipton et al. (1975) lacked a control group. Some investigators advise matching program and control participants on relevant variables, but this tends to make the groups even less equivalent on many of the variables that were not matched (Camp, 1995). Other investigators recommend using a waiting list control group, although this approach precludes long-term follow-up of the control group. In addition, keeping someone who could benefit from an intervention from participating in a program for several months to several years could be construed as unethical. In my own work, I have created control groups from offenders who had previously volunteered for a program but were transferred or released prior to being able to participate in the program.

Practical Issues

Just because a program is adequately conceptualized does not mean that it will be properly administered. A number of the programs in the Lipton et al. (1975) review were run by staff that were either inadequately trained or poorly motivated to deliver the intervention in the manner intended by the program developers. The CPAI-2000 (Gendreau & Andrews, 2001) assesses eight dimensions of correctional program integrity: (1) organizational culture, (2) program implementation/maintenance, (3) management/staff characteristics, (4) client risk/need practices, (5) program characteristics, (6) dimensions of core correctional practice, (7) inter-agency communications, and (8) evaluation. At least four of these dimensions (organizational culture, program implementation/maintenance, management/staff characteristics, inter-agency communication) relate directly to how the program is implemented and managed. From the results of their meta-analysis, French and Gendreau (2006) concluded that procedures with more therapeutic integrity achieved significantly better outcomes than procedures with less therapeutic integrity.

Measurement Issues

To properly evaluate an intervention program, multiple outcome measures should be included in the evaluation and the outcome subjected to statistical analysis. Many of the studies included in the Lipton et al. (1975) review assessed a single outcome, often over an unspecified period of time, and frequently without benefit of a statistical test. A comprehensive program review requires that multiple outcome measures be included in one's evaluation. Basing their conclusions on multiple sources of information (self-ratings versus other-ratings) and a range of dependent variables (arrests, convictions, incarcerations), meta-analytic researchers provide us with a depth of understanding that the original Lipton et al. review (1975) never could. A related issue is how well the program responds to the principles of risk, need, and responsivity such that higher-risk offenders are targeted for intervention and need variables are used to determine the interventions most likely to work with different groups of offenders.

An Example: The Lifestyle Change Program

The LCP is a three-phase intervention designed to produce a positive change in incarcerated offenders by addressing the actions and thinking patterns allegedly responsible for a criminal lifestyle. The first phase of the LCP is a 10-week psychoeducational class in which lectures, discussions, and specially designed videotapes are used to introduce participants to the criminal lifestyle concept. The 20-week intervention groups, referred to as advanced groups, constitute the second phase of the LCP. Each advanced group covers a lifestyle (e.g., criminal, drug, gambling) relevant to a large portion of the incarcerated offender population. Film segments and full-length movies are shown in each advanced group and discussed in class for the purpose of shedding light on various aspects of the particular lifestyle they are designed to address. The third phase of the LCP comprises a 40-week relapse prevention group. In the relapse prevention group, the focus is on skill development in three primary areas—(1) conditions, (2) choice, (3) cognition—and the curriculum consists of discussions, role-plays, and homework assignments.

The initial evaluation of the LCP took place after the LCP had been in effect for 5 years. Because the majority of participants had not been released from custody after the first 5 years of programming, the focus of this first follow-up

(Walters, 1999) was on assessing the LCP's ability to positively affect participants' institutional adjustment. To test this hypothesis, a group of 291 inmates who had completed one or more phases of the LCP and 82 inmates who had signed up for the LCP but were released or transferred before they could participate in the initial group session were compared. The results of this first follow-up indicated that program participants accumulated one third the number of incident reports as control inmates (0.54 versus 1.43). Furthermore, longer program exposure (phases II and III) apparently provided participants with greater benefit than shorter program exposure (phase I; see Figure 7.3), and there was a slight but nonsignificant tendency on the part of inmates with more prior incident reports to derive greater benefit from the program than inmates with fewer prior incident reports. Overall, the cognitive–behavioral program offered as part of the LCP was found to be effective in reducing disciplinary problems in program participants.

Figure 7.3   Subsequent Incident Reports Received by Control
Participants Relative to Phase I and Phase II/III Graduates
of the Lifestyle Change Program (LCP)

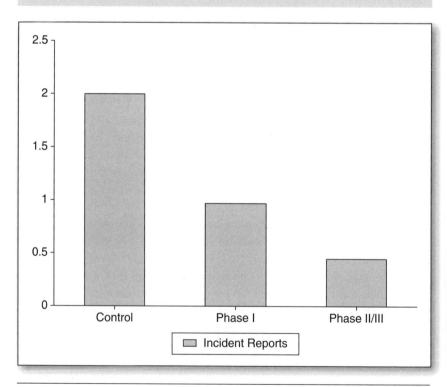

Source: Walters (1999).

Five years after the first follow-up, a second follow-up was conducted on the LCP, this one centering on recidivism. In the second follow-up, 291 program participants were compared to 89 control inmates, all of whom had been released at least 6 months before the end of the follow-up period (Walters, 2005d). The results showed that control inmates accrued significantly more subsequent arrests, were more frequently reincarcerated, and experienced a shorter latency to first arrest or incarceration than program participants. In addition, longer program exposure (phases II and III) produced larger effect sizes than shorter program exposure (phase I; see Figure 7.4). Whereas lower-risk participants (fewer than six prior arrests) seemed to benefit more from the program than higher-risk participants (six or more prior arrests) when subsequent arrests served as the outcome measure, higher-risk participants appeared to benefit more from the program than lower-risk participants when reincarceration served as the outcome measure.

Figure 7.4   Subsequent Arrests Experienced by Control Participants Relative to Phase I and Phase II/III Graduates of the Lifestyle Change Program (LCP)

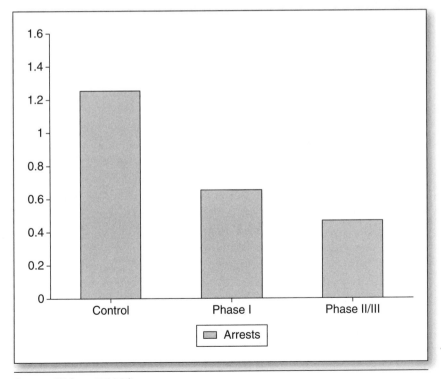

Source: Walters (2005d).

Conclusion

Programming can promote change in offenders once a philosophy of intervention is identified, a format (group or individual) is selected, the preconditions for change are addressed, the phases of change are identified, offenders are matched to interventions, specific intervention strategies are implemented, and the program is properly evaluated. As we now know, offenders are capable of change and programming can be helpful in both initiating and maintaining this change. Even Robert Martinson (1979), one of the principal architects of the "nothing works" philosophy of the mid- to late 1970s, acknowledged that some interventions do, in fact, work in a paper he wrote a year before his untimely death. The task confronting those interested in providing psychological programming to offenders is determining which programs work best for which types of offenders under which specific sets of circumstances. Although there are data indicating that behavioral and cognitive–behavioral interventions work better than nonbehavioral approaches, that our limited resources are better spent on higher-risk offenders than on lower-risk offenders, and that offender–intervention matching is an important appendage to contemporary correctional rehabilitation, there is still a great deal more that needs to be done before we can assume that we know how to facilitate change in offenders before, during, and after incarceration.

There is one other subject I would like to address before closing this chapter—the subject of evidence-based practice. Evidence-based interventions must be manualized, user-friendly, and show evidence of efficacy in controlled research. Research on interventions designed to reduce adult recidivism demonstrates that educational and vocational programs, substance abuse treatment, drug courts, sex offender programming, and cognitive behavioral therapy are all evidence-based (Przybylski, 2008). The lifestyle intervention approach outlined in this chapter would also appear to be evidence-based in that the program has a manual that guides the intervention, procedures for training program providers to administer the manualized intervention, and two controlled investigations (Walters, 1999, 2005d) attesting to the group-administered lifestyle intervention's ability to reduce short-term institutional maladjustment and long-term community recidivism above and beyond what is achieved without intervention. There are two issues that still need to be addressed, however, before the lifestyle approach can be considered evidence-based. First, random assignment of participants to the lifestyle approach and an attention-control or alternative intervention is required to rule out a placebo effect. Second, research from someone other than the founder of lifestyle theory is required to rule out an **allegiance effect** (Luborsky et al., 1999).

Key Terms and Concepts

Allegiance Effect	*Moral Philosophy*
Assisted Change	*Motivational Interviewing*
Atonement	*"Nothing Works"*
Catharsis	*Phases of Change*
Conflict Philosophy	*Placebo Effect*
Confrontation	*Precontemplation*
Contemplation	*Rehearsal*
Empathy	*Risk-Need-Responsivity*
Endorphin	*Self-Confrontation*
Evidence-Based Practice	*Shaman Effect*
Fulfillment Philosophy	*Transtheoretical Model*
Instruction	*Type II or Male-Limited Alcoholism*
Interpretation	*Unassisted Change*
Learning Philosophy	*Valuation*

8

Prevention

The Criminal Lifestyle in a High-Risk Youth Context

If you treat a man as he is, he will remain as he is; if you treat him as he ought to be and could be, he will become as he ought to be and could be.

Johann von Goethe (1749–1832)

Dennis the Menace

Dennis is a 5-year-old white male who was brought to a private psychologist by his mother for evaluation. Dennis's mother indicates that his behavior has become increasingly disruptive and unmanageable, and she is concerned not only about his unruly behavior at home but also his future school adjustment in that he is scheduled to start kindergarten in the fall. Dennis is the older of two children, and his mother reports that he frequently bullies his 3-year-old sister. His father works as a police officer in a neighboring town, and because of the small size of the department and recent staff cuts, he often has to work overtime and on weekends. Mom seems frazzled by having to deal with two energetic preschool children largely on her own. Although she looks forward to having Dennis in school half days in the fall, she is worried that he

174

will have trouble getting along with his teachers and classmates. She relates a litany of problems, which include teasing his sister, cursing at his mother, running away from home, shoplifting, setting fires, torturing animals, and stealing and drinking alcohol from his father's locked cabinet in the cellar basement.

Dennis's mother relates that Dennis incessantly teases and torments his sister and that when she tries to stop him he curses at her and runs away. Starting when he was 18 months old, Dennis made a habit of jumping out of his crib, crawling through an open window, and running around the neighborhood in his night clothes. According to his mother, he has run away from home and stayed out overnight on three separate occasions. She further states that Dennis pals around with a group of older boys (age range = 8–12 years) who steal items from local stores and businesses—anything from candy to CDs. Dennis has already been picked up by the local authorities for shoplifting. In addition, he has set fire to his sister's dollhouse and tortured the family cat by poking it with a stick and trying to cut its tail off with a knife. Dad, who is often not around, apparently views Dennis's behavior as an instance of "boys will be boys," although even he gets angry when Dennis breaks into his liquor cabinet in the cellar. It has gotten to the point where he has had to reinforce the regular lock with a chain lock. He admits that sometimes he gets so frustrated with Dennis that he hits him.

Dennis is larger than the average 5-year-old and nowhere near as angelic as his namesake. He seemed angry and indignant that his mother had brought him to see a psychologist. In fact, the first thing he said to me was "there is nothing wrong with me, except for my mother." Both of Dennis's arms were "sleeved" in play tattoos, much like the hardened criminals I worked with in the penitentiary. Dennis offered little in the way of conversation during the interview, and the test results revealed average intelligence and above average anger, hostility, and resentment toward authority. There were no signs of hyperactivity in his behavior or in his test scores. Considering that he was only 5 years old at the time of the evaluation, neither the Lifestyle Criminality Screening Form (LCSF) nor Psychological Inventory of Criminal Thinking Styles (PICTS) could be administered and even the youth version of the Psychopathy Checklist-Revised (PCL-R), the Psychopathy Checklist: Youth Version (PCL:YV) (Forth, Kosson, & Hare, 2003), requires that the child be at least 12 years old. Nonetheless, based on his outward appearance and the behavioral patterns reported by his mother, he satisfies the diagnostic criteria for early onset conduct disorder.

Primary, Secondary, and Tertiary Prevention

Rather than waiting for someone like Dennis to grow into a full-blown criminal, it would seem prudent to intervene early and try to prevent a criminal lifestyle from taking root. Prevention is ordinarily divided into three general categories: (1) **primary prevention**, (2) **secondary prevention**, and (3) **tertiary prevention**. Whereas primary prevention seeks to reduce crime by targeting and minimizing criminogenic influences in the general population, secondary prevention is directed at high-risk individuals and tertiary prevention consists of efforts to alter the course of an already existing criminal lifestyle. Primary crime prevention is normally delivered through general psychological well-being and crime prevention education programs; secondary crime prevention programs are normally delivered through predelinquent screening programs with an emphasis on early detection strategies; and tertiary crime prevention programs are normally delivered through incapacitation, punishment, and institutional treatment (Andresen & Jenion, 2008).

Primary prevention can be effective when implemented as a situational crime prevention strategy (e.g., target hardening, property marking, environmental design, neighborhood watches) (Heal & Laycock, 1986). As a person-level crime prevention strategy, however, it is expensive and of questionable validity. Despite its popularity with many police departments and school officials, there is no documented evidence of its impact on the overall crime rate. In order to reach a general audience, the preventive intervention must, by necessity, be low impact. Such an intervention is unlikely to have much of an effect on high-risk individuals like Dennis. To be fair to advocates of crime prevention education, there is no good evidence that crime prevention education does not work either. Until this area has been adequately researched, we might want to take heed of research documenting the failure of simple drug education and affective approaches (Drug Abuse Resistance Education, or DARE) to reduce alcohol and drug use in general adolescent samples (Soole, Mazerolle, & Rombouts, 2008).

Tertiary prevention is also expensive, and as we saw in Chapter 7, to be effective tertiary prevention must be of at least moderate intensity and directed at higher-risk offenders. In addition, the direct and indirect costs of chronic offending are high. We cannot simply wait for someone like Dennis to come into the system before we do something about his behavior. This suggests that secondary prevention may be the most cost-effective alternative to person-level crime prevention. By confining our preventive efforts to a relatively small group of high-risk individuals, we limit the scope of the intervention while maximizing the intensity of the intervention, a key component for success in any program, regardless of the category of prevention—primary, secondary, tertiary—being employed. The problem is finding evidence-based secondary crime prevention strategies. Two of the more popular secondary crime prevention interventions for high-risk youth, shock incarceration (correctional boot camps), and scared straight are either ineffective (boot camps) (Cullen, Blevins, Trager, & Gendreau, 2005) or harmful (scared straight) (Petrosino, Turpin-Petrosino, & Buehler, 2003). Using lifestyle theory as a guide, I will attempt to identify several secondary crime prevention strategies that may prove more helpful.

The Lifestyle Approach to Secondary Prevention

In selecting strategies for a program of secondary prevention capable of diverting high-risk youth like Dennis from a criminal lifestyle, we begin with the six developmental variables that give rise to the initiation phase of a criminal lifestyle. These six developmental variables encompass incentive (**existential fear**), opportunity (**temperament, stress, socialization, availability**), and choice (**decision making**).

Incentive

Existential Fear

Existential fear is an experience all humans share. When I first introduced this concept 20 years ago, I theorized that a high degree of existential fear drove people into a criminal lifestyle. I have since revised my views on this subject to where I now believe that existential fear plays several different roles in the development of a criminal lifestyle. I have little doubt that a high degree of existential fear can create a psychological condition or need capable of moving someone in the direction of a criminal lifestyle. The criminal lifestyle promises relief from affiliation-, control-, and status-related fears, and when combined with various life conditions (poverty, abuse, lack of parental supervision, exposure to deviant role models), these promises make crime an inviting alternative to a conventional lifestyle. Only later, and in some cases never, does the individual begin to realize that while the criminal lifestyle may deliver on these promises in the short run, it actually makes things worse in the long run. Prison is a logical consequence of a criminal lifestyle, and in prison you are forced to affiliate with people you may not like, your control over the environment is extremely limited, and your identity is the register number the government assigns you. Existential fear can also promote development of a criminal lifestyle through **fearlessness**.

Lifestyle theory attributes fearlessness, defined as a diminished autonomic response to stimuli that signal threat or danger, to a weak existential fear–physical survival bond. Attenuation of the connection between existential fear and physical survival can be the result of genetic factors, physical abuse, or desensitization caused by heavy exposure to real and symbolic criminal events, but regardless of its source it can have serious repercussions for the individual. A weak bond between existential fear and physical survival makes it easier for the individual to reattach that bond to a criminal lifestyle (or more accurately, the perceived affiliation, control/predictability, and status benefits of a criminal lifestyle). In essence, the process turns on itself to the extent that the individual places his or her physical survival at risk in order to pursue the life experiences (affiliation, control/predictability, status) that have evolved in support of an organism's physical survival. Research has identified low levels of anxiety and fear in chronic offenders—particularly those who meet the criteria for antisocial personality disorder (ASPD) and psychopathy (Arnaut, 2006; Vitale et al., 2005). Low anxiety or fearlessness has its roots in genetics and early environmental experience (Lykken, 1995) and gives rise to high pain tolerance (Reidy, Dimmick, MacDonald, & Zeichner, 2009), inability to learn from punishment (Blair, 2006), and strong sensation-seeking tendencies (Gatzke-Kopp, Raine, Loeber, Stoutheimer-Loeber, & Steinhauer, 2002), all of which correlate significantly with crime.

Adolescence is a period during which fear of death and mortality awareness are at relatively low levels (Elkind, 1967). This, in fact, may facilitate risk-taking on the part of some adolescents as exemplified by the results of a study on sexual risk-taking in male college students (Word, 1996). Risk-taking, in general, could be conducive to the development of a criminal or related (drug or gambling) lifestyle, which we know often begins in early to mid-adolescence and frequently ends in early adulthood (Moffitt, 1993; Moffitt, Caspi, Harrington, & Milne, 2002). Similarly, a masculine identity may exacerbate or mediate the fearlessness that allows a person to reattach existential fear from its original locus as a mechanism for promoting the organism's physical survival to the life experience benefits of a criminal lifestyle; this may explain, in part, why crime is more prevalent in men than women (Goodey, 1997). There are avenues other than crime available to teenage males and those with high pain tolerance, weak conditionability, or sensation-seeking tendencies. Fearlessness simply makes it more likely that people will enter crime by making it easier for them to reattach their existential fear from physical survival to the perceived affiliation, control/predictability, and status benefits of a criminal lifestyle.

Fear is a major target for secondary prevention because fearlessness is a key risk factor for future antisocial behavior (Lykken, 1995). Whereas

Cleckley (1941/1976) viewed low anxiety or fearlessness as a core component of psychopathy, Hare (2003) did not include it on the PCL-R, perhaps
because of concerns about the construct's low reliability. Other researchers
include fearlessness in their conceptualizations of psychopathy but often
disagree on its structure and function. Fearlessness in support of psychopathy
has traditionally been viewed as a limbic system deficit involving the amygdala and related structures (Blair, 2006), although a more generalized
paralimbic deficit (Kiehl, 2006) and a higher-order attention deficit
(Newman, Curtin, Bertsch, & Baskin-Sommers, 2010) have also been proposed. Some researchers favor a genetic interpretation of fearlessness etiology
(Viding, Blair, Moffitt, & Plomin, 2005), while other researchers trace the
development of fearlessness to prenatal (Mawson, 2009) and postnatal (van
Goozen & Fairchild, 2008) environmental factors. Given proactive and reactive aggression/criminality's role in lifestyle theory, an interesting biosocial
interaction surfaced in one recent study where exposure to community violence led to increased proactive but not reactive aggression in children with
low resting heart rates and increased reactive but not proactive aggression in
children with high resting heart rates (Scarpa, Tanaka, & Haden, 2008).

We can never know for sure the role existential fear plays in the life of a
specific individual. Conjecturing from what we know about Dennis, I would
argue that there are several factors that could have played a role in the weak-
ened bond that apparently exists between his existential fear and physical
survival. First, his father is a police officer, an occupation that benefits from
fearlessness and low anxiety (Lorr & Strack, 1994). Hence, heredity may
have played a role in Dennis's own fearlessness and weak existential fear–
physical survival bond. Second, according to his mother, he is sometimes the
object of his father's anger. Normally, Dennis's father ignores him, but at
times he can get so frustrated with Dennis that he becomes enraged and even
violent. Dennis's mother intimates that the father has hit Dennis on occasion, and there is some indication he may have severely beaten the boy on at
least one of these occasions. Dennis seems to have modeled his father's
aggressive behavior and may have become desensitized and callous to violence through his exposure to physical aggression early in life. Third, there
are certain personality traits that may also be contributing to Dennis's fearlessness. Sensation-seeking, novelty-seeking, and high pain tolerance, traits
Dennis would seem to possess, contribute to fearlessness and the weak bond
between existential fear and physical survival that place a person at risk for
future criminality.

Theoretically, there are at least three ways in which fearlessness could be
incorporated into a program of secondary prevention. First, we could try to
strengthen the bond between existential fear and physical survival. Second,
we could try to weaken the bond between existential fear and a fledgling

criminal lifestyle. Third, we could try to redirect the child's fearlessness into more socially acceptable channels. As we learned in Chapter 5, the existential fear–physical survival bond rebounds and the existential fear–criminal lifestyle bond weakens during the burnout/maturity phase of a criminal lifestyle. These effects occur, however, because of age and the accumulated effect of the lifestyle. Adolescents and preadolescents are much less likely to be deterred by a fear of growing old and dying in prison than an adult offender because dying in prison is a more remote possibility for a 10- or 15-year-old than it is for a 40- or 50-year-old who has spent the past 15 years in prison. Likewise, a 10- or 15-year-old is less likely to have experienced the death of a crime partner or to have lost family members over the course of his/her incarceration than a 40- or 50-year-old convict. Consequently, neither of these theoretically viable approaches to existential fear has much practical value for someone like Dennis.

Substitution may be the most practical approach to secondary prevention of person-level crime in individuals displaying a weak bond between existential fear and physical survival. What I mean by substitution is finding less destructive and more socially acceptable alternatives to crime for individuals at risk for a criminal lifestyle by virtue of low fear. Research indicates that incarcerated juveniles generally experience poorer health outcomes and weaker family support than socioeconomically comparable groups of nondelinquent youth (Forrest, Tambor, Riley, Ensminger, & Starfield, 2000). The unhealthy activities these individuals engage in during the initiation phase of a criminal lifestyle (e.g., substance use, fighting, sexual promiscuity) increase their risk of disease and future health problems. Supplying these individuals with positive outlets for their fearless impulses might not only improve their health status but also decrease their odds of entering the later phases of a criminal lifestyle. Active sports, hobbies, and pastimes may all be capable of promoting a secondary prevention effect, particularly if done with or under the supervision of family members. Perhaps enrolling Dennis in soccer, where his mother could serve as the unofficial soccer mom of the neighborhood, having him assist his father who likes to tinker with cars in the garage, and encouraging the entire family to become more active (hiking, bicycling, rock climbing) might help divert Dennis away from the criminal path he almost seems destined to follow.

Opportunity

Temperament

Broad dispositional trends in behavior interact with early environmental conditions to influence a person's reaction to environmental stimuli. The product of this interaction is referred to as temperament. Lifestyle theory proposes five temperament dimensions: (1) **sociability**, (2) **information processing speed**, (3) **novelty seeking**, (4) **activity level**, and (5) **emotionality**. Each dimension interacts with a number of other factors to increase or decrease a person's opportunities for crime. As such, they may be useful in setting goals for a program of secondary prevention. The proposed relationship among the five temperament dimensions and the three constructive strategies of existential fear management (affiliation, predictability, status) is portrayed in Figure 8.1.

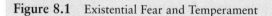

Figure 8.1 Existential Fear and Temperament

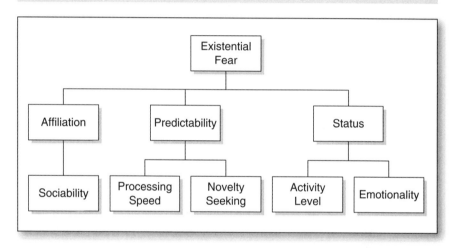

Sociability is the degree to which a person either approaches or avoids social stimuli. High sociability has been found to correlate positively with externalizing behaviors like aggression (Casiglia, Lo Coco, & Zappulla, 1998) and negatively with internalizing behaviors like depression (Rende, 1993). Carlo, Roesch, and Melby (1998) determined that low **parental support** and high child sociability predicted aggression and antisocial outcomes. In a study by Russell, Hart, Robinson, and Olsen (2003), children rated by their parents as highly sociable were more apt to receive teacher ratings of relational aggression and prosocial behavior than children rated low in sociability. A sociable temperament can lead to both increased and decreased opportunities for crime, depending on the level of other temperament dimensions and the presence of sundry environmental experiences (e.g., parental discipline and abuse). Instructing Dennis or someone like him who is at risk for future criminality in the use of prosocial skills like empathy and perspective taking can serve the secondary prevention purpose of reducing his odds of moving from crime experimentation into a criminal lifestyle.

Information processing speed is another temperament dimension central to lifestyle theory. There is a strong relationship between information processing speed and information processing efficiency (Salthouse, 1996) and between information processing speed and measured intelligence (Bates & Stough, 1998). Yet we know virtually nothing about the relationship between information processing speed and delinquency. To the extent that low information processing speed correlates with learning disabilities and learning disabilities increase opportunities for delinquency (or decrease opportunities for nondelinquency) (Morrison & Cosden, 1997) information processing speed may also help establish goals for secondary prevention. Dennis is a few weeks away from starting kindergarten, but if he experiences consistent failure due to learning difficulties this will only reinforce the negative image he has of himself, compound his other problems, and increase his odds of pursuing a criminal lifestyle. Therefore, if Dennis experiences reading or other learning disabilities as he goes through school, providing him with additional help and tutelage could serve a secondary prevention function.

Novelty seeking can be defined as the tendency to approach and seek out stimuli with which the organism is unfamiliar (Cloninger, 1987). Novelty seeking tends to correlate positively with externalizing disorders like delinquency and substance abuse (Copeland, Landry, Stanger, & Hudziak, 2004) suggesting that high novelty seeking increases opportunities for externalizing behavioral patterns. Adolescents high in novelty seeking tend to be more impulsive (Nagoshi, Walter, Muntaner, & Haertzen, 1992) and aggressive (Ruchkin, Eisemann, Hägglöf, & Cloninger, 1998) than adolescents low in novelty seeking. If high novelty seeking leads to adult antisocial stimulation-seeking behavior through the disinhibitory effects of low autonomic arousal (Raine, Venables, & Williams, 1995), then finding ways to increase autonomic arousal through conditioning or medication could serve a secondary prevention function. Substitution, modeling, and internalization, however, are more realistic methods of secondary prevention for high novelty seeking. By encouraging Dennis to engage in prosocial exciting activities (substitution), having his father model socially appropriate stimulation seeking (modeling), and helping Dennis develop self-discipline and inner-direction (internalization) we could significantly reduce his risk of entering a criminal lifestyle.

Activity level is a fourth temperament dimension with potential relevance to secondary prevention. The link between activity level and juvenile delinquency is well established (Foley, Carlton, & Howell, 1996). High activity level in children and youth has also been found to correlate with poor delay of gratification (Shoda, Mischel, & Peake, 1990), weak empathy (Rothbart, Ahadi, & Hershey, 1994), and antisocial responses on a moral dilemma task (Kochanska, Murray, & Coy, 1997). Dennis gave no behavioral indication of being hyperactive or inattentive during the testing session, and his performance on a multiscale intelligence test revealed that his attention and concentration skills are adequate. A high activity level can nonetheless be a risk factor for early conduct problems and later criminality. In cases where significant hyperactivity may put a child at risk for future involvement in a criminal lifestyle, medication (stimulant drugs like Ritalin), substitution (teaching the child to channel his or her energy into positive pursuits), and environmental manipulation (structuring the child's immediate environment to reduce the possibility of distraction) may serve secondary prevention objectives.

The fifth and final temperament dimension is emotionality. **Negative emotionality** can be defined as a tendency toward anxiety, depression, and anger—reactions commonly observed in childhood conduct disorder, adolescent delinquency, and adult criminality. A longitudinal study found that negative emotionality assessed at ages 1 to 5 predicted externalizing behavioral problems in both boys and girls at age 8 (Nelson, Martin, Hodge, Havill, & Kamphaus, 1999). A second group of researchers report that negative emotionality in adolescents correlated positively with antisocial behavior (Stice & Gonzales, 1998). Negative emotionality may also predict the persistence of antisocial behavior from childhood to adulthood (Pulkkinen, Lyrra, & Kokko, 2009). Reactive aggression and its correlates (i.e., anger, hostile attribution biases) may be more closely related to negative emotionality than proactive aggression (Vitaro, Barker, Boivin, Brendgen, & Tremblay, 2006). In developing a program of secondary prevention for negative emotionality, it is important to identify the negative emotions responsible for the negative emotionality–externalizing disorder relationship and the results of research indicate that anger is more likely to lead to antisocial behavior than anxiety or depression (Eisenberg et al., 2009). Consequently, anger management training, which is effective in reducing reactive criminal thinking (Walters, 2009a), may be of assistance to youth like Dennis who are at risk for future criminal lifestyle involvement by virtue of a high degree of angry negative emotion.

Stress

Stress is defined by lifestyle theory as a change in the internal or external environment that elicits an orienting response from the organism. The change that elicits the orienting response is referred to as a stressor. According to lifestyle theory (Walters, 2000a), there are four general categories of stressors: (1) internal approach stressors, (2) external approach stressors, (3) internal avoidance stressors, and (4) external avoidance stressors. Internal–external refers to the origin of the change, inside (internal) or outside (external) the individual, and approach–avoidance refers to the direction of the orienting response, toward (approach), or away from (avoidance) the object. A paraphilic fantasy in a juvenile sex offender is an example of an internal approach stressor, whereas an unlocked car constitutes an external approach stressor. The thought of ending up like one's father could serve as an internal avoidance stressor, and being physically abused is an example of an external avoidance stressor. All four stressors are theoretically capable of increasing opportunities for lifestyle involvement, but it is the external avoidance stressor that has received the most attention from researchers. The cumulative stressors model (recall from Chapter 2 that dimensional constructs like conduct disorder, delinquency, and the criminal lifestyle usually have an additive etiology) indicates that these various stressors add up to create a specific level of risk.

Moderating the risk of accumulated stressors can be accomplished by removing stressors, adding buffers, or improving the individual's stress-coping skills. Routinely removing everyday stressors by protecting a child from experiencing failure is not a particularly effective primary or secondary prevention strategy, however. In fact, removing everyday stressors from a child's life serves to increase the child's chances of suffering from depression and other internalizing disorders because he or she is prevented from acquiring the skills necessary to effectively cope with failure and disappointment (Seligman, 1990). Stressors that are nonroutine or serious (e.g., being physically abused at home, being bullied at school) may require a more direct approach up to and including removal of the child from the home or a change in classrooms. The value of limiting a child's exposure to serious stressors is highlighted by research showing that childhood physical abuse predicts subsequent delinquency and crime (Widom, 2003) and that a substantial minority of bullied children respond to the bullying by becoming bullies themselves (Griffin & Gross, 2004). Buffering stress with family support, new friendships, or programs like Big Brothers Big Sisters can serve a vital secondary prevention function (Cicognani, Albanesi, & Zani, 2008). Finally, teaching children to cope with stress by providing them with stress management training can be an especially effective secondary prevention strategy (Kraag, Zeegers, Kok, Hosman, & Abu-Saad, 2006).

Children exposed to high levels of stress do not necessarily suffer long-term negative consequences as a result. **Resilience** is a term used to describe good outcomes in children exposed to severe stress, marked adversity, or other threats to development (Masten, 2001). Resilience has been attributed to both person and situation variables. Person variables found to promote resilience in children exposed to abnormal levels of stress and adversity include intelligence (Fergusson & Lynskey, 1996), an easygoing temperament (Martinez-Torteya, Bogat, von Eye, & Levendosky, 2009), a strong electrodermal response (Shannon, Beauchaine, Brenner, Neuhaus, & Gatzke-Kopp, 2007), above average ego strength (Cicchetti & Rogosch, 2007), good social skills (Luthar, 1991), and an attitude of perseverence (Floyd, 1996). The results of one study showed that personal resources may not be sufficient to protect children residing in multiproblem families (Jaffee, Caspi, Moffitt, Polo-Thomás, & Taylor, 2007). Situation factors could play a leading role in these multiproblem families to the extent that early exposure to controllable stress (Garmezy, 1993), positive parenting (Werner & Smith, 1992), quality preschool education (Hall et al., 2009), and social support (Smith & Carlson, 1997) all encourage resilience in children. Given the chaotic and potentially unsupportive nature of Dennis's home life, situation factors may be required to enhance his resiliency in the face of a growing number of risk factors for criminal involvement.

Socialization

Through socialization, people acquire the beliefs, norms, values, and behaviors of a larger group or culture. Socialization can increase or decrease opportunities for crime by bringing the individual into contact with definitions congruent with crime or definitions incongruent with crime, respectively. Roger from Chapter 6 was socialized into a criminal lifestyle by his interactions with parents, peers, and the media and he subsequently learned to accept values congruent with crime and reject values incongruent with crime. Someone else could be socialized in the exact opposite manner—that is, rejecting values congruent with crime and accepting values incongruent with crime. In either case, the individual's opportunities for crime are altered by patterns of socialization. Socializing influences paramount in the formation of a criminal lifestyle and in the creation of an effective program of secondary prevention include parents, peers, and the mass media.

Parental socialization effects can be either direct or indirect. Parents socialize their children indirectly by making the children feel loved and accepted (support dimension) whereas direct socialization involves placing demands on the child (control dimension). Hoeve, Dubas, Eichelsheim, van der Laan, Smeenk, and Gerris (2009) conducted a meta-analysis of the relationship between parenting and delinquency by breaking parenting down into these two dimensions. The results of their meta-analysis revealed that parental support and control were moderately associated with delinquency and that affection, involvement, discipline, and monitoring were more important than open communication and rules setting (see Figure 8.2). Accordingly, authoritative parenting (inductive discipline) correlated with reduced levels of delinquency whereas authoritarian parenting (coercive discipline) correlated with increased levels of delinquency. In this same study, lack of warmth and support from the father promoted a higher level of delinquency than lack of warmth and support from the mother, particularly in male children. The primary implication of this meta-analysis is that parental support and control are equally potent correlates of delinquency and each should be addressed in a program of secondary prevention.

Figure 8.2   Effect Sizes (*r*) for Parental Support and Control as Predictors of Offspring Delinquency

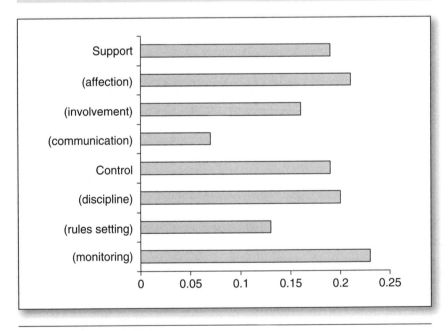

Source: Hoeve et al. (2009)

The principal focus of secondary prevention programs relevant to parental socialization is training parents to be more effective disciplinarians. Behavioral and nonbehavioral programs have been created to improve parents' child management skills using group, individual, and self-directed formats. The results of a meta-analysis on a sample of 63 peer-reviewed studies denote that parent training is effective in reducing disruptive behavior in the children of trained parents (Lundahl, Risser, & Lovejoy, 2006). Overall, the effect was strongest for younger children from nondisadvantaged homes who displayed more severe externalizing symptoms, when treatment took place using an individual rather than group format, and where only the parents received treatment (see Figure 8.3). Interestingly, behavioral and nonbehavioral programs achieved comparable results. Economically disadvantaged families benefited less from parent training than nondisadvantaged families, although when the service was delivered individually a modest treatment effect was observed even in disadvantaged families. These results indicate that the control dimension of parental socialization can be enhanced with training and may accordingly serve a secondary prevention function. More attention needs to be directed at finding ways to buttress the support dimension based on research confirming that the support dimension is just as important as the control dimension in promoting delinquency (Hoeve et al., 2009).

Parents are not the only socialization agents capable of increasing a child's opportunities for experimenting with and committing various antisocial acts. Peer and media outlets also exert a substantial influence over the initial phases of a criminal lifestyle. It is no secret that peers are instrumental in lifestyle initiation, whether the lifestyle is centered on crime, drugs, or both. Gifford-Smith, Dodge, Dishion, and McCord (2005) reviewed the literature on peers and delinquency and concluded that peers were critical in initiating, exacerbating, and maintaining delinquent behavior. The effect, they go on to say, can be attributed to direct exposure to delinquent role models and attitudes rather than to a selection bias wherein delinquents choose one another as friends because the effect persisted even after prior levels of delinquency were controlled. These authors comment that the practice of placing delinquents in environments with other delinquents (reform schools, juvenile detention) may exacerbate delinquent behavior.

The relationship between media violence and crime is more complex and controversial than the peer-delinquency relationship. Reviewing the results of five meta-analyses and one quasi-systematic review, Browne and Hamilton-Giachritsis (2005) concluded that violent images from movies, television, and computer games can lead to a substantial short-term increase in aggressive or fearful behavior in younger children, particularly boys, although the short-term effect of violent media on older children is more variable and the long-term effect on children of all ages is largely unknown. By contrast, the link between media violence and later criminality is weak at

Figure 8.3   Effect Sizes (d) of Parental Training on Disruptive Child
Behaviors

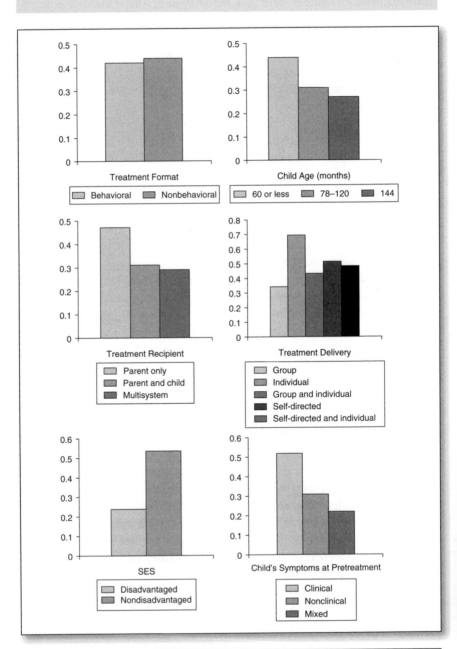

best (Savage, 2004). Even so, an angry or aggressive temperament combined with an unstable or violent home environment can potentially exacerbate the effect of media violence on childhood aggression and increase a child's odds of participating in future criminality (Browne & Pennell, 2000).

Dennis would appear to be a prime candidate for a program of secondary prevention designed to reduce opportunities for crime through altered socialization patterns. Starting with his parents, it would be helpful if both parents were enrolled in some form of parenting training. Neither parent is particularly adept or consistent in disciplining Dennis. His father seems to vacillate between authoritarian discipline and ignoring Dennis, and his mother uses an overly permissive style of parenting that allows Dennis to misbehave with impunity. **Parental control** (disciplinary style and effectiveness) is only half the battle, however. Parental support (positive parent–child relationship) also needs to be enhanced, particularly on the part of the father by involving Dennis and his dad in positive mutually reinforcing activities so that Dennis can gain a greater sense of attachment to and affection for his father. The peer portion of Dennis's secondary prevention plan should include limiting his involvement with the older and more antisocial crowd he currently associates with and encouraging him to spend more time with prosocial children closer to his own age. Creating positive peer relations with prosocial children would also provide Dennis's mother with some relief if he were to spend more time at other children's houses or in organized activities like soccer and scouting. Of course, Dennis's antisocial inclinations will need to be curbed before other parents are willing to invite him into their homes. Finally, Dennis's parents need to exercise greater control over his television viewing and video game playing habits. Given his temperament and the hectic, possibly violent, nature of his home life, he may be particularly vulnerable to media violence.

Availability

Lifestyles are composed of objects and resources that help define the lifestyle and delineate the boundaries of lifestyle activity. Various objects and resources can have important implications for criminal lifestyle development and secondary prevention by increasing or decreasing opportunities for crime, a process known as availability. On the one hand, opportunities for crime are increased as objects and resources congruent with crime become more available or objects and resources incongruent with crime become less available. On the other hand, opportunities for crime are decreased as objects and resources congruent with crime become less available or objects and resources incongruent with crime become more available. Children and early adolescents have fewer options available to them than adults and late adolescents. Unlike an adult, a child cannot seek legal recourse for a problem inside or outside the home, and unlike an older adolescent, an early adolescent cannot simply leave an abusive home environment. When conventional options are unavailable, delinquent options become more attractive (Agnew, 1992). In this section, we will consider how objects and resources congruent with crime and objects and resources incongruent with crime make crime initiation more or less available to a child and how this information can be incorporated into a program of secondary prevention.

Objects (e.g., weapons, drugs) and resources (criminal knowledge, criminal associations) can increase opportunities for criminal lifestyle involvement. The routine activities model of criminology holds that certain routine activities of everyday life can increase opportunities for crime (Cohen & Felson, 1979). Osgood, Wilson, O'Malley, Bachman, and Johnston (1996) studied routine activities in a large sample of high school students and discerned that four out of four unstructured socializing activities correlated with one or more of the following externalizing outcomes: criminal behavior, heavy alcohol use, marijuana use, other drug use, and dangerous driving. Going to parties, riding for fun, and evenings out all correlated with criminal behavior, and visiting with friends correlated with all three drug use outcomes. Encouraging the parents to keep certain objects (knives, guns, matches) away from Dennis will serve the dual purpose of protecting family members and reducing Dennis's opportunities for crime. Limiting Dennis's interactions with older neighborhood children whom the parents believe are encouraging Dennis's antisocial inclinations can also reduce opportunities for crime through decreased availability.

With reduced availability of objects and resources incongruent with crime comes enhanced opportunities for involvement in a criminal lifestyle. Lynam (1997) has advanced the concept of adolescent psychopathy and generated a body of empirical data to support the notion that psychopathy assessed in early adolescence is capable of predicting criminality in early adulthood (Lynam, Miller, Vachon, Loeber, & Stouthamer-Loeber, 2009). The problem with labeling a 5-, 13-, or 15-year-old child a psychopath given the fluidity of antisocial behavior in childhood and adolescence is that this label can decrease the labeled child's access to objects and resources incongruent with crime (e.g., school, jobs, law-abiding friends). Labeling Dennis a psychopath could also interfere with his ability to fit into regular society by creating the impression that he is "bad" and will likely remain that way in the eyes of teachers, parents, law enforcement officers, and other members of society. In fact, there is a very distinct possibility that it could become a self-fulfilling prophecy. Consequently, one component of a program of secondary prevention with someone like Dennis is to avoid using labels like psychopath or life-course-persistent (LCP) delinquent to describe his behavior.

Choice

Decision Making

Decision making can be as important as incentive and opportunity in launching a criminal career. Problem-solving deficits have been observed in children diagnosed with conduct disorder and other externalizing behaviors (Spivak & Shure, 1982). Therefore, rather than taking a pathological view of externalizing behaviors of the oppositional defiant or conduct disordered type we might instead adopt a utilitarian approach. Focusing on immediate goals and instant gratification, a strategy sometimes referred to as delinquent problem solving, can be quite effective in the short run (Brezina, 2000). The downside to delinquent problem solving, as many delinquent individuals soon learn, is the long-term problems it creates for the individual, particularly once he or she has reached the age where the consequences of social rule breaking are more severe. A child's progression through adolescence is accompanied by maturation of the frontal cortex of the brain (Hooper, Luciana, Conklin, & Yarger, 2004), increased awareness of the consequences of his/her actions (Reyna & Farley, 2006), an expanding time horizon (Nurmi, 1991), and a rise in the perceived costs of delinquent behavior (Nagin & Paternoster, 1991). Cognitive maturity results in significant improvements in problem-solving ability and accounts to some extent for the age–crime curve Hirschi and Gottfredson (1983) refer to as a brute fact of criminology. Those adolescents who do not achieve decision-making maturity by age 16 or 17 are at risk for future criminal involvement.

Interpersonal problem-solving training was introduced almost a half century ago by George Spivak as a secondary prevention method for predelinquent youth (Spivak & Levine, 1963). In collaboration with Myrna Shure (Spivak & Shure, 1982), he developed an interpersonal problem-solving approach for delinquent and predelinquent youth that has been found effective in reducing both physical and nonphysical forms of antisocial behavior (Shure, 1999). The four principal skills taught as part of the problem-solving model are (1) alternative solution thinking (brainstorming), (2) means-ends thinking, (3) consequential thinking, and (4) the weighing out of pros and cons. The development of these skills in children as young as 4 years has been found to produce results that are both meaningful and lasting (Shure, 1985). With younger children like Dennis, it may be necessary to incorporate additional strategies into the interpersonal problem-solving format. The Dina Dinosaur program provides children between the ages of 4 and 8 with training in emotional literacy, perspective taking, communication skills, anger management, school success, and interpersonal problem solving. The results of two randomized treatment studies showed that clinic-referred children with behavioral problems who completed the Dina Dinosaur program displayed significant short- and long-term improvements in behavioral adjustment relative to the control group. Combining the program with concurrent parent training, in fact, produced the strongest results (Webster-Stratton & Reid, 2003).

Dennis informed his therapist that he was upset with his sister for breaking his Game Boy handheld video-game device. His therapist asked him to work through the problem using the interpersonal problem-solving approach he had just taught Dennis. The problem-solving model and Dennis's responses to each step are reproduced in Figure 8.4. Dennis began by defining the problem as "my sister broke my Game Boy." In an effort to solve his problem, he listed seven different options: (1) Beat up sister. (2) Break something of sister's. (3) Tell mother. (4) Ask sister to pay for the damage. (5) Offer to pay half and have sister pay half for a new Game Boy. (6) Ask for a new Game Boy for Christmas. (7) Take the broken Game Boy to the next-door neighbor, Mr. Wilson, who is considered an electronics whiz around the neighborhood. In evaluating each option, Dennis soon realized that while beating up his sister or breaking something of his sister's might feel good (+5) they would also get him into trouble (−6). Telling his mother about the incident would get his sister in trouble, but this would be neutralized by the fact that he would be tattling. Asking his sister to pay for the damage or even going half-and-half with his sister on a new Game Boy is unrealistic because his sister has no money. Asking for a new Game Boy for Christmas seems like a worthwhile option (+6) but requires waiting 5 months to get a new Game Boy (−4). His seventh alternative, asking Mr. Wilson to fix the broken Game Boy, seems to be his best option in that it could result in the Game Boy being repaired (+4) against a low likelihood that Mr. Wilson will say no (−1). Dennis consequently decides to ask Mr. Wilson to fix the Game Boy, and if Mr. Wilson says no or can't repair it, he plans on telling his mother about the incident and asking for a new Game Boy for Christmas.

Conclusion

Using the six factors construed by lifestyle theory as instrumental in initiating a criminal lifestyle (i.e., existential fear, temperament, stress, socialization, availability, and choice) as guides, the current chapter identified the components of an effective program of secondary prevention. There is substantial overlap between the six factors, however, in terms of the components of secondary prevention identified by each. Whereas overlap provides cross-validation of the identified components, it also makes for redundancy and inefficiency when working directly with the six factors. Hence, a single program that contains the bulk of these components is preferable to the

Figure 8.4 Problem-Solving Model With Dennis's Responses Inserted

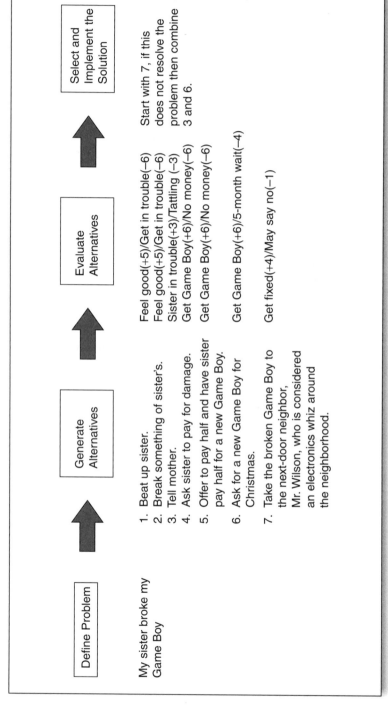

Define Problem	Generate Alternatives	Evaluate Alternatives	Select and Implement the Solution

My sister broke my Game Boy

1. Beat up sister.
2. Break something of sister's.
3. Tell mother.
4. Ask sister to pay for damage.
5. Offer to pay half and have sister pay half for a new Game Boy.
6. Ask for a new Game Boy for Christmas.
7. Take the broken Game Boy to the next-door neighbor, Mr. Wilson, who is considered an electronics whiz around the neighborhood.

Feel good(+5)/Get in trouble(−6)
Feel good(+5)/Get in trouble(−6)
Sister in trouble(+3)/Tattling (−3)
Get Game Boy(+6)/No money(−6)
Get Game Boy(+6)/No money(−6)

Get Game Boy(+6)/5-month wait(−4)

Get fixed(+4)/May say no(−1)

Start with 7, if this does not resolve the problem then combine 3 and 6.

shotgun approach employed in the current chapter to identify the relevant components of secondary prevention. Multisystematic therapy (MST) (Henggeler, 2001) is such an approach. It assesses the child in relationship to various social systems (families, schools, peer groups), targets as many of these systems as necessary, employs a small team of treatment providers, and offers a wide range of treatment services to both the child and his or her family. Many of these services were identified in the current analysis of the six developmental factors. Preliminary research on MST is encouraging (Burns, Schoenwald, Burchard, Faw, & Santos, 2000; Henggeler, Schoenwald, Borduin, Rowland, & Cunningham, 2009) and suggests that an organized program of secondary prevention can be developed and successfully implemented with high-risk youth.

Key Terms and Concepts

Activity Level

Availability

Decision Making

Emotionality

Existential Fear

Fearlessness

Information Processing Speed

Negative Emotionality

Novelty Seeking

Parental Control

Parental Support

Primary Prevention

Resilience

Secondary Prevention

Sociability

Socialization

Stress

Temperament

Tertiary Prevention

9

Mental Illness and Malingering

The Criminal Lifestyle
in an Application Context

*There is always some madness in love. But there is also always
some reason in madness.*

Friedrich Nietzsche (1844–1900)

Tattoo

Tomas is a 29-year-old Hispanic male serving a 124-month sentence for
possession of heroin with intent to distribute. His most remarkable
physical feature is that his arms and torso are covered in tattoos. Most
of the tattoos have a story to tell, and several symbolize his mental
health struggles. A prominent theme in many of the tattoos is the battle
between good and evil. Tomas indicates that he was raised in a working-
class home and that his mother was a strict disciplinarian. Being an only
child, he felt pressure from his immigrant parents to succeed in America.
They were very disappointed, then, when he brought home Cs and Ds
instead of As and Bs on his report card. In response to the pressure and
regular diet of physical abuse he suffered at the hands of his mother,
Tomas started running away from home when he was 15. He left home
for good a year later; a year after this, he dropped out of school. Tomas

eventually earned his GED in prison. Although he never married, Tomas has fathered six children with six different women. None of these relationships lasted more than a few weeks. The record reflects that he has never provided support for any of his children. Tomas has a history of criminality (five prior arrests: two for robbery and one for assault), drug abuse (marijuana, heroin), suicidal ideation and attempts, and mental illness (three prior hospitalizations ranging from 2 weeks to 3 months). He is at high risk for both criminality (Lifestyle Criminality Screening Form [LCSF] total score = 13, 88th percentile) and psychiatric relapse (was found incompetent to stand trial on two separate occasions).

There has been a long-standing debate over whether offenders with mental health difficulties are mad (psychiatric), bad (criminal), or both (Greig & Kingsley, 2002). Tomas is an example of someone who is both. On the one hand, he has been diagnosed with schizoaffective disorder, depressive type, and receives antipsychotic medication. On the other hand, he is an enforcer for one of the Hispanic prison gangs, has on occasion sold his psychotropic medication to other inmates, and was recently placed in segregation for actions that had nothing to do with his mental health difficulties. While in segregation, he stopped taking his medication and became self-injurious and self-mutilating to the point where he had to be placed on suicide watch. The institution doctor noted that Tomas was apparently careful when he self-mutilated and cut himself in a manner designed to avoid serious physical damage. Apparently, Tomas was depressed and wanted to be housed alone rather than with a cell mate. The only single cell in the institution is the suicide watch room, and so he engaged in the self-mutilating behavior to "prove" to staff that he was serious and in need of placement on suicide watch. After several days of bag lunches, Tomas grew bored with the routine of suicide watch, started taking his medication, and went back to being his usual jovial self. This illustrates how an individual with serious mental health problems can also be criminally oriented and willing to exaggerate psychiatric symptoms to get what he wants.

Mental Illness

There is a general belief among those who work in the field of corrections that the number of incarcerated offenders with serious mental health problems has increased dramatically in recent years. Mentally ill patients, who had previously been treated in the mental health system, it was reasoned, were being diverted into the criminal justice system in ever increasing numbers, a process referred to as **transinstitutionalization** (Steadman, Monahan, Duffee, Hartstone, & Robbins, 1984). Whether transinstitutionalization is a consequence of **deinstitutionalization** (replacing long-term hospitalization with community services), stress, or some other factor, it is taxing a system that has already been stretched to its limit by budget cuts and a burgeoning jail and prison population. As such, it represents an important application issue in the field of forensic psychology. The purpose of this section is to determine the **prevalence** (number of cases in a population suffering from a specific disorder at a given point in time divided by the total number of people in the population) of serious mental illness (e.g., schizophrenia, bipolar disorder, major depression) in correctional populations and apply the latent structure, diagnostic/assessment, developmental, and intervention contexts described in previous chapters to the construct of offender mental illness.

Prevalence

First generation prevalence studies on mental illness in correctional settings produced equivocal findings, with rates of serious emotional disturbance ranging from 5% (Nielson, 1979) to 69% (Guy, Platt, Zwerling, & Bullock, 1985). Most of the early studies employed unreliable measures (like self-reported prior hospitalizations or clinical impressions from a psychiatrist) instead of standardized diagnostic procedures, self-selected or staff-referred samples instead of randomized stratified samples, and pretrial detainees instead of sentenced prisoners (Diamond, Wang, Holzer, Thomas, & Cruser, 2001). More recently conducted and more methodologically sound **second generation prevalence studies** have identified a narrower range and overall lower rate of serious emotional disorder in inmate populations. In randomized stratified correctional samples of 413 to 2,185 participants administered standardized diagnostic procedures, investigators have observed a 1.5% to 4.4% rate of **schizophrenia**, 1.6% to 2.9% rate of **bipolar disorder**, and 7.2% to 13.6% rate of **major depression** (Bean, Meirson, & Pinta, 1988; California Department of Corrections, 1989; Motiuk & Porporino, 1992; Neighbors et al., 1987; Steadman, Osher, Robbins, Case, & Samuels, 2009). A recent meta-analysis of 62 surveys performed in 12 different countries with a total sample size of 22,790 male and female prisoners revealed prevalence rates of 4% for psychosis (i.e., schizophrenia, schizophreniform disorder, delusional disorder, and mania) and 10% for major depression (Fazel & Danesh, 2002). Assuming a moderate degree of overlap or **comorbidity** among the three diagnostic categories of schizophrenia, bipolar disorder, and major depression (Kessler, Chiu, Dermier, Merikangas, & Walters,

2005), the rate of serious mental disorder in second generation studies is estimated to be somewhere in the neighborhood of 10% for prison inmates and 15% for jail inmates.

Latent Structure

Taxometric research has produced conflicting results when applied to serious mental disorder in general population samples. The prevailing view is that schizophrenia and its hypothesized precursor, **schizotypy**, are categorical in nature (Blanchard, Horan, & Collins, 2005; Lenzenweger, 1999; Tyrka et al., 1995), although dimensional taxometric results have been recorded in a handful of studies examining the latent structure of schizotypy (Linscott, 2007; Rawlings, Williams, Haslam, & Claridge, 2008). There is evidence of both categorical (Ruscio, Zimmerman, McGlinchey, Chelminski, & Young, 2007) and dimensional (Prisciandaro & Roberts, 2005) latent structure in taxometric research on major depression, and at the time this chapter was being written, no published taxometric research was available for bipolar disorder. These conflicting results and findings suggest that the latent structure of serious emotional disorder is probably composed of both categorical and dimensional elements.

Walters (2010b) recently tested the latent structure of serious emotional disorder in a sample of 795 state prison inmates using the frequency and duration of psychiatric hospitalization as indicators of serious mental illness. The results disclosed evidence of categorical latent structure and produced a taxon base rate (prevalence) of 8.9%. When taxon members were compared to the top portion of the complement (all of whom had at least one prior or subsequent psychiatric hospitalization), taxon members received significantly more diagnoses of serious emotional disorder (i.e., schizophrenia or other psychosis, bipolar disorder, major depression). Assuming these results can be cross-validated in other samples using various alternate indicators of serious mental disorder it would appear that unlike criminality—which we know from Chapter 2 is dimensional in nature—mental illness is categorically organized in offender populations.

Diagnosis and Assessment

If the latent structure of mental illness in offender populations is categorical, then we would be well advised to use a categorical diagnostic system. The purpose of a categorical diagnostic system is to assign offenders to one of two mutually exclusive categories: for example, those with serious mental illness and those without serious mental illness. A categorical diagnostic system, as we learned in Chapter 3, highlights signs and symptoms, and a categorical assessment system, as we learned in Chapter 4, is composed of items that maximally differentiate between groups (i.e., the taxon and its complement). Accordingly, the signs and symptoms of the serious mental disorder taxon should display good **sensitivity**—more true positives (mentally disordered offenders correctly identified as mentally disordered) than false negatives (mentally disordered offenders incorrectly identified as non-mentally disordered); good **specificity**—more true negatives (nonmentally disordered offenders correctly identified as nonmentally disordered) than false positives (nonmentally disordered offenders incorrectly identified as mentally disordered); and adequate predictive power. A cutting score of two or more psychiatric hospitalizations in the Walters (2010b) study achieved high sensitivity and specificity and 97% accuracy. The actual criteria used to define serious mental disorder in offender samples remains to be worked out but should probably include behavioral signs (e.g., previous psychiatric hospitalizations), self-reported symptoms (e.g., command auditory hallucinations), and physical test findings (e.g., dexamethasone suppression test for serious affective disorder). Tomas satisfies the criteria for major mental disorder as represented by three prior psychiatric hospitalizations and signs and symptoms of schizoaffective disorder, depressed type.

Development

Meehl (1977, 1992) discussed four causal explanations for the discontinuity that underlies categorical constructs. First, a categorical construct could be the result of a dichotomous causal agent or **specific etiology** that all members of the taxon share in common. An example of specific etiology would be the HTT gene that is responsible for Huntington's disease. Second, a categorical construct could be the result of a **threshold model**. Cases in a threshold model are initially distributed along a continuum up to where a threshold is crossed; after which, cases above the threshold are qualitatively distinct from cases below the threshold. Scores on a defensiveness scale may reflect increasing levels (dimensions) of ego strength until a threshold is reached, above which scores signal a qualitatively different state (pathological defensiveness). A third causal explanation for categorical taxometric results is **developmental bifurcation**. Environmental mold taxa are often explained using this particular causal model. In using a developmental bifurcation model to explain the action of an alcohol taxon, dimensional differences in genetic liability for alcoholism could eventually diverge into a qualitatively distinct state from exposure to various role models or development of unusually powerful positive outcome expectancies for alcohol.

A fourth causal explanation for discontinuity is **nonlinear interaction**. Rather than a simple additive effect of multiple causal influences, as one would expect if the construct was dimensional, nonlinear interaction gives rise to a synergistic effect whereby a qualitative state above and beyond the simple additive effect of two or more variables is attained. Whereas the categorical status of mental disorder in offender populations is far from established, if a category or taxon does exist, nonlinear interaction may be the most plausible explanation. Genetics appear to play an important role in the development of serious adult mental disorder—schizophrenia, bipolar disorder, and major depression, in particular (Hanson, 2009). Two possible nonlinear interaction explanations for serious mental disorder in offender populations are **emergenesis** and **gene-environment interaction**. Emergenesis occurs when a particular behavior (e.g., serious mental disorder) is only observed when all members of a gene set are present in a single individual (Lykken, McGue, Tellegen, & Bouchard, 1992). Gene-environment interaction, as exemplified by Meehl's (1990) stress-diathesis model of schizophrenia, involves a synergy of genetic and environmental factors that promote a qualitatively distinct state that is greater than the sum of the contributing genetic and environmental factors. Either one of these nonlinear interaction models could provide a meaningful explanation for a serious mental disorder taxon, if, in fact, such a taxon exists.

Intervention

Medication is often the intervention of choice for major mental health problems. Just the same, behavioral and psychological interventions can also be effective in dealing with these disorders. Accordingly, both pharmacological and nonpharmacological interventions for schizophrenia, major depression, and bipolar disorder can be effective in treating serious mental disorder in criminal populations.

Pharmacological Intervention

Psychotropic medication can be effective in controlling the symptoms and improving the quality of life of many individuals who suffer from major mental health problems. In fact, chlorpromazine (Thorazine) started a revolution in the treatment and care of schizophrenia when it was first introduced in 1954. Common classes of medication used in the treatment of schizophrenia, major depression, and bipolar disorder are listed in Table 9.1. **Double-blind** placebo-controlled studies in which neither the subject nor investigator know whether the subject received medication or a **placebo**

(inert substance) have consistently demonstrated that these medications are superior to a placebo in the management of schizophrenia, major depression, and bipolar disorder. Even so, none of the medications are capable of "curing" serious mental disorders. There appears to be little difference in effectiveness between traditional and atypical antipsychotic agents and while both have been found to reduce the positive symptoms of schizophrenia neither has had much success with such negative symptoms as blunt affect and poverty of speech (Lieberman et al., 2005). Tricyclic, monoamine oxidase (MAO) inhibitor, and selective serotonin reuptake inhibitor (SSRI) antidepressant medications have been found effective in reducing time until recovery from depression but the effects generally do not persist once the medication is discontinued (Reimherr, Strong, Marchant, Hedges, & Wender, 2001). Antimanic medications like lithium seem to help up to 80% of the people diagnosed with bipolar disorder, but in a majority of these cases, there is only partial remission of symptoms (Prien & Potter, 1993).

People often stop taking their psychotropic medication because of the side effects. Side effects are effects other than the ones for which the medication is prescribed. Since most of the psychotropic medications currently in use affect the entire central nervous system, there are many side effects, some of which are listed in Table 9.1. Many of the side effects of psychotropic medications remain to be discovered in that a relatively large number of these medications have been on the market for less than a decade. The majority of side effects listed in Table 9.1 are mild, infrequent, and treatable. Still, some side effects can be life-threatening, and there is no such thing as a psychotropic drug without side effects. Take, for instance, the antidepressant medication trazadone, which is frequently prescribed for sleep. In addition to the insomnia rebound effect one normally gets with antidepressant treatment of primary insomnia, there is an even more serious (although admittedly rare) side effect known as **priapism**. Priapism is a prolonged, often painful, erection of the penis in the absence of sexual stimulation, which if left untreated can lead to permanent erectile dysfunction and penile necrosis. Prozac is normally considered a relatively safe antidepressant medication with few side effects. However, there is growing concern that Prozac may cause **akathisia** (extreme inner discomfort), which in a small number of cases can promote suicidal ideation and homicidal behavior (Healy, Herxheimer, & Menkes, 2006). The fact that several high-profile mass murders were perpetrated by individuals who had recently been prescribed Prozac or another SSRI is also a source of concern (Healy, 2004). The point I am trying to make here is not that these medications should be banned but that physicians must be certain that the person suffers from a significant mental health problem before prescribing them.

Table 9.1 Potential Side Effects of Psychotropic Medications

General Category	Chemical Class	Exemplar	Side Effects
ANTIPSYCHOTIC	Conventional Antipsychotics	Thorazine (chlorpromazine)	• dysphagia (difficulty swallowing)
			• extrapyramidal symptoms
			• liver damage
	Atypical Antipsychotics	Zyprexa (olanzapine)	• tardive dyskinesia (involuntary motor movements of the lips and other areas)
			• agranulocytosis (acute and potentially fatal reduction in white blood count)
			• akathisia (agitation or inner restlessness)
			• hyperglycemia (abnormal elevation of blood glucose)
			• severe weight gain
ANTIDEPRESSANT	Tricyclic Antidepressants	Elavil (amitriptytline)	• complications of heart problems
			• drowsiness/fatigue
			• inability to pass urine
			• reduced sex drive

General Category	Chemical Class	Exemplar	Side Effects
	Monoamine Oxidase Inhibitors	Parnate (tranylcypromine)	• edema (swelling) in lower extremities
			• increased appetite/weight gain
			• life-threatening interactions with foods (cheese, wine) and many over-the-counter medications
	Selective Serotonin Reuptake Inhibitors	Prozac (fluoxetine)	• akathisia (agitation or inner restlessness)
			• fine motor tremor
			• seizures
			• speech impairment
ANTIMANIC	Lithium Salt	Lithotabs (lithium carbonate)	• bradycardia (slowed heart rate)
			• hypothyroidism
			• toxicity
			• weight gain

(Continued)

203

(Continued)

General Category	Chemical Class	Exemplar	Side Effects
	Anticonvulsants	Tegretol (carbamazepine)	• bone marrow depression
			• changes in appetite; weight gain
			• liver dysfunction
ANTIANXIETY	Barbiturates	Nembutal (phenobarbitol)	• extreme sedation
			• high abuse potential
			• impaired blood pressure
			• respiratory problems
	Benzodiazepines	Xanax (alprazolam)	• ataxia (unsteady gait and other gross motor coordination problems)
			• confusion, disorientation
			• high abuse potential

Source: Physicians' Desk Reference (2009).

Nonpharmacological Intervention

Skills training programs use role-playing, modeling, and positive reinforcing to teach inmates basic social, life, and self-care skills. Such programs have been found to improve social functioning and quality of life and to reduce negative behaviors and relapse in both schizophrenic (Kopelwicz, Lieberman, & Zarate, 2002) and depressed (Segrin, 2000) patients. **Cognitive behavior therapy,** in which irrational or self-defeating cognitions are identified, challenged, and replaced, is at least as effective as antidepressant medication in reducing depressive symptoms and improving the daily adjustment of patients with major depressive disorder but without the side effects frequently observed with psychotropic medication (Hollon & DeRubeis, 2003). It was once thought that cognitive behavior therapy was inappropriate for schizophrenic patients because of the schizophrenic's disorganized thinking. However, researchers have discerned that both the positive and negative symptoms of schizophrenia respond to cognitive behavior therapy (Beck & Rector, 2000). This is particularly important because as was mentioned previously, antipsychotic medication has little impact on the negative symptoms of schizophrenia. There is also preliminary evidence that cognitive behavior therapy can be helpful in managing bipolar disorder in adolescents (Feeney, Danielson, Schwartz, Youngstrom, & Finding, 2006). Hence, social skills training and cognitive behavioral therapy alone or in combination with psychotropic medication may have value in the treatment of serious mental disorders like schizophrenia, major depression, and bipolar disorder. Because research indicates that mentally disordered offenders (Morgan, Fisher, Duan, Mandrachhia, & Murray, 2010) and civilly committed psychiatric patients (Carr, Rosenfeld, Magyar, & Rotter, 2009) have features of both mental illness and criminality, it is important that we address both the criminal and psychiatric features of mentally disordered offenders and civilly committed psychiatric patients.

Malingering

There are several reasons why criminal offenders are incorrectly diagnosed as mentally ill. For one, clinicians sometimes mistake situational distress, Axis II (personality) disorders, and features of a criminal lifestyle for an Axis I (clinical) disorder. For another, criminal offenders malinger and misrepresent symptoms for the purpose of gaining certain internal and external rewards. Malingering/exaggeration of psychiatric, neurologic, and medical symptomatology provide another example of the criminal lifestyle in application context.

Prevalence

The prevalence of malingering depends to a large extent on the rewards one can reasonably anticipate from feigning a symptom or behavior. Nonimpaired individuals who expect to receive monetary compensation from the Veteran's Administration (VA) or the Social Security Administration (SSA) will frequently fabricate a psychiatric or medical disorder to accomplish this goal. Freeman, Powell, and Kimbrell (2008) discerned that 53% of a group of Vietnam veterans enrolled in a VA residential treatment program for post-traumatic stress disorder (PTSD) and entitled to disability payments showed clear signs of symptom malingering and exaggeration on the Structured Interview of Reported Symptoms (SIRS) (Rogers, Bagby, & Dickens, 1992). Rates in excess of 50% have been reported in studies on malingering and exaggeration of psychiatric and medical symptomatology on state and federal medical disability claims (Chafetz, 2008; Chafetz, Abrahams, & Kohlmaier, 2007; Miller, Boyd, Cohn, Wilson, & McFarland, 2006) and 20% to 32% in studies on malingering and exaggeration of psychiatric symptomatology in jail and prison inmates (Pollock, Quigley, Worley, & Bashford, 1997; Rogers, Ustad, & Salekin, 1998). Malingering is further moderated by the referral question and assessment procedure. Rogers, Salekin, Sewell, Goldstein, and Leonard (1998) determined that malingering in forensic evaluations ranged from 10% to 50% depending on the individual circumstances of the evaluation and the screening measure used. Therefore, while the prevalence of malingering in various forensic contexts varies widely, it is a significant problem in nearly all of these contexts.

Latent Structure

Early taxometric research on feigned/exaggerated psychiatric symptomatology (Strong, Glassmire, Frederick, & Greene, 2006; Strong, Greene, Hoppe, Johnston, & Olesen, 1999; Strong, Greene, & Schinka, 2000) and neurocognitive deficit (Frazier, Youngstrom, Naugle, Haggerty, & Busch, 2007) showed evidence of a possible dichotomous or categorical latent structure. Many of these studies, however, suffered from significant methodological problems to include small sample sizes, admixed samples of participants with differing levels of motivation for symptom exaggeration, and unreliable (base rate consistency [BR]) or subjective (impressionistic interpretation of curve shape) analysis of taxometric results (Walters, Rogers, et al., 2008). When these methodological limitations were corrected, clear evidence of dimensional latent structure was observed in taxometric studies on feigned psychopathology (Walters, Rogers, et al., 2008), feigned neurocognitive deficit (Walters, Berry, Rogers, Payne, & Granacher, 2009), and exaggerated health complaints (Walters, Berry, Lanyon, & Murphy, 2009). These findings challenge long-standing and commonly held beliefs about malingering in offender populations, which divide those reporting mental health symptoms into mutually exclusive categories of malingerers (fakers) and genuinely disturbed individuals. The fact that there was no apparent external incentive for exaggeration of health complaints in the Walters, Berry, Lanyon, et al. (2009) study indicates that factitious disorder (exaggerating symptoms to gain attention or assume the patient role) also has a dimensional latent structure.

Diagnosis and Assessment

Dimensional latent structure means that individual differences in malingering and symptom exaggeration are a matter of degree rather than a difference in kind and that there is no such thing as a malingering type or types. Walters, White, and Greene (1988) introduced a system of malingering classification composed of four levels: Level 1 (L-1) = pure malingering with no behavioral verification of reported symptomatology; Level 2 (L-2) = significant exaggeration of symptomatology in someone with mild to moderate mental health difficulties; Level 3 (L-3) = mild to moderate exaggeration of symptomatology in someone with significant mental health difficulties; Level 4 (L-4) = significant mental health difficulties with no evidence of exaggeration. This model is congruent with the dimensional nature of symptom malingering/exaggeration but does nothing to clarify its situational nature. Walters (1988) found that inmates completing the Minnesota Multiphasic Personality Inventory (MMPI) for the purpose of determining whether they should be placed in a single cell for mental health reasons reported more severe psychological symptoms than inmates completing the MMPI within the context of a parole evaluation. Both simulation (Walters, 1995b) and known-group (Walters, 2011c) studies conducted on the Psychological Inventory of Criminal Thinking Styles (PICTS) also indicate that the reason for evaluation can have a powerful impact on the inventory's validity scale configurations. These results suggest that malingering and symptom exaggeration not only vary along a continuum but that people may change their position on the continuum in response to situational demands. Hence, whereas Tomas ordinarily functions at L-4, he may have temporarily moved down to L-2 or L-3 in order to gain access to a single cell before reconstituting himself at L-4.

As a dimensional construct, malingering should be evaluated, assessed, and diagnosed using the trends and patterns of a dimensional system instead of the signs and symptoms of a categorical system. The first step in designing a system of trends and patterns is isolating the number of dimensions in the identified malingering construct. Taxometrics is a powerful tool for differentiating between categorical and dimensional constructs, but it cannot reliably identify the number of dimensions in a dimensional construct. For that, we would need to perform an exploratory or confirmatory factor analysis. Rogers, Jackson, Sewell, and Salekin (2005) identified two dimensions in a confirmatory factor analysis of the SIRS. The first dimension, which they labeled spurious presentation, revealed content abnormalities in the feigned symptom picture (i.e., more bizarre or incongruous symptoms than are normally observed in genuine psychopathology). The second dimension, which they labeled plausible presentation, revealed magnitude abnormalities in the feigned symptom picture (i.e., broader or more severe symptom pattern than is normally observed in genuine psychopathology). Although this two-dimensional model must be considered preliminary at the present time, it could eventually serve as the foundation for a dimensional system of classification and diagnosis whereby a person's absolute position on each dimension serves as a measure of trend and a person's relative position on one dimension compared to the other serves as a measure of pattern.

Like the MMPI-2 and Personality Assessment Inventory (PAI), the PICTS come equipped with several validity scale indicators. The two original PICTS validity indicators were the Confusion-revised (Cf-r) scale (designed to identify psychosis, confusion, reading difficulties, and a "fake bad" response style) and the Defensiveness-revised (Df-r) scale (designed to identify problem denial, rigid defensiveness, and a "fake good" response style). Studies using a simulated or known-group design to assess malingering have unfortunately failed to find consistent support for the Cf-r scale as an indicator of malingering/exaggeration (Walters, 1995b, 2011c). A 10-item scale identified in a factor analysis of the PICTS item pool, however, has proven more promising. Known as the Infrequency (INF) scale because its 10 items are rarely endorsed, this scale did a better job of identifying malingering/exaggeration than the Cf-r scale using both simulation (Walters, 1995b) and known-groups (Walters, 2011c) designs. Tomas's PICTS results (see Table 9.2) reveal a highly elevated Cf-r score (Cf-r = 84) and an average INF score (INF = 51). This implies that Tomas may have been somewhat confused when taking the PICTS and still may be subject to periodic bouts of psychosis (high Cf-r) but that he was not trying to create a false impression when he completed the PICTS (average INF). A review of the composite scales is consistent with the notion that Tomas's criminal thinking is more reactive than proactive (R > P) and characterized by poor emotional control (high Co) and high distractibility (high Ds).

Table 9.2   Tomas's Psychological Inventory of Criminal Thinking
Styles Results

Psychological Inventory of Criminal Thinking Styles (PICTS)	
Validity Scales	
Confusion-Revised (Cf-r)	84
Defensiveness-Revised (Df-r)	40
Higher-Order Factor	
General Criminal Thinking (GCT)	61
Composite Scales	
Proactive Criminal Thinking (P)	57
Reactive Criminal Thinking (R)	73
Thinking Style Scales	
Mollification (Mo)	48
Cutoff (Co)	70
Entitlement (En)	48
Power Orientation (Po)	55
Sentimentality (Sn)	47
Superoptimism (So)	54
Cognitive Indolence (Ci)	58
Discontinuity (Ds)	78
Content Scales	
Current Criminal Thinking (CUR)	71
Historical Criminal Thinking (HIS)	61
Factor Scales	
Problem Avoidance (PRB)	75
Infrequency (INF)	51
Self-Assertion (AST)	60
Denial of Harm (DNH)	47

Note: PICTS scores are T-scores.

Development

As opposed to the synergistic and nonlinear interactions postulated as causes of mental disorder in offender populations, dimensional constructs are typically a consequence of many small causal influences that combine additively rather than multiplicatively. The variables that contribute to this additive effect need to be ironed out, but we could start with Walters's (2006a) seven potential motives for malingering: (1) compensation, (2) avoidance, (3) separation, (4) relocation, (5) entitlement, (6) attention, and (7) amusement. Compensation means that the individual is motivated to malinger in hopes of receiving remuneration. Avoidance illustrates how some individuals use malingering to avoid being convicted of a crime or punished for unacceptable behavior. Separation entails using malingered symptoms to create a barrier designed to protect the person from predatory inmates. Relocation is a motive for malingering by way of a person's desire to manipulate a transfer from jail or prison to a more pleasant or less restrictive environment, such as a forensic or civil psychiatric hospital. Entitlement denotes a motive for malingering based on the individual's pursuit of special privileges (e.g., single cell) or medication. Attention can also drive malingering as represented by factitious disorder or Munchausen syndrome. Amusement drives malingering by providing one with a means of passing time or relieving boredom. Of all the factors that potentially contribute to the additive effect for malingering, two that should not be included on this list, even though they are both mentioned in *Diagnostic and Statistical Manual of Mental Disorders* (*DSM–IV–TR*) (American Psychiatric Association [APA], 2000), are a history of antisocial behavior and a diagnosis of antisocial personality. Many offenders who malinger have a history of antisocial behavior but so do many offenders who do not malinger (Rogers, 2009). It would appear that malingering and crime-related constructs like psychopathy and antisocial personality fall along different dimensions rather than a common dimension.

Intervention

The psychologist's role does not necessarily end once a diagnosis of malingering or factitious disorder is made. As a dimensional construct, symptom malingering/exaggeration is a matter of degree rather than a difference in kind. Hence, a psychologist is just as likely to intervene with someone suspected of feigning mental health symptoms as he or she is to diagnose someone suspected of simulating a physical disability. There are ways to reduce a person's reliance on symptom malingering/exaggeration as a means of coping with boredom, fear, and the stresses of incarceration, three of the more popular being (1) confrontation, (2) support, and (3) providing alternatives (Walters, 2006a).

Confrontation

If a clinician believes an offender is manufacturing or exaggerating psychiatric symptomatology, he or she should address this with the offender. Otherwise, the offender will continue to use manipulation to get what he or she wants. The confrontation need not be heavy-handed, strident, or uncompromising to be effective. In fact, research indicates that techniques utilized by practitioners of motivational interviewing, from expressing empathy to rolling with the resistance and avoiding arguments (Miller & Rollnick, 2002), can enhance offender motivation for change while reducing the offender's odds of reoffending (McMurran, 2009). It is imperative that clinicians refrain from labeling the individual a malingerer and instead confront the malingering as a symptom; this is another way of saying that because malingering is a dimensional construct, individual differences on this construct are quantitative rather than qualitative. Failure to address malingering/exaggeration may be interpreted by the offender as a lack of interest or savvy on the part of the clinician, neither of which is likely to instill much confidence in the clinician. A properly conducted confrontation, on the other hand, can promote respect and trust: vital ingredients in the formation of a working assessment or therapeutic alliance.

Support

Confronting malingering and symptom exaggeration is usually not sufficient to bring about lasting change in someone who feels compelled to feign and fabricate psychiatric, neurocognitive, or physical symptoms. The confrontation must be internalized, which is another way of saying that the most effective form of confrontation is self-confrontation (Greenstein, 2007). How, we might ask, can a clinician encourage a client who is malingering/exaggerating psychiatric, neurocognitive, or physical symptoms to self-confront? The answer is that offenders are more likely to self-confront when they feel they are being supported. Because those who feign and exaggerate mental health symptoms often have legitimate problems, issues, and concerns, they need to feel that the psychologist is sensitive to these problems, issues, and concerns if they are to confront long-standing beliefs; otherwise, they will never lower their defensive shields. Providing the offender with the opportunity to explore his or her reasons for feigning or magnifying psychiatric symptomatology can consequently be of great assistance in encouraging the offender to find more constructive alternatives for dealing with the types of problems that fuel symptom malingering/exaggeration.

Providing Alternatives

Once the offender has confronted his or her malingering/exaggeration and gained a sense of support from the clinician, the next step is to help the offender find alternatives to malingering/exaggeration. A popular explanation for symptom feigning is that an individual manufactures and exaggerates psychiatric, neurocognitive, or medical symptomatology in an attempt to adapt to the stress and strain of an adversarial American criminal justice system (Rogers, Sewell, & Goldstein, 1994). Skill-based approaches like problem-solving training and coping skills instruction may be extremely helpful in getting offenders to abandon malingering/exaggeration as a strategy for dealing with the problems of everyday living in favor of more effective alternative strategies. By providing the individual with the skills necessary to find alternatives to malingering/exaggeration we are, in effect, reducing their dependence on symptom malingering/exaggeration to cope with everyday problems in living while simultaneously buttressing and nurturing their sense of self-efficacy.

Conclusion

Application means putting into practice a theoretical principle, belief, or idea. The application context for the current chapter was the overlap between mental illness and malingering in forensic populations. Borrowing principles and tenets from several individual contexts described in earlier chapters of this book (i.e., latent structure, diagnosis, assessment, development, intervention), a new context was formed. This demonstrates that not only are contexts currently unknown components of a construct waiting to be discovered but they are also possibilities in a construct waiting to be created. There are a multitude of possible application contexts for the career criminal–criminal careers schism described in the opening chapter of this book and which the current perspective seeks to resolve with the overarching criminal lifestyle construct. In the 10th and final chapter of this book, several of these possible application contexts will be discussed along with suggestions for how the first nine contexts identified in this book can be expanded.

Key Terms and Concepts

Akathisia

Bipolar Disorder

Cognitive Behavior Therapy

Comorbidity

Deinstitutionalization

Developmental Bifurcation

Double-Blind

Emergenesis

First Generation Prevalence Studies

Gene-Environment Interaction

Major Depression

Nonlinear Interaction

Placebo

Prevalence

Priapism

Psychotropic Medication

Schizophrenia

Schizotypy

Second Generation Prevalence Studies

Sensitivity

Specific Etiology

Specificity

Threshold Model

Transinsitutionalization

10

Future Contexts and Distant Horizons

The only real voyage of discovery consists not in seeking new landscapes but in having new eyes.

Marcel Proust (1871–1922)

The Second-Story Man

Mitch is a 43-year-old single Asian American male serving a 12-year sentence for burglarizing a post office. Despite growing up in a stable, middle-class home environment and having plenty of opportunities for conventional success, Mitch chose to spend his adolescence learning to burglarize homes and steal cars. This is his fourth time behind bars and his 10th year of incarceration. He estimates that he has committed at least one burglary for every day he has spent in jail or prison. If we take him at his word, this means he has participated in over 3,650 burglaries of residences, businesses, and motor vehicles in nearly every region of the United States and Canada. Although he has worked with crime partners in the past, Mitch prefers working alone; this way no one can tell on him if they get caught. In fact, almost every time he has been arrested it has been after someone with whom he had just fenced stolen goods got caught and told on him. Mitch has never been married, has never put down roots, and has never remained in the same location for more than 6 months. He believes the longer you stay in one place the easier it is for the police to catch you. Mitch has lived in practically every major city in the United States, and his biggest challenge has been finding someone to fence his stolen goods to whenever he moves to a new location. Mitch normally finds fences by talking to local prostitutes and drug addicts.

According to Mitch, his greatest downfall is heroin. He has been using heroin since the age of 17 and has "kicked the habit" eight or nine times, only to start up again several months later. Mitch has noticed that he usually does not break into cars, homes, and businesses when he is not using heroin and from this concludes that heroin is the root cause of his offending behavior. He still resists giving it up, however: "It's part of who I am," he states. Having engaged in burglary on a regular basis for the last 30 years, Mitch has become hypersensitive to criminal opportunities. Whenever he approaches a parked car, he automatically scans for objects of value (i.e., car stereo, GPS device) and whether security devices (i.e., locked door, alarm system) are in place. Whenever he visits a friend's house, his mind is working overtime and his eyes are continually scanning for objects to pilfer, though he insists that he would never steal from a friend. He was serving time in New York City when the 9/11 attacks took place, and despite the genuine horror he felt, all he kept thinking about was how the local jewelry stores would be unprotected in light of the confusion and the fact that most of the city's police officers were at the World Trade Center. Mitch, like many burglars, has trained himself to be alert to opportunities for appropriating others' property.

A trend analysis of the Lifestyle Criminality Screening Form (LCSF) denotes that Mitch has been heavily involved in a criminal lifestyle for a number of years (see Table 10.1). There is virtually no dispersion on the V-I index and scatter is minimal between the subsections of the LCSF, although his score on the irresponsibility subsection is slightly elevated above the others. The Psychological Inventory Criminal Thinking Styles (PICTS) results indicate that Mitch has extensive commitment to and identification with the criminal lifestyle. The overall trend is strong and consistent with individual trends on the General Criminal Thinking (GCT) score (> 70) and all eight of the thinking style scales (> 60). Pattern analysis reveals a tendency toward Proactive Criminal Thinking (P > R), although Reactive Criminal Thinking (R) is also high (> 70). P is manifest in Mitch's tendency to be involved in instrumental crimes like burglary and robbery, whereas P is manifest in his drug use, geographic mobility, and impulsive selection of crime targets. A review of Mitch's scores on two of the PICTS validity scales (Confusion-revised

[Cf-r] = 62; Infrequency [INF] = 57) indicates that his elevated PICTS thinking style scores are probably not the result of exaggeration. Therefore, the highly elevated PICTS profile appears to accurately reflect Mitch's level of commitment to and identification with the criminal lifestyle.

Table 10.1 Mitch's Lifestyle Criminality Screening Form and Psychological Inventory of Criminal Thinking Styles Results

Lifestyle Criminality Screening Form (LCSF)	
Overall Involvement	
Total score	15 (96th percentile)
Risk level	High
Factor Scores	
Violation (V) factor score	5
Impulse (I) factor score	6
V-I index	5:6
Subsection Scores	
Irresponsibility	5
Self-indulgence	4
Interpersonal intrusiveness	3
Social rule breaking	3
Psychological Inventory of Criminal Thinking Styles (PICTS)	
Higher-Order Factor	
General Criminal Thinking (GCT)	77
Composite Scales	
Proactive Criminal Thinking (P)	81
Reactive Criminal Thinking (R)	71

Thinking Style Scales	
Mollification (Mo)	63
Cutoff (Co)	78
Entitlement (En)	69
Power Orientation (Po)	70
Sentimentality (Sn)	65
Superoptimism (So)	79
Cognitive Indolence (Ci)	76
Discontinuity (Ds)	60

Note: LCSF scores are raw scores, and PICTS scores are T-scores.

Understanding Crime: The Prime Context

A point made throughout this book and one that I would like to reiterate here is that if we wish to predict and control crime we must first understand crime and those who commit it. However, before we can understand crime, we must first open our eyes to new possibilities, new ways of thinking, and new avenues of understanding. Because knowledge is in a constant state of change, flux, and alteration, the knowledge we possess today may be obsolete, irrelevant, or outdated tomorrow. With each new scientific discovery, previous understandings are discarded or modified, and older paradigms are replaced by newer ones. We must be receptive to new information and be willing to modify our understanding in concert with this new information if our understanding is to serve us rather than the other way around. Those who choose to serve their understanding instead of mastering it slavishly follow the path set forth by their understanding and in so doing end up endorsing belief systems in which dogma usurps science. The scientific method is accordingly essential in informing us of when our understanding is in need of modification.

Using untested postulates from Freudian theory, McDonald (1963) introduced a trio of childhood behaviors (i.e., bedwetting, fire setting, and cruelty to animals), which he believed were highly prognostic of future violence. An early study conducted on a small group of psychiatric patients revealed that significantly more aggressive patients than nonaggressive patients retrospectively recalled experiencing all three components of this so-called **ego triad** (Hellman & Blackman, 1966). More recent studies, however, have only identified cruelty to animals and to a lesser extent fire setting as predictors of future violence (Heller, Ehrlick, & Lester, 1984; Langevin, 2003; Slavin, 2001). Another recent investigation determined that cruelty to animals and fire setting are more accurately conceptualized as components of a more general antisocial syndrome and that it is the syndrome that predicts future violence, not any individual component or combination of components (Dadds & Fraser, 2006). In fact, fire setting and cruelty to animals are two of the 15 symptoms included in a *DSM-IV* diagnosis of conduct disorder (CD).

Given the preponderance of dimensional results in taxometric research on CD (Murrie et al., 2007; Walters, 2010a; Walters, Ronen, & Rosenbaum, 2010) it seems likely that an unspecified combination of CD symptoms (additive effect) rather than a specified combination of symptoms (pathognomonic sign approach) is responsible for CD. Certainly, this is true of Mitch. In addition to four burglary convictions, Mitch has also been convicted of robbery and assault. It is safe to assume then that most people would consider Mitch a violent adult offender. However, there is no record of childhood enuresis, arson, or cruelty to animals in his file, and he denied all three elements of the triad when asked about them as part of a diagnostic interview. Nevertheless, he satisfied the CD criteria for antisocial personality disorder (ASPD) when administered the *Structured Clinical Interview for DSM-IV Axis II Personality Disorders (SCID-II)* (First, Gibbon, Spitzer, Williams, & Benjamin, 1997), giving affirmative answers to starting fights, breaking into people's cars and houses, lying extensively to others, and stealing items from stores, all before the age of 15. Understanding Mitch or any offender means testing old assumptions to see if they hold up under empirical scrutiny and then modifying this understanding when reliable empirical data incompatible with our previous beliefs come into play.

Future Dimensional Contexts

As was pointed out in Chapters 2 and 9, crime-related constructs (psychopathy, antisocial personality, and criminal lifestyle) and symptom malingering/exaggeration both appear to have an underlying dimensional latent structure. This is not the final word on latent structure, however, as latent structure can be highly complex. It is not uncommon, for instance, to find categories within dimensions or vice versa (Ruscio, Haslam, & Ruscio, 2006). Some of the features of psychopathy that are not measured well or at all by the Psychopathy Checklist-Revised (PCL-R), such as fearlessness (low arousal) and repeated failure to learn from experience (weak passive-avoidance learning), need to be investigated using the taxometric method, particularly since these features seem to be at least partially genetic or biologic in origin. There is still a great deal of work that needs to be done before we can conclude that crime-related constructs and malingering/exaggeration are unqualifiedly dimensional.

In contrast to the dimensional-leaning results obtained in taxometric research on psychopathy, antisocial personality, criminal lifestyle, and symptom malingering/exaggeration, taxometric investigations on substance misuse suggest that this psychopathological construct may have a categorical latent structure. Taxometric studies on nicotine dependence (Goedeker & Tiffany, 2008) and alcohol abuse/dependence (Dana, 1990: Green, Ahmed, Marcus, & Walters, 2011; Walters, 2008a, 2009d; Walters, Diamond, & Magaletta, 2010; Walters, Hennig, Negola, & Fricke, 2009) have consistently shown evidence of categorical latent structure. Obviously, there are many more substances, to include Mitch's drug of choice, heroin, that need to be investigated before any general conclusions are reached as to the latent structure of substance misuse. In the meantime, use of Ruscio's (2007) comparison curve approach to taxometric analysis holds the promise of advancing our understanding of the latent structure of substance use disorders.

It should be noted that the Dana (1990) and Walters (2008a, 2009d; Walters, Hennig, et al., 2009; Walters, Diamond, et al., 2010) taxometric studies on alcohol abuse were performed on correctional samples. The Green et al. (2011) investigation, on the other hand, was conducted on a large epidemiological sample of nonincarcerated individuals. Like Dana and Walters, Green et al. identified a **taxon** or category of severe alcohol abuse, although it was much smaller than the taxa identified in the five previous studies. What is interesting about the Green et al. taxon is that it contained a significantly higher proportion of individuals satisfying a diagnosis of ASPD than the highest scoring segment of the complement (nontaxon). In the Dana and Walters investigations, the base rates may have been elevated because the samples contained a higher percentage of individuals with ASPD. This illustrates how a dimensional construct (ASPD) can be potentially useful in defining a taxon (i.e., alcohol dependence consistent with Cloninger's [1987] Type II alcoholism).

Future Diagnostic Contexts

Lenzenweger (2004) asserted that above all else taxometric research should be theory-driven. He maintained that a guiding model is required even when performing an exploratory taxometric analysis. However, one of the chief benefits of the taxometric method is its ability to assist in theory-building (Meehl, 1999). If we categorically dismiss taxometric research that is not theory-driven then we lose this advantage. A chief concern of Lenzenweger's (2004), with respect to exploratory taxometric analysis, is the possibility of obtaining false positive results and arriving at an erroneous conclusion about latent structure. This concern, while understandable, seems misplaced in light of the high degree of precision that is currently available to those who use Ruscio's comparison curve approach (see Ruscio, Walters, Marcus, & Kaczetow, 2010). Given a lack of consensus on whether psychopathology is dimensional, categorical, or both, all forms of psychopathology would appear to be fair game for taxometric analysis, whether theory-driven or not.

Identifying a diagnostic construct as categorical or dimensional helps determine the method by which diagnostic classifications are made. As mentioned in Chapter 3, categorical diagnostic constructs are measured with signs and symptoms whereas dimensional diagnostic constructs are measured with trends and patterns. Besides ascertaining which diagnoses are dimensional (ASPD) and which diagnoses are categorical (substance dependence), it is also important to ascertain how the two systems can be effectively integrated. How we cross signs and symptoms with trends and patterns will determine whether an integrated, meaningful, and practical diagnostic system can be developed. There are several diagnoses that can be applied to Mitch. Opiate dependence and ASPD are clearly present but so are social anxiety and **dysthymic disorder** (chronic low-grade depression). The question before us is this: How can we construct an integrated diagnostic system capable of organizing these disparate diagnoses into a meaningful whole?

Another diagnostic issue requiring further study is the notion of **diagnostic hierarchies**. A hierarchy was constructed for criminal thinking in Chapter 2, and hierarchies were constructed for the LCSF and PICTS in Chapter 3. A hierarchy for psychopathy has also been proposed. Responding to the ongoing controversy between David Cooke and his colleagues (Cooke & Michie, 2001; Cooke, Michie, & Skeem, 2007; Skeem & Cooke, 2010), on the one hand, and Robert Hare and his colleagues (Hare & Neumann, 2006, 2010), on the other hand, as to whether the structure of the PCL-R is composed of three or four factors, respectively, Blackburn (2007) postulated that psychopathy is a higher order factor made up of personality features from the *DSM-IV* Cluster B family of personality disorders (e.g., antisocial, borderline, histrionic, narcissistic). Whereas PCL-R Facets 1 (interpersonal) and 2 (affective) correlated with histrionic and narcissistic personality disorders in the Blackburn (2007) study, Facets 3 (lifestyle) and 4 (antisocial) correlated with antisocial and to a lesser extent borderline personality disorder. Exactly where the criminal lifestyle fits in this hierarchy is uncertain, although it is speculated that it has more in common with the impulsive and antisocial features of psychopathy than with the interpersonal and affective features.

Future Appraisal Contexts

As noted in Chapter 4, clinical forensic assessment serves three basic functions: (1) construct assessment, (2) risk assessment, and (3) **legal-pragmatic assessment**. Construct assessment in forensic psychology includes the assessment of psychopathy, ASPD, and criminal lifestyle. Risk assessment in forensic psychology, on the other hand, encompasses the prediction of criminal and civil outcomes related to violence, recidivism, and sexual predation. Construct and risk assessment not only serve two different forensic functions but they also rely on different assessment procedures; construct assessment on broadband procedures and risk assessment on both broadband and narrowband procedures. Therefore, while it is true that construct and risk assessment each contribute to our understanding of forensic issues, they could potentially contribute even more if they were more effectively integrated with each other and combined with an estimate of an individual's personal strengths and resources. The third function of forensic assessment, legal-pragmatic assessment, was only briefly mentioned in Chapter 4 and seeks practical answers to specific legal questions, whether of a criminal (e.g., adjudicative competence) (Zapf & Roesch, 2006) or civil (e.g., child custody) (Ackerman, 2006) nature.

Effectively integrating construct and risk forensic assessment means finding ways to successfully blend and assimilate broadband and narrowband forensic assessment procedures. A limitation of most narrowband clinical forensic assessment instruments is that they emphasize **static risk factors** (historical variables that do not change) to the detriment if not the exclusion of **dynamic risk factors** (contemporary variables that do change). Integrating construct and risk assessment, not to mention prediction-oriented and management-oriented risk assessment (Heilbrun, 1997), requires that we identify measures that contain both dynamic and static risk items (e.g., Level of Service Inventory-Revised, or LSI-R) or which integrate dynamic and static measures from the same theoretical model (e.g., PICTS and LCSF). In Mitch's case, the LSI-R identified criminal history (static), criminal attitudes/orientation (stable dynamic), and drug intoxication (acute dynamic) as prominent risk/need factors; the LCSF and PICTS identified irresponsibility (static) and proactive criminal thinking (stable dynamic) as prominent weaknesses; and a review of records identified family support and membership in the roofer's union as prominent strengths.

Future Etiological Contexts

The proactive and reactive dimensions of adult criminal thinking seem to parallel the proactive and reactive dimensions of childhood aggression. The two dimensions overlap extensively regardless of whether childhood aggression (Poulin & Boivin, 2000) or adult criminal thinking (Walters, 2008b) is examined. In addition, the same countervailing relationships are observed between the proactive–reactive dimensions and outcome expectancies–hostile attribution biases regardless of whether childhood aggression or adult criminal thinking is the focus of investigation. Specifically, proactive childhood aggression correlates with positive outcome expectancies for aggression and reactive childhood aggression correlates with hostile attribution biases for perceived challenges from other children (Crick & Dodge, 1996), whereas proactive criminal thinking correlates with positive outcome expectancies for crime and reactive criminal thinking correlates with hostile attribution biases for perceived challenges from staff and other inmates (Walters, 2008b).

The fact that research on proactive–reactive adult criminal thinking seems to parallel research on proactive–reactive childhood aggression could mean that childhood aggression and adult criminal thinking are similarly organized and perhaps even linked. However, a proper test of this **continuity hypothesis** requires a longitudinal investigation whereby the same individuals are followed and administered measures of proactive and reactive aggression in childhood and measures of proactive and reactive criminal thinking in adulthood. A significant correlation should surface between proactive childhood aggression and proactive adult criminal thinking and between reactive childhood aggression and reactive adult criminal thinking if there is continuity between proactive–reactive childhood aggression and proactive–reactive adult criminal thinking. In the event significant correlations between proactive childhood aggression and proactive adult criminal thinking or between reactive childhood aggression and reactive adult criminal thinking do not surface, then continuity is not supported as a viable explanation for the seemingly parallel results obtained in prior research and an alternate explanation needs to be found.

Congruent with the continuity hypothesis, there is evidence of continuity when Mitch's early childhood is viewed in light of his current PICTS results.

Pattern analysis of Mitch's PICTS profile (see Table 10.1) denotes that he is more likely to entertain proactive criminal thoughts than reactive criminal thoughts (P > R), although he is high on both thinking dimensions. This pattern suggests that Mitch is more likely to engage in proactive criminal offenses than reactive ones. The relationship between proactive criminal thinking and proactive criminal behavior is borne out in Mitch's criminal history, which shows five convictions for proactive offending (four burglaries, one robbery) compared to one conviction for reactive offending (one assault). Mitch's mother and sister were interviewed for the presentence investigation (PSI) report and both characterized Mitch as a calculating and devious child who planned things out before doing them. Even his angry outbursts were premeditated. These family reports are consistent with proactive childhood aggression and demonstrate a pattern of continuity from proactive childhood aggression to proactive adult criminal thinking and behavior.

Future Subjective Contexts

Qualitative research (nonnumerical data collection) was a primary method of investigation in the early years of criminology (Miller, 2005). Although it is no longer as popular as it once was, qualitative research continues to play a role in defining and testing important criminological hypotheses. Data collected qualitatively can be analyzed both qualitatively and quantitatively. In fact, the blending of qualitative and quantitative data and analytic strategies is the key to getting maximum benefit from qualitative research (Hagan & McCarthy, 1997). In the past, qualitative research has been dismissed as unscientific (Britten, 2005), but it holds the potential of shedding light on issues unamenable to quantitative data collection and analysis. Through purposive and **snowball sampling** (where existing study participants recruit future participants from their list of acquaintances), open-ended questioning, and participant-observation techniques, qualitative research has opened up new avenues of understanding that are capable of advancing the criminology, criminal justice, and forensic psychology fields. What could be more scientific than that? A great deal more could be learned, therefore, by extending the qualitative method to the criminal lifestyle.

Criminological research on offender decision making would not be possible if it were not for qualitative research. Studies conducted on the decision to shoplift (Weaver & Carroll, 1985), rob (Fenney, 1986), and burglarize (Walsh, 1986) as well as the decision to desist from crime (Cusson & Pinsonneault, 1986) have relied heavily on qualitative methods of data collection if not qualitative methods of data analysis. Weaver and Carroll (1985) followed individual novice and experienced shoplifters around a retail store and asked them to report their thoughts about stealing various items from the store while being shadowed by a student. The qualitative information provided by the shoplifters participating in this study revealed that both novice and experienced shoplifters based their decisions to shoplift on oversimplified models of the world that took into account only one or two factors at a time. Walsh (1986) interviewed 45 incarcerated burglars and 69 incarcerated robbers and discovered a fair degree of planning went into their offenses, although luck and fatalism also played a role in the criminal activities of these individuals. Like Mitch, these individuals were mostly proactive in their approach to crime but were far from methodical in executing their decisions.

Future Programmatic Contexts

Evidence-based or empirically supported psychological interventions have attracted the attention of researchers in the field of clinical psychology. Several different work groups have established criteria for evidence-based or empirically supported psychological interventions, the results of which were reviewed and summarized in a paper by Chambless and Ollendick (2001). The Chambless and Ollendick (2001) review revealed strong empirical support (well-established results from two or more work groups) for five different interventions. Cognitive behavior therapy was found to be empirically supported for use with agoraphobia/panic disorder, generalized anxiety disorder, obsessive-compulsive disorder, major depression, bulimia, rheumatic disease pain, and smoking cessation. Exposure was found to be empirically supported for use with agoraphobia and specific phobias and exposure with response prevention was found to be empirically supported for use with obsessive-compulsive disorder. Behavior therapy was empirically supported for major depression and marital discord, interpersonal therapy was empirically supported for major depression, and behavioral family therapy was empirically supported for schizophrenia.

There were no empirically supported or evidence-based psychological interventions for crime-related constructs like psychopathy, antisocial personality, and criminal lifestyle or crime-associated constructs like substance dependence in the Chambless and Ollendick (2001) review. There was modest to moderate empirical support, however, for behavior therapy as an intervention for paraphilia/sexual offending; for behavior therapy and cognitive behavior therapy as interventions for alcohol and cocaine dependence;

and for behavior therapy, cognitive therapy and brief dynamic therapy as interventions for opiate dependence. Too little is known about empirically supported interventions for criminal and antisocial behavior to offer much guidance at this point. Nevertheless, there is evidence from meta-analyses of studies spanning several decades that interventions with offenders are effective and that such interventions are most effective when they are community-based, address both risks and needs, and are cognitive-behavioral or multifaceted in nature (French & Gendreau, 2006; Gendreau & Ross, 1987; McGuire, 2001).

The evidence-based approach pushes intervention research beyond the first generation question of "which intervention is best" (e.g., Smith, Glass, & Miller, 1980) to the second generation question of "which intervention is best for which type of problem." This second generation question, although useful, could be made even more useful by expanding it to read "which intervention is best for which type of problem under which specific set of person and treatment conditions." Hence, we not only need to know which interventions are effective for offenders but also how person variables like proactive and reactive criminal thinking and treatment variables like **intervention intensity** moderate intervention efficacy. Preliminary research indicates that anger management and other skill-based approaches to intervention are capable of reducing reactive criminal thinking but have little or no impact on proactive criminal thinking (Walters, 2009a). Consequently, we must find interventions that are effective with someone like Mitch, who is high in proactive criminal thinking. Treatment variables like intervention intensity also need to be considered, particularly as they interact with certain person variables. Preliminary studies show that more intense interventions only benefit high-risk individuals and can actually be detrimental when applied to low-risk individuals (Bonta, Wallace-Capretta, & Rooney, 2000; French & Gendreau, 2006).

Future Preventive Contexts

As was noted in Chapter 8, secondary prevention may serve the goals of person-level crime prevention better than primary prevention. This does not mean, however, that person-level primary prevention has no place in a comprehensive program of crime prevention because it may still be effective under certain conditions, particularly when paired with tried and true situational crime prevention strategies like target hardening and neighborhood watches. One possible target for primary prevention of a criminal lifestyle is society's attitudes toward crime and criminals. America has formed a love–hate relationship with criminals like Roger, the individual profiled in Chapter 6. Roger, himself, notes that everyday citizens may fear crime, but they are also enthralled with certain types of criminals. People are fascinated by sophisticated bank heists, the inner workings of organized crime, and the profiling of serial killers. What the public needs to realize is that everyone is affected by crime. Car theft raises insurance rates for everyone, not just those whose cars are stolen. Murder damages everyone's sense of community, not just those who have lost a loved one to a drive-by shooting or mass murder. The general public needs to be educated about these costs and that people like Roger and Mitch are as dangerous as they are interesting. Roger claims that he tries to avoid hurting civilians, but just being around him can be dangerous by virtue of the lifestyle he leads. The message that crime does damage to the fabric of society provides more of a public service than the message that certain crimes and criminals are interesting or glamorous.

Millions of dollars are pumped into secondary prevention each year. The money is often funneled into delinquency identification, diversion, and intervention programs, yet questions persist as to the overall effectiveness of these programs. Of all the possibilities for secondary prevention mentioned in Chapter 8, only parent training for childhood conduct and oppositional defiant disorders showed signs of being evidence-based (Chambless & Ollendick, 2001). This raises the following question: What can we do for someone like Mitch when he first starts breaking into homes and businesses to prevent him from ultimately embracing a criminal lifestyle? The answer should include a variety of services, although training his parents to be better disciplinarians is the only evidence-based intervention currently available. Accordingly, a great deal more time and effort needs to be devoted to finding evidence-based interventions for childhood aggression, CD, and delinquency. Thinking back to Chapter 8, I can't help but wonder what we can do about the fearlessness (weak bond between existential fear and physical survival) that is such an important risk factor for eventual movement into a criminal lifestyle. The physical beatings these children receive at the hands of their parents and other authority figures do nothing but make them more hostile and less receptive to a law-abiding lifestyle. Strengthening the bond between the child and representatives of society requires strengthening the bond between existential fear and remnants of physical survival.

Future Application Contexts

A number of different applications could be made of the criminal lifestyle construct beyond the adult male blue-collar offenders on which this theory is based. Questions have been raised about the applicability of Gottfredson and Hirschi's (1990) general theory of crime to white-collar offending (Benson & Moore, 1992; Walters & Geyer, 2004) and of Sampson and Laub's (1993) age-graded theory of informal social control to female antisocial behavior (Thompson & Petrovic, 2009). The same criticisms could be lodged against lifestyle theory as applied to criminal behavior. It remains to be seen, for instance, how well the criminal lifestyle model applies to a range of non-blue-collar offenses such as fraud, bribery, embezzlement, identity theft, and computer crime. Sexual offending has also not been extensively examined under the microscope of lifestyle theory, although one recent study found that the PICTS correlated moderately well with the Static-99, one of the top risk assessment measures for sexual offending, in a large group of incarcerated sex offenders (Walters, Deming, & Elliott, 2009). Even traditional blue-collar offenses like burglary, Mitch's preferred crime, require further investigation within the lifestyle model. Whereas a few studies have applied the PICTS to female offenders and nonoffenders (McCoy et al., 2006; Walters & Elliott, 1999; Walters, Elliott, & Miscoll, 1998), there is still a great deal to be learned about how female offenders operate within the confines of a criminal lifestyle. There are no published reports on the use of the PICTS with juvenile offenders even though a juvenile version of the PICTS is available.

Beyond the application of the criminal lifestyle and criminal thinking constructs to different offenses and demographic groups, there is also a need to apply the lifestyle model to important process questions like the interaction of proactive and reactive criminal thinking in specific criminal events. Although research on multiple murder is still in its infancy, differences between serial and mass murder have been observed. Hence, whereas **serial murder** (killing three or more people at different times with a "cooling off" period in between murders) is characterized by a moderate to high degree of planning and organization (Canter, Alison, Alison, & Wentink, 2004), **mass murder** (killing three or more people at the same time and in the same place) is often characterized as confused and disorganized (Duwe, 2004). Emotions are vital in initiating many single homicides and are often involved in the buildup to mass murder, but they are usually absent from serial murder; the emotion in serial murder often comes after the event, while the perpetrator is reliving the act (Salfati & Bateman, 2005). Mass murderers, on average, also appear to have experienced more general life failure and social rejection than serial killers (Fox & Levin, 2003). These findings would seem to suggest the presence of a link between serial murder and instrumental aggression/proactive criminality, on the one hand, and mass murder and hostile aggression/reactive criminality, on the other hand. Even so, Meloy et al.

(2004) characterize mass murder as a predatory/instrumental act rather than an affective/hostile act based on the planning involved and the general absence of emotion in the perpetrator during the event. Perhaps it is the interaction between proactive and reactive factors that is important in differentiating between these two forms of multiple murder. A reactive spark that sets the fantasies of a serial killer into action and a proactive spark that provides the mass murderer with a plan to avenge a life of failure and disappointment, illustrate possible ways in which proactive and reactive motives interact with each other, and lead to different outcomes in superficially similar offenses.

Conclusion

As I stated in the preface, the current text is the third iteration in an effort to develop and present a lifestyle theory of crime. Hopefully, in another 10 years, I will continue this process by writing a fourth iteration. In the meantime, the focus needs to be on developing, testing, and applying the ideas and principles outlined in this most recent iteration. Alteration and change are necessary steps in theory development, but we must first understand what it is we are trying to alter before delving into the revision process. Taking the time to examine and study these principles and determine which ones have value, which ones need to be discarded, and which ones should be revised is something I plan to spend the next 10 years doing. I invite the reader to join me in this journey toward increased understanding as we set out to test and scrutinize this third iteration of a theory of crime.

Key Terms and Concepts

Continuity Hypothesis	*Legal-Pragmatic Assessment*
Diagnostic Hierarchies	*Mass Murder*
Dynamic Risk Factors	*Qualitative Research*
Dysthymic Disorder	*Serial Murder*
Ego Triad	*Snowball Sampling*
Evidence-Based	*Static Risk Ractors*
Intervention Intensity	*Taxon*

References

Ackerman, M. J. (2006). *Clinician's guide to child custody evaluations* (3rd ed.). Hoboken, NJ: John Wiley.

Adler, P. A. (1993). *Wheeling and dealing: An ethnography of an upper-level drug dealing and smuggling community* (2nd ed.). New York: Columbia University Press.

Agnew, R. (1992). Foundation for a general strain theory of crime and delinquency. *Criminology, 30*, 47–87.

Agnew, R. (2006). General strain theory: Current status and directions for further research. In F. T. Cullen, J. P. Wright, & K. R. Blevins (Eds.), *Taking stock: The status of criminological theory, advances in criminological theory* (Vol. 15, pp. 101–123). New Brunswick, NJ: Transaction Publishers.

Akers, R. L. (1991). Self-control as a general theory of crime. *Journal of Quantitative Criminology, 7*, 201–211.

American Psychiatric Association. (2000). *Diagnostic and statistical manual of mental disorders* (4th ed., text rev.). Washington, DC: Author.

Amirkhan, J., & Auyeung, B. (2007). Coping with stress across the lifespan: Absolute vs. relative changes in strategy. *Journal of Applied Developmental Psychology, 28*, 298–317.

Andresen, M. A., & Jenion, G. W. (2008). Crime prevention and the science of where people are. *Criminal Justice Policy Review, 19*, 164–180.

Andrews, D. A., & Bonta, J. (1995). *The Level of Service Inventory–Revised.* Toronto, Canada: Multi-Health Systems.

Andrews, D. A., & Bonta, J. (1998). *The psychology of criminal conduct* (2nd ed.). Cincinnati, OH: Anderson.

Andrews, D. A., & Bonta, J. (2003). *The psychology of criminal conduct* (3rd ed.). Cincinnati, OH: Anderson.

Andrews, D. A., Bonta, J., & Wormith, J. S. (2006). The recent past and near future of risk and/or need assessment. *Crime & Delinquency, 52*, 7–27.

Andrews, D. A., Zinger, I., Hoge, R. D., Bonta, J., Gendreau, P., & Cullen, F. T. (1990). Does correctional treatment work? A clinically relevant and psychologically informed meta-analysis. *Criminology, 28*, 369–404.

Archer, R. P., Buffington-Vollum, J. K., Stredny, R. V., & Handel, R. W. (2006). A survey of psychological test use patterns among forensic psychologists. *Journal of Personality Assessment, 87*, 84–94.

Arluke, A., Levin, J., Luke, C., & Ascione, F. (1999). The relationship between animal cruelty to violence and other forms of antisocial behavior. *Journal of Interpersonal Violence, 14*, 245–253.

Arnaut, G. L. Y. (2006). Sensation seeking, risk taking, and fearlessness. In J. C. Thomas, D. L. Segal, & M. Hersen (Eds.), *Comprehensive handbook of personality and psychopathology. Vol. 1: Personality and everyday functioning* (pp. 322–341). Hoboken, NJ: John Wiley.

Arneklev, B. J., Cochran, J. K., & Gainey, R. R. (1998). Testing Gottfredson and Hirschi's "low self-control" stability hypothesis: An exploratory study. *American Journal of Criminal Justice, 23*, 107–127.

Arseneault, L., Tremblay, R. E., Boulerice, B., & Saucier, J.-F. (2002). Obstetric complications and adolescent violent behaviors: Testing two developmental pathways. *Child Development, 73*, 496–508.

Austin, J. (2006). How much risk can we take? The misuse of risk assessment in corrections. *Federal Probation, 70*(2), 59–64.

Austin, J., Dedel-Johnson, K., & Coleman, D. (2003). *Reliability and validity of the LSI-R for the Pennsylvania Board of Probation and Parole.* Washington, DC: George Washington University.

Ayers, C. D., Williams, J. H., Hawkins, J. D., Peterson, P. L., Catalano, R. F., & Abbott, R. D. (1999). Assessing correlates of onset, escalation, de-escalation, and desistance of delinquent behavior. *Journal of Quantitative Criminology, 15*, 277–306.

Bagozzi, R. P., & Yi, Y. (1991). Multitrait-multimethod matrices in consumer research. *Journal of Consumer Research, 17*, 426–439.

Bandura, A. (1986). *Social foundations of thought and action: A social cognitive theory.* Englewood Cliffs, NJ: Prentice-Hall.

Bates, T., & Stough, C. (1998). Improved reaction time method, information processing speed and intelligence. *Intelligence, 26*, 53–62.

Bauer, D. J., & Curran, P. J. (2003). Distributional assumptions of growth mixture models: Implications for overextraction of latent trajectory classes. *Psychological Methods, 8*, 338–363.

Baumeister, R. F. (1997). *Evil: Inside human violence and cruelty.* New York: Freeman.

Bean, G. J., Meirson, J., & Pinta, E. (1988, June).*The prevalence of mental illness among inmates in the Ohio prison system* (Final report to the Department of Mental Health and the Ohio Department of Rehabilitation and Correction Inderdepartmental Planning and Oversight Committee for Psychiatric Services to Corrections). Columbus: Ohio State University.

Beck, A. J., & Maruschak, L. M. (2001). *Mental health treatment in state prisons, 2000* (BJSSpecial Report NCJ-188215). Washington, DC: Office of Justice Programs.

Beck, A. T., & Rector, N. A. (2000). Cognitive therapy of schizophrenia: A new therapy for the new millennium. *American Journal of Psychotherapy, 54,* 291–300.

Bengtson, S., & Långström, N. (2007). Unguided clinical and actuarial assessment of re-offending risk: A direct comparison with sex offenders in Denmark. *Sexual Abuse: Journal of Research and Treatment, 19,* 135–153.

Benson, M. L., & Moore, E. (1992). Are white-collar and common offenders the same? An empirical and theoretical critique of a recently proposed general theory of crime. *Journal of Research in Crime and Delinquency, 29,* 251–272.

Bentz, V. M., & Shapiro, J. J. (1998). *Mindful enquiry in social research.* Thousand Oaks, CA: Sage.

Bernstein, S. (1975). Can probation work? *Juvenile Justice, 26,* 20–23.

Blackburn, R. (2007). Personality disorder and antisocial deviance: Comments on the debate on the structure of the Psychopathy Checklist-Revised. *Journal of Personality Disorders, 21,* 142–159.

Blair, R. J. R. (2006). Subcortical brain structures in psychopathy: The amygdala and associated structures. In C. J. Patrick (Ed.), *Handbook of psychopathy* (pp. 296–312). New York: Guilford.

Blanchard, J. J., Horan, W. P., & Collins, L. M. (2005). Examining the latent structure of negative symptoms: Is there a distinct subtype of negative symptom schizophrenia? *Schizophrenia Research, 77,* 151–165.

Bohart, A. C., & Tallman, K. (1999). *How clients make therapy work: The process of active self-healing.* Washington, DC: American Psychological Association.

Bonta, J., Law, M., & Hanson, K. (1998). The prediction of criminal and violent recidivism among mentally disordered offenders: A meta-analysis. *Psychological Bulletin, 123,* 123–142.

Bonta, J., Wallace-Capretta, S. & Rooney, J. (2000) A quasi-experimental evaluation of an intensive rehabilitation supervision program. *Criminal Justice and Behavior, 27,* 312–329.

Boothby, J. L., & Clements, C. B. (2000). A national survey of correctional psychologists. *Criminal Justice and Behavior, 27,* 716–732.

Boss, M. (1963). *Psychoanalysis and daseinsanalysis.* New York: Basic Books.

Brezina, T. (2000). Delinquent problem-solving: An interpretative framework for criminological theory and research. *Journal of Research in Crime and Delinquency, 37,* 3–30.

Britten, N. (2005). Making sense of qualitative research: A new series. *Medical Education, 39,* 5–6.

Broidy, L. M., Nagin, D. S., Tremblay, R. E., Bates, J. E., Brame, B., Dodge, K. A., et al. (2003). Developmental trajectories of childhood disruptive behaviors and adolescent delinquency: A six-site, cross-national study. *Developmental Psychology, 39,* 222–245.

Browne, K. D., & Hamilton-Giachritsis, C. (2005). The influence of violent media on children and adolescents: A public health approach. *Lancet, 365,* 702–710.

Browne, K. D., & Pennell, A. E. (2000). The influence of film and video on young people and violence. In G. Boswell (Ed.), *Violent children and adolescents: Asking the question why* (pp. 151–168). Philadelphia: Whurr.

Bugental, J. F., & Bugental, E. K. (1984). A fate worse than death: The fear of changing. *Psychotherapy: Theory, Research, Practice, Training, 21*, 543–549.

Bulten, E., Nijman, H., & van der Staak, C. (2009). Measuring criminal thinking styles: The construct validity and utility of the PICTS in a Dutch prison sample. *Legal and Criminological Psychology, 14*, 35–49.

Burnett, R., & Maruna, S. (2004). So "prison works" does it? The criminal careers of 130 men released from prison under home secretary, Michael Howard. *Howard Journal of Criminal Justice, 43*, 390–404.

Burns, B. J., Schoenwald, S. K., Burchard, J. D., Faw, L., & Santos, A. D. (2000). Comprehensive community-based interventions for youth with severe emotional disorders: Multisystemic therapy and the wraparound process. *Journal of Child and Family Studies, 9*, 283–314.

Butcher, J. N., Graham, J. R., Ben-Porath, Y. S., Tellegen, A., Dahlstrom, W. G., & Kaemmer, B. K. (2001). *MMPI-2 (Minnesota Multiphasic Personality Inventory-2): Manual for administration, scoring, and interpretation.* Minneapolis: University of Minnesota Press.

California Department of Corrections. (1989). *Current description, evaluation, and recommendations for treatment of mentally disordered offenders.* Final report submitted to the California State Legislature. San Francisco: Standard Consulting Corporation.

Camp, B. (1995). The problem of matching. *Journal of Developmental and Behavioral Pediatrics, 16*, 54–55.

Canter, D. V., Alison, L. J., Alison, E., & Wentink, N. (2004). The organized/disorganized typology of serial murder: Myth or model? *Psychology, Public Policy, and Law, 10*, 293–320.

Carleton, R. N., Sharpe, D., & Asmundson, G. J. G. (2007). Anxiety sensitivity and intolerance of uncertainty: Requisites of the fundamental fears? *Behaviour Research and Therapy, 45*, 2307–2316.

Carlo, G., Roesch, S. C., & Melby, J. (1998). The multiplicative relations of parenting and temperament to prosocial and antisocial behaviors in adolescence. *Journal of Early Adolescence, 18*, 266–290.

Carr, W. A., Rosenfeld, B., Magyar, M., & Rotter, M. (2009). An exploration of criminal thinking styles among civil psychiatric patients. *Criminal Behaviour and Mental Health, 19*, 334–346.

Carroll, A., Houghton, S., Wood, R., Perkins, C., & Bower, J. (2007). Multidimensional self-concept: Age and gender differences in Australian high school students involved in delinquent activities. *School Psychology International, 28*, 237–256.

Casiglia, A. C., Lo Coco, A., & Zappulla, C. (1998). Aspects of social reputation and peer relationships in Italian children: A cross-cultural perspective. *Developmental Psychology, 34*, 723–730.

Castelnuovo-Tedesco, P. (1989). The fear of change and its consequences in analysis and psychotherapy. *Psychoanalytic Inquiry, 9*, 101–118.

Chafetz, M. D. (2008). Malingering on the social security disability consultative exam: Predictors and base rates. *Clinical Neuropsychologist, 22*, 529–546.

Chafetz, M. D., Abrahams, J. P., & Kohlmaier, J. (2007). Malingering on the social security disability consultative exam: A new rating scale. *Archives of Clinical Neuropsychology, 22*, 1–14.

Chaiken, J., & Chaiken, M. (1982). *Varieties of criminal behavior*. Santa Monica, CA: Rand Corporation.

Chambless, D. L., & Ollendick, T. H. (2001). Empirically supported psychological interventions: Controversies and evidence. *Annual Review of Psychology, 52*, 685–716.

Chapple, C. L., & Hope, T. L. (2003). An analysis of the self-control and criminal versatility of gang and dating violence offenders. *Violence and Victims, 18*, 671–690.

Choy, Y., Fyer, A. J., & Lipsitz, J. D. (2007). Treatment of specific phobia in adults. *Clinical Psychology Review, 27*, 266–286.

Chung, I. J., Hill, K. G., Hawkins, J. D., Gilchrist, L. D., & Nagin, D. S. (2002). Childhood predictors of offense trajectories. *Journal of Research in Crime and Delinquency, 39*, 60–90.

Cicchetti, D., & Rogosch, F. A. (2007). Personality, adrenal steroid hormones, and resilience in maltreated children: A multilevel perspective. *Development and Psychopathology, 19*, 787–809.

Cicognani, E., Albanesi, C., & Zani, B. (2008). The impact of residential context on adolescents' subjective well being. *Journal of Community and Applied Social Psychology, 18*, 558–575.

Clark, A. J. (2007). *Empathy in counseling and psychotherapy: Perspectives and practices*. Mahwah, NJ: Erlbaum.

Clark, C. M. (1992). Deviant adolescent subcultures: Assessment strategies and clinical interventions. *Adolescence, 27*, 283–293.

Cleckley, H. (1976). *The mask of sanity* (5th ed.). St. Louis, MO: Mosby. (Original work published 1941)

Cloninger, C. R. (1987). Neurogenetic adaptive mechanisms in alcoholism. *Science, 236*, 410–416.

Cloninger, C. R., & Sigvardsson, S. (1996). Type I and type II alcoholism: An update. *Alcohol Health and Research World, 20*, 18–23.

Cohen, J. (1988). *Statistical power for the behavioral sciences* (2nd ed.). Hillsdale, NJ: Erlbaum.

Cohen, L. E., & Felson, M. (1979). Social change and crime rate trends: A routine activity approach. *American Sociological Review, 44*, 588–608.

Coid, J., & Yang, M. (2008). The distribution of psychopathy among a household population: Categorical or dimensional? *Social Psychiatry and Psychiatric Epidemiology, 43*, 773–781.

Coid, J., Yang, M., Ullrich, S., Zhang, T., Sizmur, S., Roberts, C., et al. (2009). Gender differences in structured risk assessment: Comparing the accuracy of five instruments. *Journal of Consulting and Clinical Psychology, 77*, 337–348.

Conroy, M. A., & Murrie, D. C. (2007). *Forensic assessment of violence risk: A guide for risk assessment and risk management*. Hoboken, NJ: Wiley.

Cooke, D. J., & Michie, C. (2001). Refining the construct of psychopathy: Towards a hierarchical model. *Psychological Assessment, 13*, 171–188.

Cooke, D. J., Michie, C., & Skeem, J. (2007). Understanding the structure of the Psychopathy Checklist-Revised: An exploration of methodological confusion. *British Journal of Psychiatry, 190*, s39–s50.

Cooley, C. H. (1964). *Human nature and the social order*. New York: Schocken. (Original work published 1902)

Copeland, W., Landry, K., Stranger, C., & Hudziak, J. J. (2004). Multi-informant assessment of temperament in children with externalizing behavior problems. *Journal of Clinical Child and Adolescent Psychology, 33*, 547–556.

Cornell, D. G., Warren, J., Hawk, G., Stafford, E., Oram, G., & Pine, D. (1996). Psychopathy in instrumental and reactive violent offenders. *Journal of Consulting and Clinical Psychology, 64*, 783–790.

Cornish, D. B., & Clarke, R. V. (Eds.). (1986). *The reasoning criminal: Rational choice perspectives on offending*. New York: Springer-Verlag.

Cortoni, F., & Hanson, R. K. (2005). *A review of the recidivism rates of adult female sexual offenders*. Ottawa, Canada: Correctional Services of Canada.

Costa, P. T., & McCrae, R. R. (1992). *Revised NEO Personality Inventory and NEO Five-Factor Inventory (FFI): Professional manual*. Odessa, FL: Psychological Assessment Resources.

Crick, N. R., & Dodge, K. A. (1996). Social information-processing mechanisms in reactive and proactive aggression. *Child Development, 67*, 993–1002.

Cullen, F. T., Blevins, K. R., Trager, J. S., & Gendreau, P. (2005). The rise and fall of boot camps: A case study in common sense corrections. *Journal of Offender Rehabilitation, 40*, 53–70.

Cusson, M., & Pinsonneault, P. (1986). The decision to give up crime. In D. Cornish & R. Clarke (Eds.), *The reasoning criminal: Rational choice perspectives on offending* (pp. 72–82). New York: Springer-Verlag.

Dadds, M. R., & Fraser, J. A. (2006). Fire interest, fire setting and psychopathology in Australian children: A normative study. *Australian and New Zealand Journal of Psychiatry, 40*, 581–586.

Dana, D. A. (1990). Alcoholism and antisocial personality disorder: Related discrete personality variables? *Dissertation Abstracts International, 51*(04), 2056B (University Microfilms No.AAT90-24616).

Davidson, W. S., Gottschalk, R., Gensheimer, L., & Mayer, J. (1984). *Interventions with juvenile delinquents: A meta-analysis of treatment efficacy*. Washington, DC: National Institute of Juvenile Justice and Delinquency Prevention.

De Boeck, P., Wilson, M., & Acton, G. S. (2005). A conceptual and psychometric framework for distinguishing categories and dimensions. *Psychological Review, 112*, 129–158.

DeLisi, M. (2005). *Career criminals in society*. Thousand Oaks, CA: Sage.

DeLisi, M., Beaver, K. M., Vaughn, M. G., & Wright, J. P. (2009). All in the family: Gene x environment interaction between DRD2 and criminal father is associated with five antisocial phenotypes. *Criminal Justice and Behavior*, 36, 1187–1197.

Deng, X. (1995). Toward a more comprehensive understanding of crime: An integrated model of self-control and rational choice theories (Doctoral dissertation, State University of New York, Buffalo, 1994). *Dissertation Abstracts International*, 55A, 3651.

Diamond, P. M., Wang, E. W., Holzer, C. E., Thomas, C., & Cruser, D. A. (2001). The prevalence of mental illness in prison. *Administration and Policy in Mental Health*, 29, 21–40.

DiCataldo, F., & Everett, M. (2008). Distinguishing juvenile homicide from violent juvenile offending. *International Journal of Offender Therapy and Comparative Criminology*, 52, 158–174.

Doherty, E. E. (2006). Self-control, social bonds, and desistance: A test of life-course interdependence. *Criminology*, 44, 807–833.

Doležal, D., & Mikšaj-Todorović, L. (2008). Relation between the Psychological Inventory of Criminal Thinking Styles and Level of Service Inventory-Revised. *Kriminologija & Socijaina Intergracija*, 16, 25–32.

Douglas, K. S., Yeomans, M., & Boer, D. P. (2005). Comparative validity analysis of multiple measures of violence risk in a sample of criminal offenders. *Criminal Justice and Behavior*, 32, 479–510.

D'Unger, A., Land, K., McCall, P., & Nagin, D. (1998). How many latent classes of delinquent/criminal careers? Results from mixed Poisson regression analyses. *American Journal of Sociology*, 103, 1593–1630.

Duwe, G. (2004). The patterns and prevalence of mass murder in twentieth-century America. *Justice Quarterly*, 21, 729–761.

Edens, J. F., Marcus, D. K., Lilienfeld, S. O., & Poythress, N. G. (2006). Psychopathic, not psychopath: Taxometric evidence for the dimensional structure of psychopathy. *Journal of Abnormal Psychology*, 115, 131–144.

Edens, J. F., Marcus, D. K., & Vaughn, M. G. (2011). Exploring the taxometric status of psychopathy among youthful offenders: Is there a juvenile psychopath taxon? *Law and Human Behavior*, 35, 13–24.

Edens, J. F., & Petrila, J. (2006). Legal and ethical issues in the assessment and treatment of psychopathy. In C. J. Patrick (Ed.), *Handbook of psychopathy* (pp. 573–588). New York: Guilford.

Edens, J. F., Skeem, J. L., & Douglas, K. S. (2006). Incremental validity analyses of the Violence Risk Appraisal Guide and Psychopathy Checklist: Screening Version in a civil psychiatric sample. *Assessment*, 13, 368–374.

Egan, V., McMurran, M., Richardson, C., & Blair, M. (2000). Criminal cognitions and personality: What does the PICTS really measure? *Criminal Behaviour and Mental Health*, 10, 170–184.

Eggleston, D. E. (2006). Self-control, social bonds and desistance: A test of life-course interdependence. *Criminology*, 44, 807–833.

Eisenberg, N., Valiente, C., Spinrad, T. L., Cumberland, A., Liew, J., Reiser, M., et al. (2009). Longitudinal relations of children's effortful control, impulsivity, and negative emotionality to their externalizing, internalizing, and co-occurring behavior problems. *Developmental Psychology, 45,* 988–1008.

Elkind, D. (1967). Egocentrism in adolescence. *Child Development, 38,* 1025–1034.

Endrass, J., Urbaniok, F., Held, L., Vetter, S., & Rossegger, A. (2009). Accuracy of the Static-99 in predicting recidivism in Switzerland. *International Journal of Offender Therapy and Comparative Criminology, 53,* 482–490.

Epperson, D. L., Kaul, J. D., Haut, S. J., Hesselton, D., Alexander, W., & Goldman, R. (1998). *Minnesota Sex Offender Screening Tool-Revised (MnSOST-R).* St. Paul: Minnesota Department of Corrections.

Ezell, M. E., & Cohen, L. E. (Eds.). (2005). *Desisting from crime: Continuity and change in long-term crime patterns of serious chronic offenders, Clarendon Studies in Criminology.* Oxford, England: Oxford University Press.

Farrington, D. P., & West D. J. (1993). Criminal penal and life histories of chronic offenders: Risk and protective factors and early identification. *Criminal Behaviour and Mental Health, 3,* 492–523.

Fazel, S., & Danesh, J. (2002). Serious mental disorder in 23,000 prisoners: A systematic review of 62 surveys. *Lancet, 359,* 545–550.

Feeney, N. C., Danielson, C. K., Schwartz, L., Youngstrom, E. A., & Findling, R. L. (2006). Cognitive-behavioral therapy for bipolar disorders in adolescents: A pilot study. *Bipolar Disorders, 8,* 508–515.

Fenney, F. (1986). Robbers and decision-makers. In D. B. Cornish & R. V. Clarke (Eds.), *The reasoning criminal: Rational choice perspectives on offending* (pp. 53–71). New York: Springer-Verlag.

Fergusson, D. M., Horwood, L. J., & Nagin, D. S. (2000). Offending trajectories in a New Zealand birth cohort. *Criminology, 38,* 525–552.

Fergusson, D. M., Horwood, L. J., & Ridder, E. (2005). Show me the child at seven: The consequences of conduct problems in childhood for psychosocial functioning in adulthood. *Journal of Child Psychology and Psychiatry, 46,* 837–849.

Fergusson, D. M., & Lynskey, M. T. (1996). Adolescent resiliency to family adversity. *Journal of Child Psychology and Psychiatry, 37,* 281–292.

Festinger, L. (1957). *A theory of cognitive dissonance.* Evanston, IL: Row, Peterson.

Figgie Corporation. (1988). *The Figgie report, Part VI. The business of crime: The criminal perspective.* Richmond, VA: Figgie International Incorporated.

First, M. B., Gibbon, M., Spitzer, R. L., Williams, J. B., & Benjamin, L. (1997). *Structured clinical interview for DSM-IV Axis II personality disorders (SCID-II).* Washington, DC: American Psychiatric Press.

Fiske, D. W., & Campbell, D. T. (1992). Citations do not solve problems. *Psychological Bulletin, 112,* 393–395.

Floyd, C. (1996). Achieving despite the odds: A study of resilience among a group of African America high school seniors. *Journal of Negro Education, 65,* 181–189.

Foley, H. A., Carlton, C. O., & Howell, R. J. (1996). The relationship of attention deficit hyperactivity disorder and conduct disorder to juvenile delinquency: Legal implications. *Bulletin of the American Academy of Psychiatry and the Law*, *24*, 333–345.

Forrest, C. B., Tambor, E., Riley, A. W., Ensminger, M. E., & Starfield, B. (2000). The health profile of incarcerated male youths. *Pediatrics, 105*, 286–291.

Forst, B., Rhodes, W., Dimm, J., Gelman, A., & Mullin, B. (1983). Targeting federal resources on recidivists: An empirical view. *Federal Probation, 46*, 10–20.

Forth, A. E., Kosson, D., & Hare, R. D. (2003). *Psychopathy Checklist: Youth Version technical manual*. Toronto, Canada: Multi-Health Systems.

Fox, J. A., & Levin, J. (2003). Mass murder: An analysis of extreme violence. *Journal of Applied Psychoanalytic Studies, 5*, 47–64.

Frazier, T. W., Youngstrom, E. A., Naugle, R. I., Haggerty, K. A., & Busch, R. M. (2007). The latent structure of cognitive symptom exaggeration on the Victoria Symptom Validity Test. *Archives of Clinical Neuropsychology, 22*, 197–211.

Freeman, T., Powell, M., & Kimbrell, T. (2008). Measuring symptom exaggeration in veterans with chronic posttraumatic stress disorder. *Psychiatry Research, 158*, 374–380.

French, S. A., & Gendreau, P. (2006). Reducing prison misconducts: What works! *Criminal Justice and Behavior, 33*, 185–218.

Ganon, M. W., & Donegan, J. J. (2006). Self-control and insurance fraud. *Journal of Economic Crime Management, 4*(1). Retrieved from http://www.utica.edu/academic/institutes/ecii/jecm/articles.cfm?action=issue&id=19

Garmezy, N. (1993). Children in poverty: Resiliency despite risk. *Psychiatry, 56*, 127–136.

Garrett, C. J. (1985). Effects of residential treatment of adjudicated delinquents: A meta-analysis. *Journal of Research in Crime and Delinquency, 22*, 287–308.

Gatzke-Kopp, L. M., Raine, A., Loeber, R., Stouthamer-Loeber, M., & Steinhauer, S. R. (2002). Serious delinquent behavior, sensation seeking, and electrodermal arousal. *Journal of Abnormal Child Psychology, 30*, 477–486.

Ge, X., Donnellan, M. B., & Wenk, E. (2001). The development of persistent criminal offending in males. *Criminal Justice and Behavior, 26*, 731–755.

Gendreau, P., & Andrews, D. A. (2001). *Correctional Program Assessment Inventory-2000 (CPAI-2000)*. Saint John, Canada: University of New Brunswick.

Gendreau, P., Andrews, D. A., Goggin, C., & Chanteloupe, F. (1992). *The development of clinical and policy guidelines for prediction of criminal behaviour in criminal justice settings* (Programs Branch user report). Ottawa, Canada: Ministry of the Solicitor General of Canada.

Gendreau, P., Goggin, C., & Law, M. A. (1997). Predicting prison misconducts. *Criminal Justice and Behavior, 24*, 414–431.

Gendreau, P., Goggin, C., & Smith, P. (2002). Is the PCL-R really the "unparalleled" measure of offender risk? A lesson in knowledge cumulation. *Criminal Justice and Behavior, 29*, 397–426.

Gendreau, P., Little, T., & Goggin, C. (1996). A meta-analysis of the predictors of adult offender recidivism: What works! *Criminology, 34*, 575–607.

Gendreau, P., & Ross, R. R. (1987). Revivification of rehabilitation: Evidence from the 1980s. *Justice Quarterly, 4*, 349–407.

Gibbs, J. J., Giever, D., & Martin, J. S. (1998). Parental management and self-control: An empirical test of Gottfredson and Hirschi's general theory. *Journal of Research in Crime and Delinquency, 35*, 40–70.

Gifford-Smith, M., Dodge, K. A., Dishion, T. J., & McCord, J. (2005). Peer influence in children and adolescents: Crossing the bridge from developmental to intervention science. *Journal of Abnormal Child Psychology, 33*, 255–265.

Giordano, P. C., Cernkovich, S. A., & Rudolph, J. L. (2002). Gender, crime, and desistance: Toward a theory of cognitive transformation. *American Journal of Sociology, 107*, 990–1064.

Glenn, A. L., & Raine, A. (2009). Psychopathy and instrumental aggression: Evolutionary, neurobiological, and legal perspectives. *International Journal of Law and Psychiatry, 32*, 253–258.

Glueck, S., & Glueck, E. (1950). *Unraveling juvenile delinquency*. New York: Commonwealth Fund.

Goedeker, K. C., & Tiffany, S. T. (2008). On the nature of nicotine addiction: A taxometric analysis. *Journal of Abnormal Psychology, 117*, 896–909.

Gonsalves, V. M., Scalora, M. J., & Huss, M. T. (2009). Prediction of recidivism using the Psychopathy Checklist-Revised and the Psychological Inventory of Criminal Thinking Styles within a forensic sample. *Criminal Justice and Behavior, 36*, 741–756.

Goodey, J. (1997). Boys don't cry: Masculinities, fear of crime and fearlessness. *British Journal of Criminology, 37*, 401–418.

Gopnik, A., & Meltzoff, A. (1997). *Words, thoughts and theories*. Cambridge, MA: MIT Press.

Gordon, R. (1986). Folk psychology as simulation. *Mind and Language, 1*, 158–170.

Gottfredson, M. R., & Hirschi, T. (1990). *A general theory of crime*. Stanford, CA: Stanford University Press.

Graham, J., & Bowling, B. (1995). *Young people and crime*. London: HMSO.

Grasmick, H. G., Tittle, C. R., Bursick, R. J., & Arneklev, B. J. (1993). Testing the core implications of Gottfreson and Hirschi's general theory of crime. *Journal of Research in Crime and Delinquency, 30*, 5–29.

Green, B. A., Ahmed, A. O., Marcus, D. K., & Walters, G. D. (2011). The latent structure of alcohol use pathology in an epidemiological sample. *Journal of Psychiatric Research, 45*, 225–233.

Greene, M. (1997). The lived world, literature and education. In D. Vandenberg (Ed.), *Phenomenology and education discourse* (pp. 169–190). Johannesburg, South Africa: Heinemann.

Greenstein, T. N. (2007). Modifying beliefs and behavior through self-confrontation. *Sociological Inquiry, 59*, 396–408.

Greig, D. A., & Kingsley, J. (2002). *Neither bad nor mad: The competing discourses of psychiatry, law, and politics*. London: Routledge.

Gretton, H. M., Hare, R. D., & Catchpole, R. E. H. (2004). Psychopathy and offending from adolescence to adulthood: A ten-year follow up. *Journal of Consulting and Clinical Psychology, 72,* 636–645.

Griffin, R. S., & Gross, A. M. (2004). Childhood bullying: Current empirical findings and future directions for research. *Aggression and Violent Behavior, 9,* 379–400.

Groenewald, T. (2004). A phenomenological research design illustrated. *International Journal of Qualitative Methods, 3*(4). Retrieved from http://www.ualberta .ca/≈iiqm/backissues/3_1/pdf1greenwald.pdf.

Grubin, D. (1998). *Sex offending against children: Understanding the risk* (Police Research Series Paper 99). London: Home Office.

Guay, J.-P., Ruscio, J., Knight, R. A., & Hare, R. D. (2007). A taxometric analysis of the latent structure of psychopathy: Evidence for dimensionality. *Journal of Abnormal Psychology, 116,* 701–716.

Gubrium, J. F., & Holstein, J. A. (2000). Analyzing interpretive practice. In N. K. Denzin & Y. S. Lincoln (Eds.), *Handbook of qualitative research* (2nd ed., pp. 487–508). Thousand Oaks, CA: Sage.

Guy, E., Platt, J. J., Zwerling, I., & Bullock, S. (1985). Mental health status of prisoners in an urban jail. *Criminal Justice and Behavior, 12,* 29–53.

Hagan, J., & McCarthy, B. (1997). *Mean streets: Youth crime and homelessness.* Cambridge, UK: Cambridge University Press.

Hall, J., Sylva, K., Melhuish, E., Sammons, P., Siraj-Blatchford, I., & Taggart, B. (2009). The role of pre-school quality in providing resilience in the cognitive development of young children. *Oxford Review of Education, 35,* 331–352.

Hamparian, D. M., Schuster, R. Dinitz, S., & Conrad, J. P. (1978). *The violent few.* Lexington, MA: Lexington/D.C. Heath.

Haney, C., Banks, W. C., & Zimbardo, P. G. (1973). Interpersonal dynamics in a simulated prison. *International Journal of Criminology and Penology, 1,* 69–97.

Hanson, D. R. (2009). Schizophrenia and affective psychotic disorder—Inputs from a genetic perspective. In Y.-K. Kim (Ed.), *Handbook of behavior genetics* (pp. 473–486). New York: Springer.

Hanson, R. K. (1997). *The development of a brief actuarial risk scale for sexual offense recidivism* (User Report 97-04). Ottawa, Canada: Department of the Solicitor General of Canada.

Hanson, R. K., & Morton-Bourgon, K. (2004). *Predictors of sexual recidivism: An updated meta-analysis.* Public Works and Government Services Canada (Cat. No. PS3-1/2004-2E-PDF). Retrieved from http://www.psepc-sp-pcc.gc.ca/ publications/corrections/pdf/200402_e.pdf

Hanson, R. K., & Morton-Bourgon, K. E. (2009). The accuracy of recidivism risk assessments for sexual offenders: A meta-analysis of 118 prediction studies. *Psychological Assessment, 21,* 1–21.

Hanson, R. K., & Thornton, D. (2000). Improving risk assessment for sex offenders: A comparison of three actuarial scales. *Law and Human Behavior, 24,* 119–136.

Hare, R. D. (1980). A research scale for the assessment of psychopathy in criminal populations. *Personality and Individual Differences, 1,* 111–119.

Hare, R. D. (1991). *Manual for the revised Psychopathy Checklist*. Toronto, Canada: Multi-Health Systems.

Hare, R. D. (1996). Psychopathy: A clinical construct whose time has come. *Criminal Justice and Behavior, 23*, 25–54.

Hare, R. D. (1998). The Hare PCL-R: Some issues concerning its use and misuse. *Legal and Criminological Psychology, 3*, 99–119.

Hare, R. D. (2003). *The Hare Psychopathy Checklist—Revised manual* (2nd ed.). Toronto, Canada: Multi-Health Systems.

Hare, R. D., & Hervé, H. F. (1999). *Hare P-Scan: Research Version*. New York: Multi-Health Systems.

Hare, R. D., McPherson, L. M., & Forth, A. E. (1988). Male psychopaths and their criminal careers. *Journal of Consulting and Clinical Psychology, 56*, 710–714.

Hare, R. D., & Neumann, C. S. (2006). The PCL-R assessment of psychopathy: Development, structural properties, and new directions. In C. J. Patrick (Ed.), *Handbook of psychopathy* (pp. 58–88). New York: Guilford.

Hare, R. D., & Neumann, C. S. (2010). The role of antisociality in the psychopathy construct: Comment on Skeem and Cooke (2010). *Psychological Assessment, 22*, 446–459.

Harpur, T. J., Hakstian, A. R., & Hare, R. D. (1988). Factor structure of the Psychopathy Checklist. *Journal of Consulting and Clinical Psychology, 56*, 741–747.

Harpur, T. J., Hare, R. D., & Hakstian, A. R. (1989). Two-factor conceptualization of psychopathy: Construct validity and assessment implications. *Psychological Assessment, 1*, 6–17.

Harris, A., Phenix, A., Hanson, R. K., & Thornton, D. (2003). *Static-99 coding rules revised*. Ottawa, Canada: Solicitor General Canada.

Harris, G. T., Rice, M. E., Hilton, N. Z., Lalumière, J. L., & Quinsey, V. L. (2007). Coercive and precocious sexuality as a fundamental aspect of psychopathy. *Journal of Personality Disorders, 21*, 1–27.

Harris, G. T., Rice, M. E., & Quinsey, V. L. (1993). Violent recidivism of mentally disordered offenders: The development of a statistical prediction instrument. *Criminal Justice and Behavior, 20*, 315–335.

Harris, G. T., Rice, M. E., & Quinsey, V. L. (1994). Psychopathy as a taxon: Evidence that psychopaths are a discrete class. *Journal of Consulting and Clinical Psychology, 62*, 387–397.

Hart, S. D., Cox, D., & Hare, R. D. (1995). *Psychopathy Checklist: Screening Version*. Toronto, Canada: Multi-Health Systems.

Hay, C. (2004). Parenting, self-control, and delinquency: A test of self-control theory. *Criminology, 39*, 707–736.

Hay, C., & Forrest, W. (2006). The development of self-control: Examining self-control theory's stability thesis. *Criminology, 44*, 739–774.

Heal, K., & Laycock, G. K. (1986). *Situational crime prevention: From theory into practice*. London: HMSO.

Healy, D. (2004). *Let them eat prozac*. New York: New York University Press.

Healy, D., Herxheimer, A., & Menkes, D. B. (2006). Antidepressants and violence: Problems at the interface of medicine and law. *PLoS Medicine, 3*, 1478–1487.

Healy, D., & O'Donnell, I. (2006). Criminal thinking on probation: A perspective from Ireland. *Criminal Justice and Behavior, 33*, 782–802.

Heider, F. (1958). *The psychology of interpersonal relations.* New York: John Wiley.

Heilbrun, K. (1997). Prediction versus management models relevant to risk assessment: The importance of legal decision-making context. *Law and Human Behavior, 21*, 347–359.

Heller, M. S., Ehrlick, S. M., & Lester, D. (1984). Childhood cruelty to animals, firesetting and enuresis as correlates of competence to stand trial. *Journal of General Psychiatry, 100*, 151–153.

Hellman, D. S., & Blackman, N. (1966). Enuresis, firesetting and cruelty to animals: A triad predictive of adult crime. *American Journal of Psychiatry, 122*, 1431–1435.

Henggeler, S. W. (2001). Multisystemic therapy. *Residential Treatment for Children and Youth, 18*(3), 75–85.

Henggeler, S. W., Schoenwald, S. K., Borduin, C. M., Rowland, M. D., & Cunningham, P. B. (2009). *Multisystemic therapy for antisocial behavior in children and adolescents* (2nd ed.). New York: Guilford.

Higgins, G. E., Fell, B. D., & Wilson, A. L. (2006). Digital piracy: Assessing the contributions of an integrated self-control theory and social learning theory using structural equation modeling. *Criminal Justice Studies: A Critical Journal of Crime, Law and Society, 19*, 3–22.

Hirschi, T., & Gottfredson, M. (1983). Age and the explanation of crime. *American Journal of Sociology, 89*, 552–584.

Hoeve, M., Dubas, J. S., Eichelsheim, V. I., van der Laan, P. H., Smeenk, W., & Gerris, J. R. M. (2009). The relationship between parenting and delinquency: A meta-analysis. *Journal of Abnormal Child Psychology, 37*, 749–775.

Hoffman, P. B., & Beck, J. L. (1985). Recidivism among released federal prisoners: Salient factor score and five year follow-up. *Criminal Justice and Behavior, 12*, 501–507.

Hoffman, P. B., & Stone-Meierhoefer, B. (1980). Reporting recidivism rates: The criterion and follow-up issues. *Journal of Criminal Justice, 8*, 53–60.

Hollon, S. D., & DeRubeis, R. (2003, August). *Cognitive therapy for depression.* Presentation at the annual conference of the American Psychiatric Association, Philadelphia, PA.

Hooper, C. J., Luciana, M., Conklin, H. M., & Yarger, R. S. (2004). Adolescents' performance on the Iowa Gambling Task: Implications for the development of decision making and ventromedial prefrontal cortex. *Developmental Psychology, 40*, 1148–1158.

Horner, R. H., & Day, H. M. (1991). The effects of response efficiency on functionally equivalent competing behaviors. *Journal of Applied Behavior Analysis, 24*, 719–732.

Hughes, M. (1998). Turning points in the lives of young inner-city men forgoing destructive criminal behaviors: A qualitative study. *Social Work Research, 22,* 143–151.

Irwin, J. (1970). *The felon.* Englewood Cliffs, NJ: Prentice-Hall.

Isen, J. D., Baker, L. A., Raine, A., & Bezdjian, S. (2009). Genetic and environmental influences on the Junior Temperament and Character Inventory in a preadolescent twin sample. *Behavior Genetics, 39,* 36–47.

Izzo, R. L., & Ross, R. R. (1990). Meta-analysis of rehabilitation programs for juvenile delinquents: A brief report. *Criminal Justice and Behavior, 17,* 134–142.

Jaffee, S. R., Caspi, A., Moffitt, T. E., Polo-Thomás, M., & Taylor, A. (2007). Individual, family, and neighborhood factors distinguish resilient from non-resilient maltreated children: A cumulative stressors model. *Child Abuse and Neglect, 31,* 231–253.

Jeglum-Bartusch, D., Lynam, D., Moffitt, T. E., & Silva, P. A. (1997). Is age important? Testing general versus developmental theories of antisocial behavior. *Criminology, 35,* 13–47.

Kessler, R. C., Chiu, W. T., Dernier, O., Merikangas, K. R., & Walters, E. E. (2005). Lifetime prevalence and age-of-onset distributions of DSM-IV disorders in the National Comorbidity Survey replication. *Archives of General Psychiatry, 62,* 593–602.

Kiehl, K. A. (2006). A cognitive neuroscience perspective on psychopathy: Evidence for paralimbic system dysfunction. *Psychiatry Research, 142,* 107–128.

Kiesler, C. (1971). *The psychology of commitment: Experiments linking behavior to belief.* New York: Academic Press.

Kochanska, G., Murray, K., & Coy, K. C. (1997). Inhibitory control as a contributor to conscience in childhood: From toddler to early school age. *Child Development, 68,* 263–277.

Konstam, A. (2006). *Blackbeard: America's most notorious pirate.* Hoboken, NJ: John Wiley.

Kopelowicz, A., Lieberman, R. P., & Zarate, R. (2002). Psychosocial treatments for schizophrenia. In P. E. Nathan & J. M. Gorman (Eds.), *A guide to treatments that work* (pp. 201–228). New York: Oxford University Press.

Kraag, G., Zeegers, M. P., Kok, G., Hosman, C., & Abu-Saad, H. H. (2006). School programs targeting stress management in children and adolescents: A meta-analysis. *Journal of School Psychology, 44,* 449–472.

Kroner, D. G., & Mills, J. F. (2001). The accuracy of five risk appraisal instruments in predicting institutional misconduct and new convictions. *Criminal Justice and Behavior, 28,* 471–489.

Kropp, P. R., & Hart, S. D. (2000). The Spousal Assault Risk Assessment (SARA) Guide: Reliability and validity in adult male offenders. *Law and Human Behavior, 24,* 101–118.

Kropp, P. R., Hart, S. D., Webster, C. W., & Eaves, D. (1994). *Manual for the Spousal Assault Risk Assessment Guide.* British Columbia: British Columbia Institute on Family Violence.

Kruttschnitt, C., Uggen, C., & Shelton, K. (2000). Predictors of desistance among sex offenders: The interaction of formal and informal social controls. *Justice Quarterly, 17,* 61–87.

Kuhns, J. B. (2005). The dynamic nature of the drug use/serious violence relationship: A multicausal approach. *Violence and Victims, 20,* 433–454.

Kyvsgaard, B. (2003). *The criminal career: The Danish longitudinal study.* Cambridge, UK: Cambridge University Press.

Langan, P. A., & Levin, D. J. (2002). *Recidivism of prisoners released in 1994* (Bureau of Justice Statistics Special Report: NCJ-193427). Washington, DC: Office of Justice Programs.

Langevin, R. (2003). A study of the psychosexual characteristics of sex killers: Can we identify them before it is too late? *International Journal of Offender Therapy and Comparative Criminology, 47,* 366–382.

Langton, C. M., Barbaree, H. E., Harkins, L., Peacock, E. J., & Arenovich, T. (2008). Further investigation of findings reported for the Minnesota Sex Offender Screening Tool-Revised. *Journal of Interpersonal Violence, 23,* 1363–1379.

Langton, L., Piquero, N. L., & Hollinger, R. C. (2006). An empirical test of the relationship between employee theft and low self-control. *Deviant Behavior, 27,* 537–565.

Laub, J. H., Nagin, D. S., & Sampson, R. J. (1998). Trajectories of change in criminal offending: Good marriages and the desistance process. *American Sociological Review, 63,* 225–238.

Laub, J. H., & Sampson, R. J. (1988). Unraveling families and delinquency: A reanalysis of the Gluecks' data. *Criminology, 26,* 355–380.

Laub, J. H., & Sampson, R. J. (2003). *Shared beginnings, divergent lives: Delinquent boys to age 70.* Cambridge, MA: Harvard University Press.

LeBel, T. P., Burnett, R., Maruna, S., & Bushway, S. (2008). The "chicken and egg" of subjective and social factors in desistance from crime. *European Journal of Criminology, 5,* 131–159.

Le Blanc, M., & Fréchette, M. (1989). *Male criminal activity from childhood through youth: Multilevel and developmental perspectives.* New York: Springer-Verlag.

Leistico, A. M. R., Salekin, R. T., DeCoster, J., & Rogers, R. (2008). A large-scale meta-analysis relating the Hare measures of psychopathy to antisocial conduct. *Law and Human Behavior, 32,* 28–45.

Lenzenweger, M. F. (1999). Deeper into the schizotypy taxon: On the robust nature of maximum covariance analysis. *Journal of Abnormal Psychology, 108,* 182–187.

Lenzenweger, M. F. (2004). Consideration of the challenges, complications, and pitfalls of taxometric analysis. *Journal of Abnormal Psychology, 113,* 10–23.

Levenson, M. R., Kiehl, K. A., & Fitzpatrick, C. M. (1995). Assessing psychopathic attributes in a noninstitutionalized population. *Journal of Personality and Social Psychology, 68,* 151–158.

Levine, J. D., Gordon, N. C., & Fields, H. L. (1979). The role of endorphins in placebo analgesia. In J. J. Bonica, J. C. Liebeskind, & D. Albe-Fessard (Eds.), *Advances in pain research and therapy* (Vol. 3, pp. 547–551). New York: Raven.

Lewis, M., & Brooks-Gunn, J. (1979). *Social cognition and the acquisition of the self.* New York: Plenum.

Lieberman, J. A., Stroup, T. S., McEvoy, M. S., Swartz, R. A., Rosenheck, D. O. et al. (2005). Effectiveness of antipsychotic drugs in patients with chronic schizophrenia. *New England Journal of Medicine, 353,* 1209–1223.

Lilienfeld, S. O., & Andrews, B. P. (1996). Development and preliminary validation of a self-report measure of psychopathic personality traits in noncriminal populations. *Journal of Personality Assessment, 66*, 488–524.

Linscott, R. J. (2007). The latent structure and coincidence of hypohedonia and schizotypy and their validity as indices of psychometric risk for schizophrenia. *Journal of Personality Disorders, 21*, 225–242.

Lipton, D., Martinson, R., & Wilks, J. (1975). *The effectiveness of correctional treatment: A survey of treatment evaluation studies.* New York: Praeger.

Lorr, M., & Strack, S. (1994). Personality profiles of police candidates. *Journal of Clinical Psychology, 50*, 200–207.

Lowenkamp, C. T., Holsinger, A. M., Brusman-Lovins, L., & Latessa, E. J. (2004). Assessing the inter-rater agreement of the Level of Service Inventory-Revised. *Federal Probation, 68*(3), 34–38.

Luborsky, L., Diguer, L., Seligman, D. A., Rosenthal, R., Krause, E. D., Johnson, S., et al. (1999). The researcher's own therapy allegiances: A "wild card" in comparisons of treatment efficacy. *Clinical Psychology: Science and Practice, 6*, 95–106.

Lundahl, B., Risser, H. J., & Lovejoy, M. C. (2006). A meta-analysis of parent training: Moderators and follow-up effects. *Clinical Psychology Review, 26*, 86–104.

Luthar, S. S. (1991). Vulnerability and resilience: A study of high-risk adolescents. *Child Development, 62*, 600–616.

Lykken, D. T. (1995). *The antisocial personalities.* Hillsdale, NJ: Lawrence Erlbaum.

Lykken, D. T., McGue, M., Tellegen, A., & Bouchard, T. J. (1992). Emergenesis: Genetic traits that may not run in families. *American Psychologist, 47*, 1565–1577.

Lynam, D. R. (1997). Pursuing the psychopath: Capturing the fledgling psychopath in a nomological net. *Journal of Abnormal Psychology, 106*, 425–438.

Lynam, D. R., Caspi, A., Moffitt, T. E., Wikström, P.-O., Loeber, R., Novak, S. et al. (2000). The interaction between impulsivity and neighborhood context on offending: The effects of impulsivity are stronger in poorer neighborhoods. *Journal of Abnormal Psychology, 109*, 563–574.

Lynam, D. R., Miller, D. J., Vachon, D., Loeber, R., & Stouthamer-Loeber, M. (2009). Psychopathy in adolescence predicts official reports of offending in adulthood. *Youth Violence and Juvenile Justice, 7*, 189–207.

Marcus, D. K., John, S. L., & Edens, J. F. (2004). A taxometric analysis of psychopathic personality. *Journal of Abnormal Psychology, 113*, 626–635.

Marcus, D. K., Lilienfeld, S. O., Edens, J. F., & Poythress, N. G. (2006). Is antisocial personality disorder continuous or categorical? A taxometric analysis. *Psychological Medicine, 36*, 1571–1581.

Marcus, D. K., Ruscio, J., Lilienfeld, S. O., & Hughes, K. T. (2008). Converging evidence for the latent structure of antisocial personality disorder: Consistency of taxometric and latent class analysis. *Criminal Justice and Behavior, 35*, 284–293.

Marks, I. M. (1987). *Fears, phobias, and rituals: Panic, anxiety, and their disorders.* New York: Oxford University Press.

Martinez-Torteya, C., Bogat, G. A., von Eye, A., & Levendosky, A. A. (2009). Resilience among children exposed to domestic violence: The role of risk and protective factors. *Child Development, 80*, 562–577.

Martinson, R. (1979). New findings, new views: A note of caution regarding sentencing reform. *Hofstra Law Review, 7*, 243–258.

Mason, W. A., & Windle, M. (2002). Gender, self-control, and informal social control in adolescence: A test of three models of the continuity of delinquent behavior. *Youth and Society, 33*, 479–514.

Massoglia, M., & Uggen, C. (2007). Subjective desistance and the transition to adulthood. *Journal of Contemporary Criminal Justice, 23*, 90–103.

Masten, A. S. (2001). Ordinary magic: Resilience processes in development. *American Psychologist, 56*, 227–238.

Matthews, B. A., & Norris, F. H. (2002). When is believing "seeing"? Hostile attribution bias as a function of self-reported aggression. *Journal of Applied Social Psychology, 32*, 1–32.

Maughan, B., Pickles, A., Rowe, R., Costello, E. J., & Angold, A. (2000). Developmental trajectories of aggressive and non-aggressive conduct problems. *Journal of Quantitative Criminology, 16*, 199–221.

Mawson, A. R. (2009). On the association between low resting heart rate and chronic aggression: Retinoid toxicity hypothesis. *Progress in Neuro-Psychopharmacology and Biological Psychiatry, 33*, 205–213.

Mazerolle, P., & Maahs, J. (2002).*Developmental theory and battery incidents: Examining the relationship between discrete offender groups and intimate partner violence* (Final report). Washington, DC: Office of Justice Programs.

McCartan, L. M., & Gunnison, E. (2007). Examining the origins and influence of low self-control. *Journal of Crime and Justice, 30*, 35–62.

McCoy, K., Fremouw, W., Tyner, E., Clegg, C., Johansson-Love, J., & Strunk, J. (2006). Criminal-thinking styles and illegal behavior among college students: Validation of the PICTS. *Journal of Forensic Sciences, 51*, 1174–1177.

McDermott, B. E., Edens, J. F., Quanbeck, C. D., Busse, D., & Scott, C. L. (2008). Examining the role of static and dynamic risk factors in the prediction of inpatient violence: Variable- and person-focused analyses. *Law and Human Behavior, 32*, 325–338.

McDonald, J. M. (1963). The threat to kill. *American Journal of Psychiatry, 120*, 125–130.

McGuire, J. (2001). What works in correctional intervention? Evidence and practical implications. In G. A. Bernfeld, D. P. Farrington, & A. W. Leschied (Eds.), *Offender rehabilitation in practice: Implementing and evaluating effective programs* (pp. 25–43). New York: John Wiley.

McMurran, M. (1994). *The psychology of addiction*. Washington, DC: Taylor & Francis.

McMurran, M. (2009). Motivational interviewing with offenders: A systematic review. *Legal and Criminological Psychology, 14*, 83–100.

Mead, G. H. (1934). *Mind, self, and society*. Chicago: University of Chicago Press.

Meehl, P. E. (1977). Specific etiology and other forms of strong influence: Some quantitative meanings. *Journal of Medicine and Philosophy, 2,* 33–53.

Meehl, P. E. (1990). Toward an integrated theory of schizotaxia, schizotypy, and schizophrenia. *Journal of Personality Disorders, 4,* 1–99.

Meehl, P. E. (1992). Factors and taxa, traits and types, differences of degree and differences in kind. *Journal of Personality, 60,* 117–174.

Meehl, P. E. (1995). Bootstraps taximetrics: Solving the classification problem in psychopathology. *American Psychologist, 50,* 266–275.

Meehl, P. E. (1999). Clarifications about taxometric method. *Journal of Applied and Preventive Psychology, 8,* 165–174.

Meehl, P. E. (2004). What's in a taxon? *Journal of Abnormal Psychology, 113,* 39–43.

Meehl, P. E., & Yonce, L. J. (1994). Taxometric analysis: I. Detecting taxonicity with two quantitative indicators using means above and below a sliding cut (MAMBAC procedure). *Psychological Reports, 74,* 1059–1274.

Meehl, P. E., & Yonce, L. J. (1996). Taxometric analysis: II. Detecting taxonicity using covariance of two quantitative indicators in successive intervals of a third indicator (MAXCOV procedure). *Psychological Reports, 78,* 1091–1227.

Meloy, J. R., Hempel, A. G., Gray, B. T., Mohendie, K., Shiva, A., & Richards, T. C. (2004). A comparative analysis of North American adolescent and adult mass murderers. *Behavioral Sciences & the Law, 22,* 291–309.

Menzies, R. G., & Clarke, J. C. (1995). The etiology of phobias: A nonassociative account. *Clinical Psychology Review, 15,* 23–48.

Miller, D. T., & Ross, M. (1975). Self-serving biases in the attribution of causality: Fact or fiction? *Psychological Bulletin, 82,* 213–225.

Miller, J. (2005). *The status of qualitative research in criminology.* Proceeding from the National Science Foundation's Workshop on Interdisciplinary Standards for Systematic Qualitative Research.

Miller, L. S., Boyd, M. C., Cohn, A., Wilson, J. S., & McFarland, M. (2006, February). *Prevalence of sub-optimal effect in disability applicants.* Poster session presented at the 34th annual meeting of the International Neuropsychological Society, Boston.

Miller, W. R. (1985). Motivation for treatment: A review with special emphasis on alcoholism. *Psychological Bulletin, 98,* 84–107.

Miller, W. R., Benefield, R. G., & Tonigan, J. S. (1993). Enhancing motivation for change in problem drinking: A controlled comparison of two therapist styles. *Journal of Consulting and Clinical Psychology, 61,* 455–461.

Miller, W. R., & Rollnick, S. (2002). *Motivational interviewing: Preparing people for change* (2nd ed.). New York: Guilford.

Mitchell, O., & MacKenzie, D. L. (2006). The stability and resiliency of self-control in a sample of incarcerated offenders. *Crime and Delinquency, 52,* 432–449.

Moffitt, T. E. (1993). Adolescence-limited and life-course-persistent antisocial behavior: A developmental taxonomy. *Psychological Review, 100,* 674–701.

Moffitt, T. E. (2007). A review of research on the taxonomy of life-course persistent versus adolescence-limited antisocial behavior. In D. J. Flannery, A. T. Vazdonyi,

& I. D. Waldman (Eds.), *The Cambridge handbook of violent behavior and aggression* (pp. 49–74). New York: Cambridge University Press.

Moffitt, T. E., & Caspi, A. (2001). Childhood predictors differentiate life-course persistent and adolescence-limited pathways among males and females. *Development and Psychopathology, 13,* 355–375.

Moffitt, T. E., Caspi, A., Harrington, H., & Milne, B. (2002). Males on the life-course persistent and adolescence-limited antisocial pathways: Follow-up at age 26. *Development and Psychopathology, 14,* 179–207.

Moffitt, T. E., Lynam, D., & Silva, P. A. (1994). Neuropsychological tests predict persistent male delinquency. *Criminology, 32,* 101–124.

Morey, L. C. (2007). *The Personality Assessment Inventory (PAI): Professional manual* (2nd ed.). Lutz, FL: Psychological Assessment Resources.

Morgan, R. D., Fisher, W. H., Duan, N., Mandracchia, J. T., & Murray, D. (2010). Prevalence of criminal thinking among state prison inmates with serious mental illness. *Law and Human Behavior, 34,* 324–336.

Morrison, G. M., & Cosden, M. A. (1997). Risk, resilience, and adjustment of individuals with learning disabilities. *Learning Disability Quarterly, 20,* 43–60.

Motiuk, L. L., & Porporino, F. J. (1992). *The prevalence, nature and severity of mental health problems among federal male inmates in Canadian penitentiaries.* Ottawa, Canada: Correctional Services of Canada.

Murrie, D. C., Marcus, D. K., Douglas, K. S., Lee, Z., Salekin, R. T., & Vincent, G. (2007). Youth with psychopathic features are not a discrete class: A taxometric analysis. *Journal of Child Psychology and Psychiatry, 48,* 714–723.

Muslin, H. (1992). Adolph Hitler: The evil self. *Psychohistory Review, 20,* 251–270.

Muthén, L. K., & Muthén, B. O. (2007). *Mplus user's guide* (5th ed.). Los Angeles: Authors.

Nagin, D. S. (1999). Analyzing developmental trajectories: A semiparametric group-based approach. *Psychological Methods, 4,* 139–157.

Nagin, D. S., Farrington, D. P., & Moffitt, T. E. (1995). Life-course trajectories of different types of offenders. *Criminology, 33,* 111–139.

Nagin, D. S., & Land, K. C. (1993). Age, criminal careers, and population heterogeneity: Specification and estimation of a nonparametric, mixed Poisson model. *Criminology, 31,* 327–362.

Nagin, D. S., & Paternoster, R. (1991). The prevalence effects of the perceived risk of arrest: Testing an expanded conception of deterrence. *Criminology, 29,* 561–587.

Nagin, D. S., & Paternoster, R. (2000). Population heterogeneity and state dependence: State of the evidence and directions for future research. *Journal of Quantitative Criminology, 16,* 117–144.

Nagoshi, C. T., Walter, D., Muntaner, C., & Haertzen, C. A. (1992). Validation of the Tridimensional Personality Questionnaire in a sample of male drug users. *Personality and Individual Differences, 13,* 401–409.

Natsuaki, M., Ge, X., & Wenk, E. (2008). Continuity and change in the developmental trajectories of criminal career: Examining the roles of timing of first arrest and high school graduation. *Journal of Youth and Adolescence, 37,* 431–444.

Neighbors, H. W., Williams, D. H., Gunnings, T. S., Lipscomb, W. D., Broman, C., & Lepkowski, J. M. (1987). *The prevalence of mental disorder in Michigan prisons.* Final report submitted to the Michigan Department of Corrections. Lansing, MI: Department of Corrections.

Nelson, B., Martin, R. P., Hodge, S., Havill, V., & Kamphaus, R. (1999). Modeling the prediction of elementary school adjustment from preschool temperament. *Personality and Individual Differences, 26,* 687–700.

Newman, J. P., Curtin, J. J., Bertsch, J. D., & Baskin-Sommers, A. R. (2010). Attention moderates the fearfulness of psychopathic offenders. *Biological Psychiatry, 67,* 66–70.

Newman, J. P., & Schmitt, W. A. (1998). Passive avoidance in psychopathic offenders: A replication and extension. *Journal of Abnormal Psychology, 107,* 527–532.

Nielson, E. D. (1979). Community mental health services in community jail. *Community Mental Health Journal, 15,* 27–32.

Nurmi, J.-E. (1991). How do adolescents see their future? A review of the development of future orientation and planning. *Developmental Review, 11,* 1–59.

Osgood, D. W., Wilson, J. K., O'Malley, P. M., Bachman, J. G., & Johnston, L. D. (1996). Routine activities and individual deviant behavior. *American Sociological Review, 61,* 635–655.

Otter, Z., & Egan, V. (2007). The evolutionary role of self-deception enhancement as a protective factor against antisocial cognitions. *Personality and Individual Differences, 43,* 2258–2269.

Palmer, E., & Hollin, C. (2003). Using the Psychological Inventory of Criminal Thinking Styles with English prisoners. *Legal and Criminological Psychology, 8,* 175–187.

Palmer, E., & Hollin, C. (2004a). Predicting reconviction using the Psychological Inventory of Criminal Thinking Styles with English prisoners. *Legal and Criminological Psychology, 9,* 57–68.

Palmer, E., & Hollin, C. (2004b). The use of the Psychological Inventory of Criminal Thinking Styles with English young offenders. *Legal and Criminological Psychology, 9,* 253–263.

Petrosino, A., Turpin-Petrosino, C., & Buehler, J. (2003). Scared Straight and other juvenile awareness programs for preventing juvenile delinquency: A systematic review of the randomized experimental evidence. *Annals of the American Academy of Political and Social Science, 589,* 41–62.

Physicians' desk reference. (63rd ed.). (2009). Montvale, NJ: Thomson PDR.

Piaget, J. (1963). The attainment of invariants and reversible operations in the development of thinking. *Social Research, 30,* 283–299.

Piquero, A. R. (2008). Taking stock of developmental trajectories of criminal activity over the life course. In A. Liberman (Ed.), *The long view of crime: A synthesis of longitudinal research* (pp. 23–78). New York: Springer-Verlag.

Piquero, A. R., Brame, R., & Lynam, D. (2004). Studying criminal career length through early adulthood among serious offenders. *Crime and Delinquency, 50,* 412–435.

Piquero, A. R., Daigle, L. E., Gibson, C., Piquero, N. L., & Tibbetts, S. G. (2007). Are life-course-persistent offenders at risk for adverse health outcomes? *Journal of Research in Crime and Delinquency, 44*, 185–207.

Piquero, A. R., Paternoster, R., Mazerolle, P., Brame, R., & Dean, C. W. (1999). Onset age and offense specialization. *Journal of Research in Crime and Delinquency, 36*, 275–299.

Pollock, P., Quigley, B., Worley, K., & Bashford, C. (1997). Feigned mental disorder in prisoners referred to forensic mental health services. *Journal of Psychiatric Mental Health Nursing, 4*, 9–15.

Poulin, F., & Boivin, M. (2000). Reactive and proactive aggression: Evidence of a two-factor model. *Psychological Assessment, 12*, 115–122.

Pratt, T. C., & Cullen, F. T. (2000). The empirical status of Gottfredson and Hirschi's general theory of crime: A meta-analysis. *Criminology, 38*, 931–964.

Pratt, T. C., Turner, M. G., & Piquero, A. R. (2004). Parental socialization and community context: A longitudinal analysis of the structural sources of low self-control. *Journal of Research in Crime and Delinquency, 41*, 219–243.

Prien, R. F., & Potter, W. Z. (1990). NIMH workshop report on treatment of bipolar disorder. *Psychopharmacology Bulletin, 26*, 409–427.

Prisciandaro, J. J., & Roberts, J. E. (2005). A taxometric investigation of unipolar depression in the National Comorbidity Survey. *Journal of Abnormal Psychology, 114*, 718–728.

Prochaska, J. O., & DiClemente, C. C. (1992). Stages of change in the modification of problem behaviors. In M. Hersen, R. M. Eisler, & P. M. Miller (Eds.), *Progress in behavior modification* (pp. 184–214). Sycamore, IL: Sycamore.

Prochaska, J. O., DiClemente, C. C., & Norcross, J. C. (1992). In search of how people change: Applications to addictive behavior. *American Psychologist, 47*, 1102–1114.

Przybylski, R. (2008). *What works: Effective recidivism reduction and risk-focused prevention programs.* Denver: Colorado Division of Criminal Justice.

Pulkkinen, L., Lyrra, A.-L., & Kokko, K. (2009). Life success of males on nonoffender, adolescence-limited, persistent, and adult onset antisocial pathways: Follow-up from age 8 to 42. *Aggressive Behavior, 35*, 117–135.

Quinsey, V. L., Harris, G. T., Rice, M. E., & Cormier, C. A. (1998). *Violent offenders: Appraising and managing risk.* Washington, DC: American Psychological Association.

Raine, A., Moffitt, T. E., Caspi, A., Loeber, R., Stouthamer-Loeber, M., & Lynam, D. (2005). Neurocognitive impairments in boys on the life-course persistent antisocial path. *Journal of Abnormal Psychology, 114*, 38–49.

Raine, A., Venables, P., & Williams, M. (1995). High autonomic arousal and electrodermal orienting at age 15 years as protective factors against criminal behavior at age 29 years. *American Journal of Psychiatry, 152*, 1595–1600.

Rawlings, D., Williams, B., Haslam, N., & Claridge, G. (2008). Taxometric analysis supports a dimensional latent structure for schizotypy. *Personality and Individual Differences, 44*, 1640–1651.

Reidy, D. E., Dimmick, K., MacDonald, K., & Zeichner, A. (2009). The relationship between pain tolerance and trait aggression: Effect of sex and gender role. *Aggressive Behavior, 35,* 422–429.

Reimherr, F. W., Strong, R. E., Marchant, B. K., Hedges, D. W. & Wender, P. H. (2001). Factors affecting return symptoms 1 year after treatment in a 62-week controlled study of fluoxetine in major depression. *Journal of Clinical Psychiatry, 62,* 16–23.

Rende, R. D. (1993). Longitudinal relations between temperament traits and behavioral syndromes in middle childhood. *Journal of the American Academy of Child and Adolescent Psychiatry, 32,* 287–290.

Reyna, V. F., & Farley, F. (2006). Risk and rationality in adolescent decision making: Implications for theory, practice, and public policy. *Psychological Science in the Public Interest, 7,* 1–44.

Rhee, S. H., & Waldman, I. D. (2002). A meta-analytic review of twin and adoption studies examining antisocial behavior. *Psychological Bulletin, 128,* 490–529.

Rice, M. E., & Harris, G. T. (2005). Comparing effect sizes in follow-up studies: ROC area, Cohen's *d*, and *r. Law and Human Behavior, 29,* 615–620.

Roberts, C. F., Doren, D. M., & Thornton, D. (2002). Dimensions associated with assessments of sex offender recidivism risk. *Criminal Justice and Behavior, 29,* 569–589.

Rogers, R. (2009). Detection strategies for malingering and defensiveness. In R. Rogers (Ed.), *Clinical assessment of malingering and deception* (3rd ed., pp. 14–35). New York: Guilford.

Rogers, R., Bagby, R. M., & Dickens, S. E. (1992). *The SIRS test manual.* Odessa, FL: Psychological Assessment Resources.

Rogers, R., Jackson, R. L., Sewell, K. W., & Salekin, K. L. (2005). Detection strategies for malingering: A confirmatory factor analysis of the SIRS. *Criminal Justice and Behavior, 32,* 511–525.

Rogers, R., Salekin, R. T., Sewell, K. W., Goldstein, A., & Leonard, K. (1998). A comparison of forensic and nonforensic malingerers: A prototypical analysis of explanatory models. *Law and Human Behavior, 22,* 353–367.

Rogers, R., Sewell, K. W., & Goldstein, A. M. (1994). Explanatory models of malingering: A prototypical analysis. *Law and Human Behavior, 18,* 543–552.

Rogers, R., Ustad, K. L., & Salekin, R. T. (1998). Convergent validity of the Personality Assessment Inventory: A study of emergency referrals in a correctional setting. *Assessment, 5,* 3–12.

Rosenman, S., Korten, A., Medway, J., & Evans, M. (2003). Dimensional vs. categorical diagnosis in psychosis. *Acta Psychiatrica Scandinavica, 107,* 378–384.

Rothbart, M. K., Ahadi, S. A., & Hershey, K. L. (1994). Temperament and social behavior in childhood. *Merrill-Palmer Quarterly, 40,* 21–39.

Rozycki-Lozano, A. T., Morgan, R. D., Murray, D. D., & Varghese, F. (2011). Prison tattoos as a reflection of the criminal lifestyle. *International Journal of Offender Therapy and Comparative Criminology, 55,* 509–529.

Ruchkin, V. V., Eisemann, M., Hägglöf, B., & Cloninger, C. R. (1998). Interrelations between temperament, character, and parental rearing in male delinquent adolescents in northern Russia. *Comprehensive Psychiatry, 39*, 225–230.

Ruscio, J. (2007). Taxometric analysis: An empirically-grounded approach to implementing the model. *Criminal Justice and Behavior, 34*, 1588–1622.

Ruscio, J., Haslam, N., & Ruscio, A. M. (2006). *Introduction to the taxometric method: A practical guide.* Mahwah, NJ: Lawrence Erlbaum.

Ruscio, J., & Ruscio, A. M. (2002). A structure-based approach to psychological measurement: Matching measurement models to latent structure. *Assessment, 9*, 4–16.

Ruscio, J., Ruscio, A. M., & Meron, M. (2007). Applying the bootstrap to taxometric analysis: Generating empirical sampling distributions to help interpret results. *Multivariate Behavioral Research, 42*, 349–386.

Ruscio, J., Walters, G. D., Marcus, D. K., & Kaczetow, W. (2010). Comparing the relative fit of categorical and dimensional latent variable models using consistency tests. *Psychological Assessment, 22*, 10–19.

Ruscio, J., Zimmerman, M., McGlinchey, J. B., Chelminski, I., & Young, D. (2007). Diagnosing major depressive disorders XI: A taxometric investigation of the structure underlying DSM-IV symptoms. *Journal of Nervous and Mental Disease, 195*, 10–19.

Russell, A., Hart, C. H., Robinson, C. C., & Olsen, S. F. (2003). Children's sociable and aggressive behavior with peers: A comparison of the US and Australia and contributions of temperament and parenting styles. *International Journal of Behavioral Development, 27*, 74–86.

Sable, P. (1989). Attachment, anxiety, and loss of a husband. *American Journal of Orthopsychiatry, 59*, 550–556.

Salfati, C. G., & Bateman, A. L. (2005). Serial homicide: An investigation of behavioural consistency. *Journal of Investigative Psychology and Offender Profiling, 2*, 121–144.

Salthouse, T. A. (1996). The processing-speed theory of adult age differences in cognition. *Psychological Review, 103*, 403–428.

Sampson, R. J., & Laub, J. H. (1993). *Crime in the making.* Cambridge, MA: Harvard University Press.

Sampson, R. J., & Laub, J. H. (2003). Life-course desisters? Trajectories of crime among delinquent boys followed to age 70. *Criminology, 41*, 555–592.

Sampson, R. J., & Laub, J. H. (2005). A life-course view of the development of crime. *Annals of the American Academy, 602*, 12–45.

Sampson, R. J., Laub, J. H., & Wimer, C. (2006). Does marriage reduce crime? A counterfactual approach to within-individual causal effects. *Criminology, 44*, 465–508.

Savage, J. (2004). Does viewing violent media really cause criminal violence? A methodological review. *Aggression and Violent Behavior, 10*, 99–128.

Scarpa, A., Tanaka, A., & Haden, S. C. (2008). Biosocial bases of reactive and proactive aggression: The roles of community violence exposure and heart rate. *Journal of Community Psychology, 36*, 969–988.

Schroeder, R. D., Giordano, P. C., & Cernkovich, S. A. (2007). Drug use and desistance processes. *Criminology, 45*, 191–222.

Segrin, C. (2000). Social skills deficits associated with depression. *Clinical Psychology Review, 20*, 379–403.

Seligman, M. E. P. (1971). Phobias and preparedness. *Behavior Therapy, 2*, 307–320.

Seligman, M. E. P. (1990). Why is there so much depression today? The wasting of the individual and the waning of the commons. In R. E. Ingram (Ed.), *Contemporary psychological approaches to depression: Theory research, and treatment* (pp. 1–9). New York: Plenum.

Shannon, K. E., Beauchaine, T. P., Brenner, S. L., Neuhaus, E., & Gatzke-Kopp, L. (2007). Familial and temperamental predictors of resilience in children at risk for conduct disorder and depression. *Development and Psychopathology, 19*, 701–727.

Shannon, L. W. (1982). *Assessing the relationship of adult criminal careers to juvenile careers: A summary*. Washington, DC: Office of Juvenile Justice and Delinquency Prevention.

Shear, M. K., Greeno, C., Kang, J., Ludewig, D., Frank, E., Swartz, H. A., et al. (2000). Diagnosis of nonpsychotic patients in community clinics. *American Journal of Psychiatry, 157*, 581–587.

Shelden, R. G. (2004). The imprisonment crisis in America: Introduction. *Review of Policy Research, 21*, 5–12.

Shipley, T. E. (1988). Opponent-processes, stress, and attributions: Some implications for shamanism and the initiation of the healing relationship. *Psychotherapy, 25*, 593–603.

Shoda, Y., Mischel, W., & Peake, P. K. (1990). Predicting adolescent cognitive and self-regulatory competencies from preschool delay of gratification: Identifying diagnostic conditions. *Developmental Psychology, 26*, 978–986.

Shover, N. (1996). *Great pretenders: Pursuits and careers of persistent thieves*. Oxford, England: Westview.

Shure, M. B. (1985). *Problem-solving and mental health of ten- to twelve year olds* (Final Report #MH-35989). Washington, DC: National Institute of Mental Health.

Shure, M. B. (1999). *Preventing violence the problem-solving way* (Juvenile Justice Bulletin). Washington, DC: Office of Juvenile Justice and Delinquency Prevention.

Simons, L. G., Simons, R. L., & Conger, R. D. (2004). Identifying the mechanisms whereby family religiosity influences the probability of adolescent antisocial behavior. *Journal of Comparative Family Studies, 35*, 547–563.

Simons, R., Wu, C., Conger, R., & Lorenz, F. (1994). Two routes to delinquency: Differences between early and late starters in the impact of parenting and deviant peers. *Criminology, 32*, 247–275.

Simourd, D. J. (1997). The Criminal Sentiments Scale—Modified and Pride in Delinquency Scale: Psychometric properties and construct validity of two measures of criminal attitudes. *Criminal Justice and Behavior, 24*, 52–70.

Simourd, D. J., & Hoge, R. D. (2000). Criminal psychopathy: A risk-and-need perspective. *Criminal Justice and Behavior, 27*, 256–272.

Simourd, L., & Andrews, D. A. (1994).Correlates of delinquency: A look at gender differences. *Forum on Correctional Research, 6,* 26–31.

Skeem, J. L., & Cooke, D. J. (2010). Is criminal behavior a central component of psychopathy? Conceptual directions for resolving the debate. *Psychological Assessment, 22,* 433–445.

Skelton, A., Riley, D., Wales, D., & Vess, J. (2006). Assessing risk for sexual offenders in New Zealand: Development and validation of a computer-scored risk measure. *Journal of Sexual Aggression, 12,* 277–286.

Skilling, T. A., Harris, G. T., Rice, M. E., & Quinsey, V. L. (2002). Identifying persistently antisocial offenders using the Hare Psychopathy Checklist and DSM antisocial personality disorder criteria. *Psychological Assessment, 14,* 27–38.

Skilling, T. A., Quinsey, V. L., & Craig, W. M. (2001). Evidence of a taxon underlying serious antisocial behavior in boys. *Criminal Justice and Behavior, 28,* 450–470.

Slavin, M. L. (2001). Enuresis, firesetting, and cruelty to animals: Does the ego triad show predictive validity? *Adolescence, 36,* 461–465.

Smith, C., & Carlson, B. E. (1997). Stress, coping and resilience in children and youth. *Social Science Review, 71,* 231–256.

Smith, M. L., Glass, G. V., & Miller, T. J. (1980). *The benefits of psychotherapy.* Baltimore: John Hopkins University Press.

Smithmyer, C. M., Hubbard, J. A., & Simons, R. F. (2000). Proactive and reactive aggression in delinquent adolescents: Relations to aggression outcome expectancies. *Journal of Clinical Child Psychology, 29,* 86–93.

Sommers, I., Baskin, D. R., & Fagen, J. (1994). Getting out of the life: Crime desistance by female street offenders. *Deviant Behavior, 15,* 125–149.

Soole, D. W., Mazerolle, L., & Rombouts, S. (2008). School-based drug prevention programs: A review of what works. *Australian and New Zealand Journal of Criminology, 41,* 259–286.

Spivak, G., & Levine, M. (1963).*Self-regulation in acting-out and normal adolescents* (Report M-4531). Washington, DC: National Institute of Mental Health.

Spivak, G., & Shure, M. B. (1982). Interpersonal cognitive problem solving and clinical theory. In B. Lahey & A. E. Kazdin (Eds.), *Advances in clinical psychology* (Vol. 5, pp. 323–372). New York: Plenum.

Sprock, J. (2003). Dimensional versus categorical classification of prototypic and nonprototypic cases of personality disorder. *Journal of Clinical Psychology, 59,* 991–1014.

Stattin, H., & Magnusson, D. (1991). Stability and change in criminal behavior up to age 30. *British Journal of Criminology, 31,* 327–346.

Steadman, H. J., Monahan, J., Duffee, B., Hartstone, E., & Robbins, P. C. (1984). The impact of state mental hospital deinstitutionalization on United States prison populations, 1968–1978. *Journal of Criminal Law and Criminology, 75,* 474–490.

Steadman, H. J., Osher, F. C., Robbins, P. C., Case, B., & Samuels, S. (2009). Prevalence of serious mental illness among jail inmates. *Psychiatric Services, 60,* 761–765.

Stice, E., & Gonzales, N. (1998). Adolescent temperament moderates the relation of parenting to antisocial behavior and substance use. *Journal of Adolescent Research, 13*, 5–31.

Stich, S., & Nichols, S. (2003). Folk psychology. In S. Stich & T. A. Warfield (Eds.), *The Blackwell guide to philosophy of mind* (pp. 235–255). Oxford, England: Basil Blackwell.

Strong, D. R., Glassmire, D. M., Frederick, R. I., & Greene, R. L. (2006). Evaluating the latent structure of the MMPI-2 F(p) scale in a forensic sample: A taxometric analysis. *Psychological Assessment, 18*, 250–261.

Strong, D. R., Greene, R. L., Hoppe, C., Johnston, T., & Olesen, N. (1999). Taxometric analysis of impression management and self-deception on the MMPI-2 in child-custody litigants. *Journal of Personality Assessment, 73*, 1–18.

Strong, D. R., Greene, R. L., & Schinka, J. A. (2000). A taxometric analysis of MMPI-2 infrequency scales [F and F(p)] in clinical settings. *Psychological Assessment, 12*, 166–173.

Sykes, G., & Matza, D. (1957). Techniques of neutralization: A theory of delinquency. *American Sociological Review, 22*, 664–670.

Taxman, F. S., Shepardson, E., & Byrne, J. M. (2004). *Tools of the trade: A guide to incorporating science into practice.* Washington, DC: National Institute of Corrections.

Taylor, P. J., Russ-Eft, D. F., & Chan, D. W. L. (2005). A meta-analytic review of behavior modeling training. *Journal of Applied Psychology, 90*, 692–709.

Thompson, M., & Petrovic, M. (2009). Gendered transitions: Within-person changes in employment, family, and illicit drug use. *Journal of Research in Crime and Delinquency, 46*, 377–408.

Thornberry, T. P., Huizinga, D., & Loeber, R. (1995). The prevention of serious delinquency and violence: Implications from the program of research on the causes and correlates of delinquency. In J. C. Howell, B. Krisberg, J. D. Hawkins, & J. J. Wilson (Eds.), *Sourcebook on serious, violent, and chronic juvenile offenders* (pp. 213–237). Thousand Oaks, CA: Sage.

Tibbetts, S., & Piquero, A. (1999). The influence of gender, low birth weight and disadvantaged environment on predicting early onset of offending: A test of Moffitt's interactional hypothesis. *Criminology, 37*, 843–878.

Tice, D. M. (1992). Self-concept change and self-presentation: The looking glass is also a magnifying glass. *Journal of Personality and Social Psychology, 63*, 435–451.

Tillich, P. (1952). *The courage to be.* New Haven, CT: Yale University Press.

Tracy, P. E., Wolfgang, M. E., & Figlio, R. M. (1990). *Delinquency careers in two birth cohorts.* New York: Plenum.

Tremblay, R. E., Nagin, D., Seguin, J. R., Zoccolillo, M., Zelazo, P. D., Boivin, M. et al. (2004). Physical aggression during early childhood: Trajectories and predictors. *Pediatrics, 114*, e43–e50.

Tucker, M., & Oei, T. P. S. (2007). Is group more cost effective than individual cognitive behaviour therapy? The evidence is not solid yet. *Behavioural and Cognitive Psychotherapy, 35*, 77–91.

Turner, K., Miller, H. A., & Henderson, C. E. (2008). Latent profile analyses of offense and personality characteristics in a sample of incarcerated female sexual offenders. *Criminal Justice and Behavior, 35*, 879–894.

Turner, M. G., Hartman, J. L., & Bishop, D. M. (2007). The effects of prenatal problems, family functioning, and neighborhood disadvantage in predicting life-course-persistent offending. *Criminal Justice and Behavior, 34*, 1241–1261.

Turner, M. G., & Piquero, A. R. (2002). The stability of self-control. *Journal of Criminal Justice, 30*, 457–471.

Turner, M. G., Piquero, A. R., & Pratt, T. C. (2005). The school context as a source of self-control. *Journal of Criminal Justice, 33*, 327–339.

Tyrka, A. R., Cannon, T. D., Haslam, J., Mednick, S. A., Schulsinger, F., Schulsinger, H., & Parnas, J. (1995). The latent structure of schizotypy: I. Premorbid indicators of a taxon of individuals at risk for schizophrenia-spectrum disorders. *Journal of Abnormal Psychology, 104*, 173–183.

Ullrich, S., Borkenau, P., & Marneros, A. (2001). Personality disorders in offenders: Categorical versus dimensional approaches. *Journal of Personality Disorders, 15*, 442–449.

Valle, S. K. (1981). Interpersonal functioning of alcoholism counselors and treatment outcome. *Journal of Studies on Alcohol, 42*, 783–789.

van Goozen, S. H. M., & Fairchild, G. (2008). How can the study of biological processes help design new interventions for children with severe antisocial behavior? *Development and Psychopathy, 20*, 941–973.

Vasey, M. W., Kotov, R., Frick, P. J., & Loney, B. R. (2005). The latent structure of psychopathy in youth: A taxometric investigation. *Journal of Abnormal Child Psychology, 33*, 411–429.

Vaughn, M. G., & DeLisi, M. (2008). Were Wolfgang's chronic offenders psychopaths? On the convergent validity between psychopathy and career criminality. *Journal of Criminal Justice, 36*, 33–42.

Viding, E., Blair, J. R., Moffitt, T. E., & Plomin, R. (2005). Evidence for substantial genetic risk for psychopathy in 7-year-olds. *Journal of Child Psychology and Psychiatry, 46*, 592–597.

Vignoles, V. L., Manzi, C., Regalia, C., Jemmolo, S., & Scabini, E. (2008). Identity motives underlying desired and feared possible future selves. *Journal of Personality, 76*, 1165–1200.

Vitale, J. E., Newman, J. P., Bates, J. E., Goodnight, J., Dodge, K. A., & Pettit, G. S. (2005). Deficient behavioral inhibition and anomalous selective attention in a community sample of adolescents with psychopathic traits and low anxiety traits. *Journal of Abnormal Child Psychology, 33*, 461–470.

Vitaro, F., Barker, E. D., Boivin, M., Brendgen, M., & Tremblay, R. E. (2006). Do early difficult temperament and harsh parenting differentially predict reactive and proactive aggression? *Journal of Abnormal Child Psychology, 34*, 685–695.

Walker, F. O. (2007). Huntington's disease. *Lancet, 369*, 218–228.

Waller, N. G., & Meehl, P. E. (1998). *Multivariate taxometric procedures: Distinguishing types from continua.* Thousand Oaks, CA: Sage.

Waller, N. G., & Ross, C. A. (1997). The prevalence and biometric structure of pathological dissociation in the general population: Taxometrics and behavior genetic findings. *Journal of Abnormal Psychology, 106,* 499–510.

Walsh, D. (1986). Victim selection procedures among economic criminals: The rational choice perspective. In D. B. Cornish & R. V. Clarke (Eds.), *The reasoning criminal: Rational choice perspectives on offending* (pp. 39–52). New York: Springer-Verlag.

Walters, G. D. (1988). Assessing dissimulation and denial on the MMPI in a sample of maximum security, male inmates. *Journal of Personality Assessment, 52,* 465–474.

Walters, G. D. (1990). *The criminal lifestyle: Patterns of serious criminal conduct.* Newbury Park, CA: Sage.

Walters, G. D. (1991). Predicting the disciplinary adjustment of maximum and minimum security prison inmates using the Lifestyle Criminality Screening Form. *International Journal of Offender Therapy and Comparative Criminology, 35,* 63–71.

Walters, G. D. (1992). A meta-analysis of the gene-crime relationship. *Criminology, 30,* 595–613.

Walters, G. D. (1995a). The Psychological Inventory of Criminal Thinking Styles: Part I. Reliability and preliminary validity. *Criminal Justice and Behavior, 22,* 307–325.

Walters, G. D. (1995b). The Psychological Inventory of Criminal Thinking Styles: Part II. Identifying simulated response sets. *Criminal Justice and Behavior, 22,* 437–445.

Walters, G. D. (1996). The Psychological Inventory of Criminal Thinking Styles: Part III. Predictive validity. *International Journal of Offender Therapy and Comparative Criminology, 40,* 105–112.

Walters, G. D. (1997a). A confirmatory factor analysis of the Lifestyle Criminality Screening Form. *Criminal Justice and Behavior, 24,* 294–308.

Walters, G. D. (1997b). Predicting short-term release outcome using the LCSF and PICTS. *Journal of Mental Health in Corrections Consortium, 43,* 18–25.

Walters, G. D. (1998). Planning for change: An alternative to treatment planning with sexual offenders. *Journal of Sex and Marital Therapy, 24,* 217–229.

Walters, G. D. (1999). Short-term outcome of inmates participating in the Lifestyle Change Program. *Criminal Justice and Behavior, 26,* 322–337.

Walters, G. D. (2000a). *Beyond behavior: Construction of an overarching psychological theory of lifestyles.* Westport, CT: Praeger.

Walters, G. D. (2000b). *The self-altering process: Exploring the dynamic nature of lifestyle development and change.* Westport, CT: Praeger.

Walters, G. D. (2001). The shaman effect in counseling clients with alcohol problems. *Alcoholism Treatment Quarterly, 19*(3), 31–43.

Walters, G. D. (2002). *Criminal belief systems: An integrated-interactive theory of lifestyles.* Westport, CT: Praeger.

Walters, G. D. (2003a). Predicting criminal justice outcomes with the Psychopathy Checklist and Lifestyle Criminality Screening Form: A meta-analytic comparison. *Behavioral Sciences & the Law*, 21, 89–102.

Walters, G. D. (2003b). Predicting institutional adjustment and recidivism with the Psychopathy Checklist factor scores: A meta-analysis. *Law and Human Behavior*, 27, 541–558.

Walters, G. D. (2004). Changes in positive and negative crime expectancies in inmates exposed to a brief psychoeducational intervention: Further data. *Personality and Individual Differences*, 37, 505–512.

Walters, G. D. (2005a). *Assessing world-view beliefs with a simple four-dimensional rating scale*. Unpublished manuscript.

Walters, G. D. (2005b). How many factors are there on the PICTS? *Criminal Behaviour and Mental Health*, 15, 273–283.

Walters, G. D. (2005c). Predicting institutional adjustment with the Lifestyle Criminality Screening Form and Psychological Inventory of Criminal Thinking Styles. *International Journal of Forensic Mental Health*, 4, 63–70.

Walters, G. D. (2005d). Recidivism in released Lifestyle Change Program participants. *Criminal Justice and Behavior*, 32, 50–68.

Walters, G. D. (2006a). Coping with malingering and exaggeration of psychiatric symptomatology in offender populations. *American Journal of Forensic Psychology*, 24(4), 21–40.

Walters, G. D. (2006b). *The PICTS composite scales and recidivism: Predicting release outcome in inmates previously enrolled in psychological programming*. Unpublished manuscript.

Walters, G. D. (2006c). Risk-appraisal versus self-report in the prediction of criminal justice outcomes: A meta-analysis. *Criminal Justice and Behavior*, 33, 279–304.

Walters, G. D. (2006d). Use of the Psychological Inventory of Criminal Thinking Styles to predict disciplinary adjustment in male inmate program participants. *International Journal of Offender Therapy and Comparative Criminology*, 50, 166–173.

Walters, G. D. (2007a). Correlations between the Psychological Inventory of Criminal Thinking Styles and World-View Rating Scale in male federal prisoners. *Criminal Behaviour and Mental Health*, 17, 184–188.

Walters, G. D. (2007b). The latent structure of the criminal lifestyle: A taxometric analysis of the Lifestyle Criminality Screening Form and Psychological Inventory of Criminal Thinking Styles. *Criminal Justice and Behavior*, 34, 1623–1637.

Walters, G. D. (2007c). Measuring proactive and reactive criminal thinking with the PICTS: Correlations with outcome expectancies and hostile attribution biases. *Journal of Interpersonal Violence*, 22, 371–385.

Walters, G. D. (2008a). The latent structure of alcohol use disorders: A taxometric analysis of structured interview data obtained from male federal prison inmates. *Alcohol and Alcoholism*, 43, 326–333.

258   Crime in a Psychological Context

Walters, G. D. (2008b). Self-report measures of psychopathy, antisocial personality, and criminal lifestyle: Testing and validating a two-dimensional model. *Criminal Justice and Behavior, 35*, 1459–1483.
Walters, G. D. (2009a). Anger management training in incarcerated male offenders: Differential impact on proactive and reactive criminal thinking. *International Journal of Forensic Mental Health, 8*, 214–217.
Walters, G. D. (2009b). Latent structure of a two-dimensional model of antisocial personality disorder: Construct validation and taxometric analysis. *Journal of Personality Disorders, 23*, 647–660.
Walters, G. D. (2009c). The Psychological Inventory of Criminal Thinking Styles and Psychopathy Checklist: Screening Version as incrementally valid predictors of recidivism. *Law and Human Behavior, 33*, 497–505.
Walters, G. D. (2009d). Taxometric analysis of alcohol dependence in male prisoners: Measuring latent structure with indicators from DSM-IV. *Addiction Research and Theory, 17*, 372–380.
Walters, G. D. (2010a). *The Psychological Inventory of Criminal Thinking Styles (PICTS): Professional manual.* Allentown, PA: Center for Lifestyle Studies.
Walters, G. D. (2010b). *Serious mental disorder in prison inmates: Category or continuum.* Unpublished manuscript.
Walters, G. D. (2011a). The latent structure of life-course-persistent antisocial behavior: Is Moffitt's developmental taxonomy a true taxonomy? *Journal of Consulting and Clinical Psychology, 79*, 96–105.
Walters, G. D. (2011b). Predicting recidivism with the Psychological Inventory of Criminal Thinking Styles and Level of Service Inventory-Revised: Screening Version. *Law and Human Behavior, 35*, 211–220.
Walters, G. D. (2011c). Screening for malingering/exaggeration of psychiatric symptomatology in prison inmates using the PICTS Confusion and Infrequency scales. *Journal of Forensic Sciences, 56*, 444–449.
Walters, G. D., Berry, D. T. R., Lanyon, R. I., & Murphy, M. P. (2009). Are exaggerated health complaints continuous or categorical? A taxometric analysis of the Health Problem Overstatement scale. *Psychological Assessment, 21*, 578–594.
Walters, G. D., Berry, D. T. R., Rogers, R., Payne, J. W., & Granacher, R. P. (2009). Feigned neurocognitive deficit: Taxon or dimension? *Journal of Clinical and Experimental Neuropsychology, 31*, 584–593.
Walters, G. D., Brinkley, C. A., Magaletta, P. R., & Diamond, P. M. (2008). Taxometric analysis of the Levenson Self-Report Psychopathy scale. *Journal of Personality Assessment, 90*, 491–498.
Walters, G. D., & Chlumsky, M. L. (1993). The Lifestyle Criminality Screening Form and antisocial personality disorder: Predicting release outcome in a state prison sample. *Behavioral Sciences & the Law, 11*, 111–115.
Walters, G. D., & Cosgrove, E. (1997). Recidivism rates in federal probationers. Unpublished raw data.
Walters, G. D., Deming, A., & Elliott, W. N. (2009). Assessing criminal thinking in male sex offenders with the Psychological Inventory of Criminal Thinking Styles. *Criminal Justice and Behavior, 36*, 1025–1036.

Walters, G. D., Diamond, P. M., & Magaletta, P. R. (2010). What is the latent structure of alcohol use disorders? A taxometric analysis of the Personality Assessment Inventory Alcohol Problems scale in male and female prison inmates. *Psychology of Addictive Behaviors*, 24, 26–37.

Walters, G. D., Diamond, P. M., Magaletta, P. R., Geyer, M. D., & Duncan, S. A. (2007). Taxometric analysis of the antisocial features scale of the Personality Assessment Inventory in federal prison inmates. *Assessment*, 14, 351–360.

Walters, G. D., & Di Fazio, R. (2000). Psychopathy and the criminal lifestyle: Similarities and differences. In C. B. Gacono (Ed.), *The clinical and forensic assessment of psychopathy* (pp. 369–384). Mahwah, NJ: Erlbaum.

Walters, G. D., Duncan, S. A., & Mitchell-Perez, K. (2007). The latent structure of psychopathy: A taxometric investigation of the Psychopathy Checklist-Revised in a heterogeneous sample of male prison inmates. *Assessment*, 14, 270–278.

Walters, G. D., & Elliott, W. N. (1999). Predicting release outcome and disciplinary outcome with the Psychological Inventory of Criminal Thinking Styles: Female data. *Legal and Criminological Psychology*, 4, 15–21.

Walters, G. D., Elliott, W. N., & Miscoll, D. (1998). Use of the Psychological Inventory of Criminal Thinking Styles in a group of female offenders. *Criminal Justice and Behavior*, 25, 125–134.

Walters, G. D., Frederick, A. A., & Schlauch, C. (2007). Postdicting arrests for proactive and reactive aggression with the PICTS proactive and reactive scales. *Journal of Interpersonal Violence*, 22, 1415–1430.

Walters, G. D., & Geyer, M. D. (2004). Criminal thinking and identity in male white-collar offenders. *Criminal Justice and Behavior*, 31, 263–281.

Walters, G. D., & Geyer, M. D. (2005). Construct validity of the Psychological Inventory of Criminal Thinking Styles in relationship to the PAI, disciplinary adjustment, and program completion. *Journal of Personality Assessment*, 84, 252–260.

Walters, G. D., Gray, N. S., Jackson, R. L., Sewell, K. W., Rogers, R., Taylor J., et al. (2007). A taxometric analysis of the Psychopathy Checklist: Screening Version (PCL:SV): Further evidence of dimensionality. *Psychological Assessment*, 19, 330–339.

Walters, G. D., & Heilbrun, K. (2010). Violence risk assessment and facet 4 of the Psychopathy Checklist: Predicting institutional and community aggression in two forensic samples. *Assessment*, 17, 259–268.

Walters, G. D., Hennig, C. L., Negola, T. D., & Fricke, L. A. (2009).The latent structure of alcohol dependence in female federal prisoners. *Addiction Research and Theory*, 17, 525–537.

Walters, G. D., & Knight, R. A. (2010). Antisocial personality disorder with and without antecedent childhood conduct disorder: Does it make a difference? *Journal of Personality Disorders*, 24, 165–178.

Walters, G. D., Knight, R. A., Grann, M., & Dahle, K.-P. (2008). Incremental validity of the Psychopathy Checklist facet scores: Predicting release outcome in six samples. *Journal of Abnormal Psychology*, 117, 396–405.

Walters, G. D., Knight, R. A., & Thornton, D. (2009). The latent structure of sexual violence risk: A taxometric analysis of widely used sex offender actuarial risk measures. *Criminal Justice and Behavior, 36,* 290–306.

Walters, G. D., & Kotch, S. T. (2007). *Instructing federal probation officers in the use of the Lifestyle Change model with substance-abusing probationers.* Unpublished manuscript.

Walters, G. D., & Mandell, W. (2007). Incremental validity of the Psychological Inventory of Criminal Thinking Styles and Psychopathy Checklist: Screening Version in predicting disciplinary outcome. *Law and Human Behavior, 31,* 141–157.

Walters, G. D., Marcus, D. K., Edens, J. F., Knight, R. A., & Sanford, G. M. (2011). In search of the psychopathic sexuality taxon: Indicator size does matter. *Behavioral Sciences and the Law, 29,* 23–39.

Walters, G. D., & McCoy, K. (2007). Taxometric analysis of the Psychological Inventory of Criminal Thinking Styles in incarcerated offenders and college students. *Criminal Justice and Behavior, 34,* 781–793.

Walters, G. D., & McDonough, J. R. (1998). The Lifestyle Criminality Screening Form as a predictor of federal parole/probation/supervised release outcome: A 3-year follow-up. *Legal and Criminological Psychology, 3,* 173–181.

Walters, G. D., Revella, L., & Baltrusaitis, W. (1990). Predicting parole/probation outcome with the aid of the Lifestyle Criminality Screening Form: Preliminary data. *Psychological Assessment, 2,* 313–316.

Walters, G. D., Rogers, R., Berry, D. T. R., Miller, H. A., Duncan, S. A., McCusker, P. J., et al. (2008). Malingering as a categorical or dimensional construct: The latent structure of feigned psychopathology as measured by the SIRS and MMPI-2. *Psychological Assessment, 20,* 238–247.

Walters, G. D., Ronen, T., & Rosenbaum, M. (2010). The latent structure of childhood aggression: A taxometric analysis of self-reported and teacher-rated aggression in Israeli schoolchildren. *Psychological Assessment, 22,* 628–637.

Walters, G. D., & Ruscio, J. (2009). To sum or not to sum: Taxometric analysis with ordered categorical assessment items. *Psychological Assessment, 21,* 99–111.

Walters, G. D., & Schlauch, C. (2008). The Psychological Inventory of Criminal Thinking Styles and Level of Service Inventory-Revised: Screening Version as predictors of official and self-reported disciplinary infractions. *Law and Human Behavior, 31,* 141–157.

Walters, G. D., White, T. W., & Denney, D. (1991). The Lifestyle Criminality Screening Form: Preliminary data. *Criminal Justice and Behavior, 18,* 406–418.

Walters, G. D., White, T. W., & Greene, R. L. (1988). Use of the MMPI to identify malingering and exaggeration of psychiatric symptomatology in male prison inmates. *Journal of Consulting and Clinical Psychology, 56,* 111–117.

Walters, G. D., Wilson, N. J., & Glover, A. J. J. (2011). Predicting recidivism with the Psychopathy Checklist: Are factor score composites really necessary? *Psychological Assessment, 23,* 552–557.

Walters, S. T., Clark, M. D., Gingerich, R., & Meltzer, M. L. (2007). *Motivating offenders to change: A guide for probation and parole* (NIC #022253). Washington, DC: National Institute of Corrections.

Warr, M. (1998). Life-course transitions and desistance from crime. *Criminology, 37*, 479–514.

Weaver, F. M., & Carroll, J. S. (1985). Crime perceptions in a natural setting by expert and novice shoplifters. *Social Psychology Quarterly, 48*, 349–359.

Webster, C. D., Douglas, K. S., Eaves, D., & Hart, S. D. (1997). *HCR-20: Assessing risk for violence* (Version 2). Burnby, British Columbia, Canada: Simon Fraser University, Mental Health, Law and Policy Institute.

Webster, C. D., Harris, G. T., Rice, M. E., Cormier, C., & Quinsey, V. L. (1994). *The violence prediction scheme: Assessing dangerousness in high risk men.* Toronto, Canada: University of Canada, Centre of Criminology.

Webster-Stratton, C., & Reid, M. J. (2003). Treating conduct problems and strengthening social and emotional competence in young children: The Dina Dinosaur treatment program. *Journal of Emotional and Behavioral Disorders, 11*, 130–143.

Weiner, B. (1990). Attribution in personality psychology. In L. A. Pervin (Ed.), *Handbook of personality: Theory and research* (pp. 465–485). New York: Guilford.

Werner, E. E., & Smith, R. S. (1992). *Overcoming the odds: High risk children from birth to adulthood.* Ithaca, NY: Cornell University Press.

Wexler, H. K., Melnick, G., & Cao, Y. (2004). Risk and prison substance abuse treatment outcomes: A replication and challenge. *Prison Journal, 84*, 106–120.

Weyant, J. M., Dembo, R., & Ciarlo, J. A. (1981). The influence of group versus individual and family versus individual therapy on client outcomes. *Evaluation of the Health Professions, 4*, 347–364.

Whitehead, J. T., & Lab, S. P. (1989). A meta-analysis of juvenile correctional treatment. *Journal of Research in Crime and Delinquency, 26*, 276–295.

Widom, C. S. (2003). Understanding child maltreatment and juvenile delinquency: The research. In J. Wiig, C. S., Widom, & J. A. Tuell (Eds.), *Understanding child maltreatment and juvenile delinquency: From research to effective program, practice, and systemic solutions.* Washington, DC: Child Welfare League of America.

Wiesner, M., & Capaldi, D. M. (2003). Relations of childhood and adolescent factors to offending trajectories of young men. *Journal of Research in Crime and Delinquency, 40*, 231–262.

Williams, K. E., Chambless, D. L., & Ahrens, A. (1997). Are emotions frightening? An extension of the fear of fear construct. *Behaviour Research and Therapy, 35*, 239–248.

Wolfgang, M. E., Figlio, R., & Sellin, T. (1972). *Delinquency in a birth cohort.* Chicago: University of Chicago Press.

Woodworth, M., & Porter, S. (2002). In cold blood: Characteristics of criminal homicides as a function of psychopathy. *Journal of Abnormal Psychology, 111*, 436–445.

Word, S. (1996). Mortality awareness and risk-taking in late adolescence. *Death Studies, 20*, 133–148.

Wright, J. P., & Beaver, K. M. (2005). Do parents matter in creating self-control in their children? A genetically informed test of Gottfredson and Hirschi's theory of low self-control. *Criminology, 43*, 1169–1202.

Yochelson, S., & Samenow, S. E. (1976). *The criminal personality: Vol. 1. A profile for change.* New York: Aronson.

Yochelson, S., & Samenow, S. E. (1977). *The criminal personality: Vol. 2. The change process.* New York: Aronson.

Xiaogang, D., & Lening, Z. (1998). Correlates of self-control: An empirical test of self-control theory. *Journal of Crime and Justice, 21*, 89–110.

Zapf, P. A., & Roesch, R. (2006). Competency to stand trial: A guide for evaluators. In I. B. Weiner & A. K. Hess (Eds.), *The handbook of forensic psychology* (3rd ed., pp. 305–331). New York: John Wiley.

Index

SAGE Research Methods Online

The essential tool for researchers

**Sign up now at
www.sagepub.com/srmo
for more information.**

An expert research tool

- An **expertly designed taxonomy** with more than 1,400 unique terms for social and behavioral science research methods

- **Visual and hierarchical earch tools** to help you iscover material and link to related methods

- Easy-to-use navigation tools
- Content organized by complexity
- Tools for citing, printing, and downloading content with ease
- Regularly updated content and features

A wealth of essential content

- The most comprehensive picture of quantitative, qualitative, and mixed methods available today

- More than **100,000 pages of SAGE book and ference material** on research methods as well as litorially selected material from SAGE journals

- More than **600 books** available in their entirety online

Launching 2011!

⑤SAGE research methods online